SWEET TALKERS

SWEET TALKERS

KATHLEEN K.

First Richard Kasak Book Edition 1994

First printing July 1994

ISBN 1-56333-192-6

Cover Art © by Judy Simonian
Cover Design by Steve Powell

Manufactured in the United States of America
Published by Masquerade Books, Inc.
801 Second Avenue
New York, N.Y. 10017

A RICHARD KASAK BOOK

THIS BOOK IS DEDICATED TO MY PARTNER, M.

This is a book about life in the 1980s, and about a "love-line" telephone business which operated in the Pacific Northwest from July 1, 1987 through June 30, 1988, providing a whisper-smooth voice in the privacy of a caller's imaginary sexscape. Much of this book is based upon re-creations of telephone conversations, derived from diary entries like the samples provided here. Dialogue is always subject to various interpretations when read. Don't fight the feelings (not mine, not theirs, not yours).

I'm due on the phones in thirty-two minutes. I'm in the checkout line at the grocery with a salad and a six-pack of pop. I've got to get gas for the car and deal with the kittens when I get home (feed them, remove results of earlier feedings). These two sister cats keep me company and, in my absence, entertain each other. Relative to the phone business, my name is Jamie; theirs are Jane Grey and Patsy Brown. My phone-y personality as Down'n'Dirty contrasts delightfully with my Little Miss Neatness style at home: dishes always done, fresh flowers on the dining-room table, porch swept. To hear me tell it on the phones, I live in my bedroom, making frequent forays to the bathtub....

I blast onto the line right on time, teeth brushed and lipstick on, act as if I had nothing on my mind but the fantasies of my callers but, in truth, I'm thinking of this book, the taping of my first guest appearance on a TV show (topic: telephone sex and unauthorized access by minors) and why, oh, why, these darling kittens can't learn to keep their little cat-butts over the litter and not over the side of the pan.

The operator on the line before me says it's been busy, but we both know that is just chat between us. You can't predict the traffic on the line from hour to hour. Sometimes men stampede in response to factors we simply can't imagine. The general pattern seems obvious: before and after work, before and after going to the bars/clubs, before and after working out on the weekends, before and after actual sex acts, making this a round-the-clock business. In one shift, from midnight to six Saturday morning, I get the following calls:

12:03–11 gen'l advice re: dating; 12:12–20 is twenty-six yrs. old, nice-girl syndrome, why not wild girl (too much risk); 12:21–23 Tim, divorced, twenty-three, one kid, half-life recovery after split (i.e., five yr. recovery on ten-year marriage), AIDS; 12:23–25 kids, moan/groan, I send Tim away; 12:28 hang up; 12:42–?? silent??; 12:46–55 Tim back, raised by elder relatives, masturbating is taboo, skinny girls are too shallow so plump is better as less perfect; 12:57–1:06 wetness factors in women, acne as disability; 1:07–09 bathing each other and jerking off; 1:10–16 Tim, acne and stress (he's never been kissed on the cheek...); 1:15–16 pussy eating; 1:16–25 eleven-inch cock problems, it's great to look at, hard to ride; 1:25–34 him in teddy (beige), when shopping calls ahead to lingerie store to verify his welcome; 1:45–54 striptease, mutual masturbation, why people so shy?; 1:56–2:02 Jack (previous), would I ever masturbate on phone, how, why, when?; 2:02–12 shy about fantasies, in elevator, face fuck; 2:36–46 dancer gal-pal w/ Ph.D. earns more at peep show than straight job, he's a regular here, likes my articulate discussion of sexual politics, tell him about upcoming TV show; 2:49 hang up; 2:50–54 gal-pal bisex goings on observed at party house, likes tough "top" and sweet "bottom"; 3:02–03 silent; 3:07–16 couldn't hear him, he would not dial back so we limped through confusing array of "say what?"; 3:16–25 faint voice, gen'l topics; 3:26–29 big titties, 3:29–32 Dan, eight-inch cock, he was listening in, liked my style; 3:??–32 hang up; 3:35 hang up; 3:46–56 had been playing cards, male bonding, celibate three years, AIDS prevention to the max, no more hustle, married at twenty for twelve years; 4:15 Disconnected after click; 4:25 hang up; 4:26–27 whisperer, wants pussy; 4:27–37 on/off love life, never too weird, liked threesome talk, espec. "hold open for buddy" fuck; 4:45–46 silent; 5:13–14 silent; 5:19–29 twenty-two, 5'9", 160 pounds, match weight class for best sex, back to basics, older ladies; 5:29–39 previous back, still ready but muted; 5:32–37 6'3", pubic hair (long) fetish, various positions; 5:47–56 on/off machine fuzz; 5:56 silent; 6:02–12 very frank discussion of all wild ways (mine) and incredulity (his); *Due off at six!!* As of 6:14 operator no show, no answer phone; 6:15 operator arrives. I get extra quarter hour pay. Off to bed.

The preceding is not out of the ordinary, a little slow, in fact. My comments are cryptic because it all happens so fast. I don't need to remember specifics because I can reroll exchanges in my memory almost verbatim as needed and it protects the anonymity if I smudge the record at the start. Times and topics are for real, but there is so much richness of detail committed solely to my mind that it will reap me rewards for the rest of my life. A "hang up" call means they were on less than thirty seconds after the intro tape, a "silent" call is someone who listens past my hello but will not acknowledge me or provide age ID via his voice. We've reduced the shifts to a four-hour maximum in most cases, more often two- or three-hour stretches. When we started the business, we were more overtly sexual to the unspeaking listener. Now our policy is that we can't start without them (diminishes risk of performing for minors). Note the gaps in time—ten minutes here, forty minutes there. As long as the operator listens in, she is "free" to pass the quiet times quietly.

"…sliding in and out of…"
    "Hi? Hi?"
    "—my mouth…. Hello! This is Jamie. Who's this?"
    "Jamie, this is, umm, Bob."
    "Got yourself something to play with over there, Bob?"
    "Uh, um-hum…yeah, yes, I do."
    "Going to fall asleep when we get done?"
    "Uh, um-hum…yes, I am."

"I'm thinking of you laying in bed, Bob, are you in bed? I thought so. I'm stretched out in my bed, looking in the mirror. I'm fleshy, curvaceous, long, strong legs spread wide, both my hands are free, I'm feeling my curves, the smooth skin."

"Talk about your tits."

"Big, firm, fleshy breasts, pink nipples all puckered up, I'd like to dangle them right in front of you, shake them in your face. Like to get your hands on these big titties, baby? Firm, round."

"Oh, I want to suck them…"

"Put your lips on me. Taste the nipple, feel it on your tongue, suck it right in, it changes in your mouth. Squeeze those tits together, crush them in your hands. Now, stroke that dick and think about me, Bob. Think about Jamie, about my long, curly brown hair and pale white skin, imagine my big titties pressed up against your face…"

"Oh, Jamie…I'm so hard it's killlling me."

"Tug at that prick, sweetheart, pretend it was sliding up between my legs, hot and sweet, the two of us moving, those pointy nipples between your teeth, I'm moaning with the passion."

"Uh, oh…"

"Wrap my arms and legs around you…feel all that woman flesh around you…you're pumping now, pumping it."

"Jamie!"

"Now, stroke that cock for Jamie, stroke it for me, let me have it now, lover-boy…yes, yes, give it to me *now*."

"Oh…uh…yeahhh…thanks, wow."

"Sleep tight, darling, and call us back sometime, you hear?" *Click.*

"…I want to curl my fingers around—"

"Hello?"

"—that cock.…Hi, this is Jamie. How are you today?"

"Who were you talking to? Did I interrupt?"

"Nah, I've been waiting here for you, stroking myself and fantasizing out loud. I'd like to get my hands on your cock, feel my fingers curl around it one by one…"

"I'm not one of those guys who jacks off on the phone."

"Whoops, so sorry. Let me shift gears here. You don't *have* to jack off when you call...wanna talk?"

"Doesn't it give you the creeps, all these guys calling?"

"No, it gives me a job. I know they're going to fuck their fists anyway; this way I get a little excitement, too. It's fantasy time, I'm your secret girlfriend, the one no one knows about."

"Do you think you're weird—I mean, because you do this?"

"No, I don't. It turns me on to be involved in a man's private passion."

"That's a pretty way to describe them dribbling come on their own bellies."

"Fucking isn't all that glamorous either, you know, when you get down to the hydraulics."

"But at least you've got two people trying to relate to each other."

"I reach out this way."

"It's so empty."

"Not to us. Those guys have fresh fantasies when they hang up the phone, a new shape to consider; vivid language ringing in their ear, a real voice, an impression, a hope, a feeling of possibility..."

"You make it sound almost romantic. You do sound very real to me."

"I'm just a whisper away, your big-titted wide-hipped bitch...stroking the firm flesh between my legs, it's hot and moist, smells sweet, my finger glides right down the slit..."

"Big tits?"

"Fill your hands up, baby. Heavy and smooth, cool, yes, female flesh, nipples puckered up, erect, think of them between your lips, your tongue licking that bumpy flesh, responsive to your touch."

"You're getting to me. You know that, don't you?"

"Running my hands up and down the smooth skin of my thighs, you think about crawling up between my legs, burying your face in my wet cunt. I'd grind right against your face, hold your head tight between my legs; drink me in, lover, it's open wide."

"Gee...I love oral sex."

"Lick it sweet for me, baby. Stick that tongue into me, taste that juice, sweet honey, my soft thighs around your ears…. Then I'd haul you up on top of me, kiss my juice right off your face, suck your tongue and taste myself, and you'd be slipping that dick into me, wouldn't you? Slide it in, every inch, spread my legs and open me up for your cock…make me take it, let me have it…"

"Fuck you, bitch, I'm going to fuck you."

"Come on, fucker, shut me up, bang it in there, pound me, come on, you fuck, you hot, hot cock, fuck me."

"Jesus! Jesus! Oh, my dear God! How did you do that?"

"Sweet talk, that's all it takes; now, listen, thanks for calling, bye-bye, baby, sleep tight."

We call that coming and going.

"Hi, this is Jamie, and you bet I feel like sweet-talking tonight."

Click.

The message machine is clicking in the phone room off the kitchen. The ad for operators is running again, and we have to sort through the cranks and the timid for the clear-voiced open-minded females who might seriously consider working for us.

Some are young mothers. Infants and toddlers devour their time. These women snatch at this precious income because it is earned at home, working short shifts, lots of flexibility, and you don't ever, ever, ever have to touch anybody, ever. Some are office workers with a taste for extra spending money. They pack in fifteen hours a week early in the morning or right after work, eavesdrop on the fantasies of men they'll never meet. Others are lazy and horny. They bullshit for hours on the phone with the guys and think it's a gas that we'll pay them for it.

Phone-fantasy services work many different ways. Ours involves no commission on callback so the operator has no reason to hustle the call. No credit cards, no names—just a per-minute charge by the phone company on the customer's bill and a per-hour rate for the operators.

She plugs into the line through her home phone for her shift, chats away the hours, not always knowing if she's got one of the many "silent strokers" who never speak. Sometimes you hear a distant moan, and of course the click (or clatter) when the phone hangs up. Other callers speak right up. In either case, it is safe and anonymous fantasy contact. The operators are more actress than whore, never have to "put up or shut up." The callers are looking for a mindfuck because there is no chance to meet the operators. Of course, the guys ask, beg, try tricks, begging and flattery...sometimes it gets tense. The operators explain they are fantasy friends only, a voice whispering the secret passwords into your ear.

There is an art to sweet talk, to getting a man's attention, helping him focus his energy and bring it to a climax, listening closely for changes in his voice, in his breathing, in his longer and longer silences...each of them has his own style, a way they pace themselves, what they want to hear or say.

The best operator is almost telepathic: a question or two, and she is flying into the guy's head, rattling his thoughts, making his mind leap and twitch, triggering old associations and making new connections with him. She echoes in his head for days. Exact phrases she chooses to hiss at him through the phone, of all the words she might have picked, seem to electrify his imagination.

The caller may want to know about the operator's sexual history. When did she bloom? Who was the first? How was it? When did she start blowing cock, letting a man lick her? How was her premiere at an orgy? Married? Kids? Did her first gal-pal go all the way with her, or what? How many men has she had? Ever been a prostitute? Exotic dance? Special massage? Swing? Would she do a movie? Who has the privilege of loving her now? Is that a long-term arrangement? What are his chances of meeting her, someone like her?

Many find the operator the most fascinating of creatures: the bad girl, the one who'll let you have your way with her, who enjoys being the object of your hottest fantasies, admits to you that your lust attracts her, your naughtiness encourages her own. There is a certain distance, at times, as if the caller feels it would be impossible to take the operator seriously, but he can certainly engage in a bit of repartee...some believe they've gotten a hold of a pipeline into the women's hideaway and use it as a research tool into their most baffling counterpart.

The majority of operators are housewives or office workers, but a few have been retired prostitutes, pregnant dancers, or have given special massage. Nothing is going to bother them on the phone; they know the lingo, recognize the characters. They are good operators because they relish the privacy. No one can see them, no one can reach out and invade their space and, once given the freedom of safety, these women know no bounds. When their shift is over, they hang up the phone and resume their "real" lives.

Some men are sure that if the operator met him, she would give up this life of senseless pleasure for security—as if she might not be wrapped up tight by some man already, or that her ability to simulate sex verbally means she can and would deliver it physically. In truth, there are some operators who are at stages of their lives when such a man might truly "rescue" them in the sense that he would provide focus for a change she wished to pursue—but it does not appeal to the usual motives of the average operator and remains the same long shot as "reforming" or "deprogramming" anybody else from a currently-held belief to a new one.

Admittedly, some portion of the operator pool thinks this is not a nice thing to do. They do it for the money—specifically, the chance to earn money at home whether the reason to stay home is kids or a disinclination to commute or lack of other marketable skills, and surely one of their fantasies is a knight with a job to accept her burden as his own. It doesn't always show in their performance (although when it does, they are disengaged, as even subtle negativism booms over the line to the hypersensitive listener who may be all too familiar with rejection and the undermining of his manhood and/or the lust for his big wallet). Most operators would be offended by anyone presuming the fact that they were phone-fantasy females indicated anything else than the fact they were females who fantasized on the phones.

"...red high heels, black stockings, long-legged woman with a fleshy ass—"

"In your ass."

"Bent over, spreading my cheeks for you, bent almost in half, you're nudging your dick at the hole, it's too tight! You poke your finger in my asshole, open it, ease your dickhead in. I'm moaning, your cock is too big for me, it hurts, you keep pushing, no, I can't, I can't, you shove it, you can't stop, gotta fill it, that first two inches is so tight around your cock...you finally get all the way in, my asshole clamped around the base of your cock. I'm shaking, you start to move, I moan and move, too, your cock is in my ass, you're butt-fucking me, and I like it, I like that big cock filling me up, yes, want your cock, come on, that's it, deeper and harder...you're rocking now, rocking in and out of that ass, sweet white ass you're fucking, come on, come on, come deep inside me, thrust hard, that's my man, you're there now, feel that come spurting, that's right, that's right, ohh, it's the best...best..."

Click.

"...is Jamie, I'm your sweet-talking lady this morning. Now, come on, being the strong silent type doesn't work too well on the phone..."

"Is this live?"

"The liveliest, angel. I am right here, waiting to talk to you. My name is Jamie."

"What do you want to talk about?"

"Anything. We let the customer choose."

"So what are my choices?"

"Wide-open choices. If you're over eighteen, you can talk about anything that's legal."

"Legal?"

"No drugs. No sex talk about kids, animals, blood relatives, or dead things. Got that?"

"That's weird. Why would I want to talk about those things?"

"Beats me, but we can talk about anything else. Like we can talk about me if you like."

"I don't know you."

"You have somebody on your mind, somebody you do know?"

"Nope."

"Hmmm. So, now what? You know I'm Jamie and I know you don't know why you called."

"My friend gave me the number. I didn't know what it was all about."

"Do you know you'll be billed one dollar per minute on your phone bill for this?"

"Of course. I know what 976 means, I just never called this one. I usually call that CHAT one, but it's full of kids."

"We're the adult alternative."

"I have to go now."

"Thanks for calling. Sweet dreams, darling."

"You're welcome. I mean, good night, 'bye, good-bye—that's what I meant."

Click.

Local paper won't run the operator ad anymore, claim they got complaints. Wonder how many of our first 1,700 callers buy the paper; let them stack that against their supposed mountain of concerned citizens. Our guys vote with their dollars when they dial; it isn't theory to us. We can hardly advertise anywhere, but still they call—dare we call it word of mouth? Damn the papers. They are the only classifieds in town (big population, small town attitude). They claim they can't support that type of employment; guess they're too busy kowtowing to the franchise insta-food chains paying minimum wage. I consider *that* obscene! Our competitive wage, the freedom to work at home, short flexible shifts, supplanting the incomes of young families and clerical workers, and who cares who as long as the money gets back into the economy; why should they support such a thing? The supposedly "alternative" paper discontinued running operator ads even though we had hired some good operators through it and had no direct complaints. From word one we had spoken honestly and frankly to each applicant, not pretending to be anything but what we are: a local phone-fantasy service.

The business is always on the edge of failing for lack of traffic, which may have something to do with the narrowness of our advertising options to acquire talent; we happen to obey the community-norm standard and do not advertise for operators or callers where we are not welcome, don't hand out business cards to minors (or anyone else—we don't have them for this business), only moved to TV advertising for a limited-time experiment based in part on changing regulations, like using a loophole before it closes—which is a corporate decision, not ours.

My partner M. and I co-manage the business, each concentrating on our areas of expertise. The Californiacs who own the business are his relatives, ergo his province. I can be an emergency fill-in operator while he cannot—although he'll jump on the line and warn callers off if there is no operator, thus reducing their lost dollars). It can be a profitable business for some, and in the sense that our management fee is guaranteed for as long as the business exists, it has been a dependable income source to us. Overall, if this were truly our own business we would never have even started it. The equipment, up-front tech costs, and unrelenting payroll would have crushed a cash-poor start-up effort.

We've always hung on by the slimmest margin, and even TV advertising doesn't turn us into a household name. It is definitely a specialized service, appreciated by those who appreciate it and who will seek it out. Experimental new-call contacts do result from tv ad, but of those, only a certain percentage turn into regulars. It has been for us a slide into the sex industry for a bit of a look-see and never was intended as more than that. It could not have been any more successful than it is because it is what it is and this city is this city and the times are the times. We might have expected a little steadier stream of business. The newspaper blackout was not unexpected, but the narrow-mindedness of the alternative paper did hurt. From first day to last day, men called.

Our best and most loyal advertiser, a local free music magazine, was being pressured by a local drug/variety chain to remove ads for the phone fantasy industry altogether which surely resulted in a toning down of the ones that approached salacity, but we object that any logo per se is banned. Ours is a modest image that creatively embodies the nature and sense of our business: clothed woman on phone on floor on stomach, legs crossed in the air behind her, old-fashioned, smudgy, impressionistic. It looks chatty, relaxed, personal.

It offends us that the moralists reduce themselves to secular methods like boycotting "good" business A if they advertise in "neutral" magazine X which contains ads for "naughty" business B. This pressure on "neutral" magazine X denies legal business B the right to pay for and use ad space in accordance with established magazine policy all because of the moralists' interpretation of some old book like a bible or a Koran (which if accepted at all must be as a guide to attainment of spiritual goals like balance, love, harmony, patience and consideration for all life). Issues of taste and decorum are valid on personal levels, but this is inappropriate manipulation. The appropriate (and effective) action is to attempt to confine all businesses to the law and to change those laws if they do not serve the public. If these people are convinced they are right, isn't the force of their faith the key to changing the world? Must they stoop to name calling and stereotyping? Do they really believe I am a cause, rather than evidence? If the law does not serve, then lobbying, action committees and electioneering seem in order, not exaggerating the purported peril to confuse the real issue which is one of freedom for privacy within the law. They don't say to the magazine, "Don't advertise for them; because it is illegal." They say, "We represent more advertising income; thus we are more right than they are."

"Why'd you hang up on me?"

"I didn't, darlin'. The machine cut us off. You get ten minutes. It keeps you from racking up more charges than you expect—you know, phonus interruptus!"

"So we better hurry, huh?"

"Just think, we can build back up to it. You still on your back? That's my boy. Now, I want you absolutely flat. Stretch out those legs, press your back against the bed, shift those hips forward so your cock has a nice platform, show it off for me, raise up. Come on, Jerry, tense those legs, pull in that ass, make that hot cock big for me, stand it up, does it look good, baby?"

"Yes, Jamie, yes...I can see it in the mirror."

"Look at it, touch it for me. Think! Think of me, my lips wrapped around it. You lift it up to me, present me with that beautiful dick, show me how stiff it is, my long, curly hair tickles your belly, you feel my breasts on your thigh, think!"

"Jamie, I want you so bad."

"Focus, Jerry, coax that come to the head of your cock, bring it to Jamie, give it to her."

"Yes, I can feel it."

"It's burning, isn't it, fire-hot, hot cock, good man, big man, my man, come on, coax that come to the head of your cock."

"Here it comes, it's coming…shit! Oh…Jamie…"

"Ahh, Jerry, my friend, breathe deep, relax, let yourself drift away…but hang up that phone first, you hear?"

"Yeahh, yeahhhh. 'Night. Thanks. 'Night, Jamie, honey."

"Sweet dreams."

Click.

"—feel like talking, just say hi. Sometimes it helps if you have a mental picture of the person you're talking to… I'm 5'7", 136 pounds, long brown curly hair, green eyes, pale skin with freckles, my name is Jamie and I'm thirty years old."

"Is this for real? I never called before. You really look like you say?"

"I'm looking in the mirror when I talk, kid."

"I'm not a kid, I'm twenty-four."

"Gee, that's too bad. I sure do like to gobble up the young dudes."

"You do? Well, I'm really twenty-two, but I look twenty-four."

"You sound like a cutie. I love guys your age—they're full of all that energy. Ever-ready. Recover quick, you know. And they are so eager to learn new things."

"You make it sound like school."

"Would you get A's or F's?"

"I'd say I'm a B+ and working on it."

"Is this a special project, perhaps?"

"I guess it is. I wanted to find out what would happen."

"And what is?"

"I'm interested, I guess. You know, keep talking…"

The machine that makes these phone connections possible is best described this way: On the left side, five, and later, six lines that charge for access; dial the 1–976–#### number and for each minute or portion thereof you stay on the line you are charged one dollar. The phone company imposes ten dollars per connection ceiling on charges, our machine cuts the connection at 11.4 (later 10.5) minutes, giving the caller a "volume discount" for loyal listening. A tape plays when they connect: "Hi, thanks for calling Sweet Talkers, the conversational party line for adults only." Party-line connection—i.e., conference call: all callers hear each other and operator simultaneously.

On the right side, two lines with no charge access. Dial one of the local numbers, and you are joined to the conference at no cost with no time limit. Operator on one line, other line used by monitor/manager to listen in to and/or demonstrate line (or by disgruntled former operators disrupting the line as if we couldn't guess who it was).

Usually one caller speaks at a time. The others listen or call back in the hopes that the hostess will be free to concentrate on them later. Some callers will never speak no matter how you entice them, but you can go to the central machine and see three lines active, yet hear only the operator talking (supposedly) to herself. This is an aspect of the service that intrigues me most. I presume some are too young and know if they spoke up we'd shoo them away; others may be cops or competitors. Some men are rude and will speak up over the caller already engaging the hostess, but the good hostess stays with her original caller, advising the other to wait his turn or call back later, or she might turn the call into a "be watched" scene. It all depends.

Out of our first 986 callers, 985 were men; the one woman who called thought it might be a way to meet men. I caught the call and dissuaded her from hustling the guys which is, after all, what those cops and outside spies are just waiting to hear.

Why don't women call? I don't know. I suspect a few reasons, chief among them being women's distaste for depersonalized sex, fighting as they have been for recognition of personhood in spite of the pigeonholing by gender. The zipless-fuck concept might be fine for fantasy literature and popular novels but is rarely acted upon, so the appeal of phone sex escapes them. To some degree their concern is valid; more effective intervention would look to the creation of the demand rather than the inevitable supply once the demand exists.

Most women have an aversion to prick teasing. Men may bleat about being victims of it, but on the whole women think this is unbecoming—even dangerous—and to many of them this service would appear to be the ultimate tease. To dissuade them of this opinion, you have to explore the masturbation element and the ability of men to adapt to reality and, conversely, to their imagination, which allows disembodied sex to physically move them.

Some women prefer to believe that the sex industry doesn't exist; thus the men in their lives (spouse/brother/son) aren't potential participants, hence she need not consider this side of them nor the corresponding (or contrasting) side in her. Characterizing men as horny all the time is one thing; admitting they actually spend real money on it is something else. The heart of the matter is discounting the real drives in people and how those drives are manipulated.

Many women don't realize that phone sex can be fun. The guys are usually in a good mood, full of vim and vigor, and ready to talk. If they weren't allowed to stimulate themselves overtly, they would still consider the opportunity to have a frank discussion valuable. (They will glean images for later fantasy and/or maybe learn something to help their actual relations.)

The operators who have proven reliable don't want to meet the men. Either they can't simply because their families/interests don't allow the time or because they are so vastly different from their description on the line it would be a shock to any caller they met. Contrary to the stereotype, not all are fat/old women with deceptively beautiful voices, although some are. Most have boyfriends/spouses who don't mind other guys desiring their mate as long as they can't actually get to them. Pay-to-stay-at-home is a big motive, as is a weekly paycheck.

"...turns on my lesbian fantasies, to feel that lacy slip against your warm skin, those silky stockings under my hand as I touch your thigh, I kiss your lips, run my hands through your hair. The lingerie itself turns us on, doesn't it, for you to wear it and for me to see you in it? And hidden there for my secret pleasure is that big cock, isn't it? Throbbing and huge in those silky-slick panties. My prettiest boy, my darling, you know how it turns me on that you trust me."

"No one else knows."

"Jim, why should they? Is it relevant, are they trying to get you off? Do they care if your cock aches? I understand simply because I *do* understand. Who cares *why* it works if it does? All your life you've been fascinated by women's underwear, with the goal of getting them out of it, right? Stealing peeks of it, dreaming of it, feeling it on women when you first touched their bodies. Of course this stuff has erotic associations."

"But I like to *see* myself *in* it, for God's sake!"

"You're probably in front of the mirror, right? A vision of loveliness except the big bulge in the crotch of your slip, right?"

"Well, yeah, that's about it."

"Tell me, Jim, do you like what you see? Tell me."

"Yes."

"So, what's the problem?"

"It bugs me, I guess. I don't want to like it."

"Good observation. OK. You can give it up and let it haunt you or you can try to extinguish it by letting it flare up and then burn out…see? I'm just saying, OK, you want to get dressed up in ladies lingerie and see yourself in the mirror. OK. So, do it. Big deal. The world is still spinning. You are a healthy young man. It is time to explore; denial is probably the worst way to deal with an obsession. Now, listen, cutie pie, you're almost out of time."

"I'll call back in a little while."

"You look in the mirror and think of me behind you, wrapping my arms around you from the back, feeling your bra beneath the slip, rubbing up against your ass, my prettiest boy, sweet and innocent, so different than the beast inside, the hard-fucking woman-loving man you are…"

"You always know what to say."

"I say what's in my heart, baby. Talk to you later."
Click.

"This is Sweet Talkers. My name is Jamie and I'll be here until

5:00. After that you can talk to Stacy; you just missed Rosalie, she was here until midnight...there's always someone here to talk to you.... Hello, this is Jamie...if you feel like talking, just say hi, then you can fall back on the pillow...baby doll, I know you're out there...now, come on, let me know you're out there...oohh, you're a stubborn one. Well, darling, I hope I luck onto a topic you like—I'll never know what you want if you don't tell me...I might talk about eating pussy when you want to hear about fucking cunt...and I'd hate to disappoint you...it's late at night, we're all alone, no reason to be shy with me, hell, I'm practically naked, stroking myself, smiling into the mirror...I like what I see: round, firm breasts with pointy nipples, black patch of pubic hair, curly, long, soft, my legs spread wide, this firm juicy pussy open wide, waiting for a hard cock like yours...I'd take it from you, honey, take it all, take it deep...sweet cock in my hole...push it hard, harder...I want it all, all of it...such a good dick, stroking in deep, filling me up, letting me have it..."

"Take it, you bitch!"

"Ride me, you fucker, get on top and stick it to me, force it deep between my legs, feel that cunt clench tight around your dick, milking the come, nothing like it. Ride your bitch."

"Bitch, you beautiful bitch."

"Hot bitch, good fucking, ride me, baby, let me have it."

"Turn over, on your hands and knees. Show me, show me."

"She-bitch, spread for you, let the sight of it inflame you, you jam forward, your belly at her ass, cock in her hole, reach around and crush those boobs in your hand, mama's breasts, bitch tits, big and heavy. All the while you shove that cock forward, really push it, use your ass, push with it, shove it."

"I'm making you hot—you're going to come."

"I'm going to come, fucker, you feel my ass getting tight, my moans are low in my throat, I'm out of control, humping back at you, wild for your cock. I'm so close, so close to coming, do me, darling, come on, finish it, make it happen, make me come, give me pleasure, share that cock."

"Here I come, bitch, you beautiful bitch."

"I'm your bitch, baby, your bad girl, wants your cock, takes your cock, eats it up, fuck-fuck-fucks it. Yes, that's it, spill it, shoot it for me, pump that come up out of your cock for me, let it go, feel it pumping, that's my man. Empty it out, sweetheart, let it go, such a good cock."

"Got it."

Click.

Dead times on the line are odd. Like a firefighter, you never know if it'll be five minutes or an hour before the next alarm. You have to stay alert, but not tire yourself in case a real call comes in…you can usually hear a caller coming on due to the machine's background noise. There is no warning beep or anything, it's just experience and the sound of some pretty subtle clicks and whirs. In the dead times you're supposed to speak up, introduce yourself, be inviting, but twenty minutes of that and you feel like the last living soul on the planet. Some times of the day are slow as molasses; others click right along. I like late nights because the callers are usually talkative and relaxed; the pre-work jerk-offs tend to get right down to business while the dinner-hour callers are for the most part the slowest to come. You just never know…that next call could be a live one!

Working at home offers an operator certain advantages. First of all, she is in a safe location with familiar objects; she can feel confident and expansive. She doesn't have to worry about commuting or buying clothes or including time to dry her hair after a shower before work; she can sit in her favorite chair, lounge around in her well-worn robe, have a pot of homemade coffee on hand. Lie back and yackety-yak. Indulge herself in those romance novels she never found time to read…think up new ways to spend the extra money.

If her home environment is chaotic, she may have some trouble establishing the required peace and privacy necessary to the job. Kids are one problem, men another. Maybe she has a housemate who plays the piano or a dog that barks. One operator lived near a popular dock, and the motorboats made it hard for her to hear at times. It is sometimes difficult, but we consider it a part of their performance; if we hear distractions in the background, we know the callers hear them too. At a premium price, the callers deserve exclusive attention.

One annoying error the operators make is having people with them (sometimes operator-friends visit each other and toss the phone back and forth) which, from one point of view isn't gruesome, as there are periods of inactivity. But unfortunately the sounds of a new caller are so subtle that when the operator is gabbing she can miss it. Her job is to be 100 percent available, whether there is a caller audible or not, and we are quick to explain that we require a solitary sense between the caller and operator, as if they were connected.

A technological pain in the ass is the call-waiting feature that signals another call. We ask operators to disable the feature. These ladies are paid by the hour, not by the call. They are compensated for instant availability, which can be achieved only by constant attention to the line. Quiet activities like handicrafts and light reading (e.g., you can put it down), journal writing, manicures, puzzles, and daydreaming are all fine; we don't expect them to twiddle their thumbs for hours at a time.

Our hourly rate exceeds the going rate of downtown clerical work for the generally skilled. The average part-time operator earns between $90 and $180 a week, a nice boost to her financial situation. It isn't a fortune, but it is fair compensation, considering that much of the time is spent accomplishing her own pursuits at our expense. For instance, I wrote this book.

We also pay by the week, another advantage. A little money in your pocket at the end of every week can really smooth things in a budget; it allows a bit of maneuvering room for the weekend. For some it represents one big monthly item—car payment or rent—which frees up their "real" income for living. We mail the checks, unless they want to pick them up after noon on Wednesday at my house. If requested, veteran employees may receive pay advances, deducted from their next check(s). We've never messed around with the payroll. (We promised to pay on Fridays, voluntarily took to mailing checks on Wednesdays, so they'd arrive on Fridays, then felt bad we mailed them "late" one Thursday out of fifty-two.) We are serious about paying promptly—no one likes their earnings delayed by administrative crap or management failure.

Which brings us to the money side. We don't know where

the money goes; we are paid our management fee and payroll/adver-
tising expenses. We can track the number of calls, and now, with
new equipment, the actual connected minutes. But that is only a
gross approximation of actual income because we don't know
(a) what portion of collected charges the phone company retains,
    but rumor has it between 5 and 40 percent;
(b) the percentage of collection, although the grapevine pegs it
    as low as 50 percent;
(c) the costs of doing business other than our fees and expens-
    es to our corporate owners—e.g., the cost of the suite which
    houses the equipment;
(d) the access charges and technical support costs associated
    with the high-tech wiring;
(e) taxes and licensing fees.

But we do know that even if they got 75 percent of 75 percent
of the connected minutes, they wouldn't be churning income dollars through this particular line.

[Note: The following is a rough guesstimate, for general informational purposes, and is not provided as an auditable document.] In a twenty-four-hour period we may have anywhere from
125 to 500 calls, connected from one minute to ten, average
5.2, depending on the day and depending on our advertising.
At one dollar per minute, that is anywhere from $600 to $2,500
per day of potential income. If 75 percent is collected, of which
we get 75 percent, then $1,000 of potential income would be
$562.50 of actual gross income, minus expenses like payroll and
other costs listed above. There is a pure income potential of
$7,200/day, which is our five party lines engaged twenty-four
hours a day at one dollar per minute. Costs are fixed, so net
income rises in direct relation to increased traffic. We have the
machinery and the operator waiting whether or not callers call, to
assure we are always there when they do call.

Our corporate contacts are business people. They must see a
profit or a way to use any loss to offset other profits. They elect
to continue—which, in context of their success overall, indi-
cates that this operation fits into their master plan for now. There
are family ties to my partner which may nudge them to continue this line where, with another manager, they might not. They

run general "chat" lines primarily, and we may shift in that direction as time passes, de-emphasizing the overt sex. But that would be an entirely different enterprise.

"Jamie, do you remember me? This is Tony. I called you three times last Friday night."

"Sure, Tony. How's that broken leg?"

"I get a walking cast next week. I can finally get out of bed."

"Gee, I hope you'll go back and visit it once in a while…"

"Ha-ha. The way I feel, if I never see another bed, it's fine with me. I'm going to do all my screwing on the couch from now on. I hate beds."

"I'm lying on the floor, on my stomach, that pretty ass is in plain view. Tight blue panties barely cover the cheeks. Wish you could get over here and spank me, Tony, get me over your knee, feel that flesh beneath the palm of your hand."

"Jamie, get out that dildo—you know the one."

"The anal one? Sure, honey. You got yours?"

"Ready, baby. Now, go on, you know what I want."

"Slide your dildo in, and as you do, think of mine going up my butt, think of that tight hole resisting the dildo, just like yours…now come on, baby, relax, it feels good, my ass clenches, I force myself to relax. It feels so good, come on, Tony, take it slow, all the way in, yeahh, that's my baby."

"Ohh, Jamie, pretend it's my cock in your ass."

"Pretend that dildo is much bigger, made of flesh, full of come…think of it forcing itself into my hole, I'm open for you, that dildo got me ready, now your dick slides right in. I'm tight but you fit so good, feel so good, you know, you've got one up your own ass, you're taking it in, imagining how I'd feel with your dick inside me, filling me up. Now move that dildo in and out, slowly, slowly and pretend you're fucking my ass, my luscious ass."

"Oh, yes, my precious, yes, take it from your bad boy."

"Yes, Tony is my bad boy, my assfreak, that cock would feel so good, deep and hot in my ass, buggering your pretty girl, taking her ass and making it yours. Now shove that dildo deep, take it all in, come on, Tony, Tony, take that dildo up your ass."

"Yes, it feels good, like I would feel inside you, up your ass, Jamie. I'd be deep in your ass, wouldn't I?"

"Thrust up to the hilt, all the way, you bad boy, making your bitch take it this way, bad...such a bad boy."

"My bitch, my ass-fucking darling, oh, my ass is so hot, my cock is rock hard, ohhh, ohhh, I can feel it, I can really feel it!"

"Great, baby, finish it, give it to me, come on."

"Oh, Jamie, you're the best, I think I love you."

"I love you, too, Tony...roll over and dream of me, darling."

Click.

"Doesn't that fruit shit turn you off, really?"

"Putting him down won't raise you in my eyes. Quite the opposite. Now, shall we start over? This is Jamie."

"Fred. And, come on, a dildo up *his* ass?"

"You ever butt-fucked anyone?"

"Women, yeah..."

"Basic anatomy's the same for him, for you, for me, a tight hole, the right sized dildo and some privacy...some people enjoy it, whether you can believe it or not."

"Don't you ever do it the regular way?"

"You mean missionary position for five minutes, that's what you like? Nah, I'm saving up those for when I'm old and lazy."

"You're pissed, aren't you?"

"I guess so. I feel like that guy's a friend of mine and you've insulted him, it's hard to get comfortable. Maybe you ought to call back when there's another operator on. After seven, OK? No big deal."

"Oh, well, sure. Yeah, OK."

Click.

Men masturbate more often, with more ritual, for more reasons than most women and many men will admit. That is one reason this business is misunderstood. Dial-a-dream is not a substitute for intercourse; it is the enhancement of an essentially solitary mental pursuit to which phone-y sex is particularly suited. Seeing dancers (for instance) requires getting dressed, leaving home, being observed while responding to the stimulation, then driving home, getting undressed, and trying to re-create the sensation…tele-erotic females are right there in his bed with him, in a caller's ear, sharing a creative experience with him, yet leaving him free of obligation. Nothing for him to worry about—just a sweet talker who appreciates him and charges that are masked by the ubiquitous phone company envelope detailing his other personal contacts. (Why do you think wiretapping is illegal? Phones are a private resource of the adult individual like closets and cars.)

Once you admit the frequency of men's masturbation, it isn't difficult to understand why a business like ours flourishes. It is *not* a cover for prostitution; it isn't a device to con men out of credit card numbers. It is what it is…no more and definitely no less. Denying a fact doesn't disprove it; bottling up one outlet forces the creation of another. Passion is a nice word for lust, for the drive, more intense than desire; the human need to express this portion of their psychosexual energies.

We have a lot of repeat business. Far from being disappointed at the simple service, the callers seem delighted. They are accepted and listened to, encouraged to speak their minds. There is an air of collusion and secrets, breathy pleas, deep sighs of satisfaction and wonder. They could spend more money going to a club and have less of a chance of such frank and honest contact with a live female. But it's all talk! They *want* to talk; they *pay* to talk!

Married men call (at least they claim to be married). Some say their wives fulfill their fantasies; others do not feel this way. The variation in response is interesting in and of itself, as in the old joke of the husband saying, "She never wants sex, maybe three-four times a week," and the wife saying, "He's always after sex, every other day!" Again, expectation determines satisfaction: if you are set for a $30,000 windfall, you might be "disappointed" if it were "only" $15,000; if you expect to lose your hand and lose "only" a finger, isn't that "good"? Sometimes the married man sneaks the calls (especially if he's the type to control the money so she never sees the phone-bill evidence). Some lucky husbands have their wives' cooperation ("Baby, let's budget fifty dollars a month for phone fantasy"; "OK, darling, and how about fifty dollars for something special for me each month?"). Some husbands aren't sure what their wives would think (which is most curious of all to me—shouldn't they have some idea?).

No matter what you think of lust in the heart, there is no denying the passion of their desire. They could not fake the yearning in their voices, after hearing hundreds of hours of men's sexual dreams and accomplishments, their fascination with feminine form and feeling, their desire to possess in some manner the loving energy of partner(s)ship. I am *not* repelled by them, as has been suggested as the inevitable result of doing this sort of work. We dodge the seamier side of the business by emphasizing a sweet-talking service. We don't intend to add to the negative imagery out there, but by word and attitude convey an accepting, passionate atmosphere where dreams can be discussed in detail. As such, it might be easier to preserve a sense of balance; the topic may be cocks, but the voices are human. The callers are touchingly ordinary.

I believe operators must have had good contacts with men in their lives in order to do the job well, which doesn't mean they have all been deliriously and continuously happy, but rather that they are sexually confident and understanding of human desires. Like any courtesan, successful phone friends project an air of interest and challenge; they allow the man to define his dream-space and their place in it.

A bad operator can be too friendly, attempting to extend her phone personality into a real-life meeting. But all she would discover is that the "person" sought is the phone persona and not the flesh-and-blood being that creates the voice which embodies the fantasy. When you put a face on an imaginary character, it disappoints people; their Cleopatra wouldn't look like that. It is the operator's job to be unreal, fantastic, a character.

I doubt anyone ever expects to see me after reading my work, or hearing it…. I'm always shorter/taller than they thought, and it surprises them when I'm not funny, or when I am. I've corresponded with people for years who couldn't pick me out of a lineup. I'm very aware of the actual presence of another *mind* in other people's lives, it is not all that different on the phone lines, where half the time I'm doing monologue entertainment anyway. "Jamie, it's me again, Jim. I'm all dressed up now, like you said I should be."

"Tell me, you beautiful man, what did you decide to wear for me this time?"

"I bought a red bra and garter belt, fishnet stockings, and of course my black heels."

"Don't lie to me now. You came in the car after you bought those new things, didn't you?"

"I kept thinking of you, that I'd call you and well, I looked down and my jeans were wet—I hadn't even felt it."

"You just vented some steam, I don't call that coming! We're on an adventure together. It's new, babe, it's sharpest now, you've waited a long time; enjoy yourself, have fun with it, it'll fade, become less important…it's the things we deny ourselves which haunt us, don't you know?"

"Jamie, really, you would fuck a man who did this?"

"Would fuck, have fucked, hope to fuck again. Known a couple guys…the first was awkward because I didn't understand, you know? That's all…you gotta admit the stereotype is bad, but the reality is quite different: I've had the holy fuck banged out of me by a guy in a slip! But each of my guys admitted it was a phase, the desire came over them and once they indulged it, it faded. Transsexuals are not looking for a girl like me…"

"I must be in bloom or something. I walk around at work and wonder what the guys would say. My God, I lay brick! No jokes, please."

"I think that's part of the thrill. You've always been a naughty boy, secretly sneaking into your mom's panty drawer after hitting a home run at Little League."

"How did you know?"

"Educated guess…you like ladies, like their underwear, have imprinted it with sexual symbolism…you're probably healthy and fit and actually look fine in the stuff, that hard cock jutting out from the garter belt, that flat belly below the bra, long lean legs in high heels, essentially attractive, am I right? You look good in men's clothes, no clothes and—surprise, surprise—women's clothes."

"I can get partners for the usual stuff, but not one I can ask to unhook my bra for me!"

"Honey, we're out here. Rare, but all the more precious when you find us. I know it's tough. But at least you can talk about it, and that's half the battle. It's not as weird as you think."

"Jamie, Jamie, Jamie...if only you were real."

"Yeah, isn't it amazing what they're doing with robots these days..."

"You know what I mean—you're better than a friend, you're like a psychiatrist with a sexy voice."

"Well, get on my couch, pretty boy, your time is running out...."

"Uh, Jamie?"

"Hi, this is Jamie. Do you have a name?"

"Fred, you know, the guy from before, you didn't like something I said, remember, you said I could call back later."

"Sure I remember. Sorry if I came on strong, but I have to follow my instincts, things didn't sound right to me. Delilah will be here after seven, you can call back then...sorry you wasted another buck."

"I called you, I mean, you know, I heard you the first time. Now, come on, were you really pissed 'cause I called a guy you don't even really know a fruit?"

"Why pay to insult somebody? You can walk down the street and do it free, unless you're worried you'll get popped for it. That man pays the same kind of cash you do. From here you look the same to me—he deserves my consideration."

"That's what got me—you stood up for a guy like that! All right, I can respect that. I was out of line. I can think it's wacky, but I'm not supposed to say so."

"That's one big step on the road to maturity, Fred. May the rest of your journey be less expensive..."

"So, what do you look like?"

"Long-legged, wide-hipped, big-breasted woman."

"Could you repeat that?"

"Long-legged, the kind that wrap right around your ass; wide-hipped for a long, comfortable ride; firm round titties to press against your chest."

"I *thought* that's what you said. Boy, do I have a picture of you! You ever try it on top?"

"I'll crawl right up on you, babe, slide these knees around your hips and tease that cock with my moist firm pussy, rock back until my ass is on your thighs. You can watch my boobs while I fuck your brains out."

"From the back?"

"Like a dog, if you like, hands and knees, or do you mean standing up, legs braced wide, bent at the waist?"

"The first."

"You want to take a bitch, grab a handful of hair and yank her head back, feel her ass on your belly, force that cock deep inside."

"Push, let me push."

"I can take it, baby, I want it from you, don't hold back, I can take it, come on, show me, shove it, lover, flex that muscle, move for Jamie, push it, push it in, all the way in."

"Say more! Say more!"

"I want your cock, Fred, sweet and hot, Fred…all of it, don't hold back, come on, you fucker, you like it tough, you want it hard, push, you fucker, bang me, come on, fuck me, come on, do it, don't hold back, I can take it."

"Ohh, yeah, good talking, yeah, oh, yeah…oh, yeah."

"Glad you called back?"

"This was worth it. I must say I never paid to get lectured about my manners before. But I won't forget it. Gotta go, Jamie. 'Bye."

"Farewell, Fred, you're all right… Hi, this is Jamie. Anybody feel like talking? Or listening? I'm right here, baby, waiting for you."

Click.

Many of the new operators chicken out on their first shift. They call with either ridiculous excuses or firm pronouncements that they simply cannot do the job. They've heard the line (it's part of the training process), and we've had talks in which I've introduced most sexual topics known. But suddenly they get the shakes. I can understand, I felt the same way; anybody with a new job or who has had a date can understand. It's just performance anxiety. I suggest they do an hour for me while I hunt up a substitute. I call a friend and have him call in and do a gentle but good scene. I get on the line 45 minutes later and see if she can hang on just a bit longer since I'm waiting for her substitute to call back or else I'll take the line myself. They almost always volunteer to stay. If they don't, they don't belong there. I never ever push, but I tell them if it's just nerves, they ought to at least try it.

The phrase "satisfied customer" often comes up when they explain to me why they decided to stay after all. And it isn't always just my confederate caller. These women often turn into great operators because they care about it in the first place. Their vivid imagination of failure quickly changes to a vision of success.

How does it feel to talk to strangers about sex? Fine, thank you. You have to remember the essential privacy of the service, the fact most men are stretched out on their very own couch or lounging on their personal bed when they call. They are at home for the most part (I quit sweet-talking a caller if I figure out they aren't footing the bill themselves). The callers have usually been preparing themselves for the call, psyching themselves up (some pump up their cock in advance to save money). The nervousness in face-to-face conversations is generally lacking; the intoxication of solitude adds to the sexiness of the situation; the operator *could* be anybody. I coax them into admitting what's on their minds: they long to lick a breast, they've got pussy on their minds, would I pretend he was my boyfriend peeking into the bathroom as I get ready for bed; if he put it in my butt would I pretend to resist him, saying it was way, way, *way* too big? These calls are easier to deal with: I have somewhere to start.

The harder calls are the type who say, "Oh, well, I don't know...." when you ask what's on their mind, what turns them on, is there anything special I could discuss....

Either way, I'm so used to describing the acts of love that I can close my eyes and it isn't me, it's memories, it's Jamie with the inexhaustible supply of desire, able to inspire the man to a great performance. I've gotten dizzy when I've solo-spun the fantasy with very little interaction, a breathless silent concentration from the caller is palpable, but offers no relief in the sense I just spin and spin and spin...

We get calls from workplaces ("Gotta go, here comes the boss!"), one car-phone call from a man watching joggers in a city park who was very excited by the long, striding legs of shorts-clad runners; they call to run up the bill on a roommate who has the phone in his name but is dodging other expenses. They're playing a joke on a newlywed friend by getting these charges on the phone for the new bride to find. (This particular trio conducted a great nonarousing sex ethics discussion with me for several sessions' worth while their soon-to-be-married buddy went for [more] beer. The three of them were taking turns with the two phones in the love nest. I believed their promise to pay the bill when the joke was over plus dinner for the wedded ones, to which I was invited but, alas, had to decline).

"You slut! How can you do this job? You might as well walk the streets."

"You kidding, lady? It's much cozier in here. Hey, guys, we got us a tight-ass mama here. Say hello, tightie! I have the feeling there's some bible verse coming, something from Leviticus, perhaps; hang up till she runs out of money...about a minute from now."

"*Hussy.* I'll tie you up all day and night."

"Sounds kinky! What you mean to say, if I might show some charity, is you want to tie up my five phone lines. Right, tightie? Let's talk about your fantasy. At a dollar a minute per line, that's $7,200 a day...the meter's running, tightie, so...you want to talk, or what? It's obvious your mind is made up. I think it's made up of rock, but, hey, you're paying for my next car, so let's not argue. I think I like you."

"Liar, it is not really that expensive."

"It's a buck a minute, tightie, and here on the planet Earth there are sixty minutes to an hour, twenty-four hours a day, that's $1,440...then we've got those five lines. You better hang up and call your accountant, have her figure it out for you. Can't rack that up on your rosary, hon."

Click.

"...is Jamie, if you feel like talking..."
Click.

We've tried to get a handle on the local ordinances and statutes that might apply to this business. You can't just walk into the attorney general's office and ask for a pamphlet on phone-sex rules; you have to guide yourself by the general tone of other sex-oriented businesses, read the stuffy language, and try to imagine how a judge might apply that. Read between the lines once you find the lines to read. Lawyers are cautious, they have reputations at stake, and I've had trouble finding one with the right expertise. I finally found one young lawyer who will do the research for me, as long as I promised never to associate his name with the business.

One ethical consideration for a lawyer is the idea of "enabling" an illegal activity: i.e., aiding a client to break the law, rather than using the law to shape the client's behavior. I make it clear that I want to find out the law to comply with it. I can structure this business any way I like: we can put on sterner warnings, provide more delay between the connection and the graphic language (although in a party-line situation, of course, the caller joining midstream is dumped right into the hot stuff). The closest description I can find in (what I think are) the regulations is "operating a moral nuisance," like an X-movie theater, and those are not outright prohibited, merely controlled in every aspect from location to hours.

We don't solicit the callers other than the discreet print ads in adult magazines. They dial us up and can disconnect at any time, stopping the charges; we can't call them back, chase them down, harass or annoy them. It takes a court order to even try to get their number (but it can be done); they seem to want to talk to women about sex, direct and uncensored, in a fantasy situation. If it *is* illegal, it probably shouldn't be.

I sometimes worry about legal action; good intentions don't always sway justice, but a spotless record ought to help. My main worry is for the operators. I don't want them hassled, and if the fat hits the fire, I'm taking the blame. But, in all honesty, I don't believe this is wrong. It might be a statement of the evolutionary progress of our race; but as long as we're still using sex to sell stuff, people will turn to less-than-animate partners. In the face of relentless stimulation of a fundamental urge, people will always be drawn to release. Besides, we operators are really women, and we're really there. Yet we really can't bug them. What a perfect outlet for certain people or certain times!

The primary advantage of phone sex for the caller seems to be the ability to control access to their life; it is a one-way street down which they travel when, if, and as often as they wish. We can never intrude on them, instigate a connection, or summon sexual imagery uninvited. There is no guarantee that the caller can get a specific operator at a particular time but there will be an operator on at all times.

Fantasy is a necessary element in our culture because much of what is "offered" to us conceptually is not actually available: the mere facts that advertising is an industry and promotion is a career prove our fascination with illusion and promise. We know the gorgeous gal/guy doesn't deliver the can of engine oil and a darling kid doesn't pop out of your cereal box; those models are selected because they are extraordinary.

As a phone-fantasy service, we act as a release of tension, a break from the real. The caller may project any image, request any role in a sexual drama, act out verbally, indulge himself; it's Walter Mitty on the telephone. In its simplest form, it is a harem of female voices and styles, a private tool to be used in accordance with personal taste.

People like to talk; the sociability of this service is its redeeming quality. I am told so many stories and hear so many memories and dreams that I have become like a personal therapist, creating an environment where directness and brevity are prized; venting ideas to a responsive being can create changes in thought. Timed right, even a casual remark can be pivotal, so when the caller is sexually reflective and the operator is willing to offer an opinion, it often hits the spot. Sometimes its value is in the unwitting reiteration of advice from another source; when heard from a stranger out of context it can be striking.

More than once after rendering an opinion to him, a caller has said to me, "You sound just like my [wife] [friend] [family]." I remind him that I'm probably quite unlike his [wife] [friend] [family], yet I have arrived at a similar conclusion. I do admit it might be in his presentation of a situation, and when I do offer a conflicting interpretation, some callers are fascinated by that; it is fresh information to be sifted. Even if my idea is ultimately rejected, it can serve to strengthen their own view. Sexual ethics are so rarely discussed that almost any opening of the topic is valued.

My "survey" of the male mind is limited by geography, by time and place, by the nature of the business itself, but still and all it does represent a peek into the locker room, a tape recorder under their beds. Each contact is of interest and, when cataloged one after another, they are fascinating to me.

Noon to 4:00 P.M. on a Wednesday in February:
    12:02 Relieve Helen; 12:04 silent; 12:06 silent; 12:16 silent; 12:29–30 how's your pussy?; 12:32–33 silent; 12:42 silent; 12:59–1:08 interview style, graphic technique; 1:??–12 do you do girls? same caller, slow to interact; 1:13 silent; 1:19–26 5'10", 165, has girlfriend, masturbation; 1:28–29 new caller, couple of questions; 1:30–31 blow job; 1:34–35 background ahems to a provocative but discreet come-on from me; 1:36–40 1st call, kind of different, might like a moaner; 1:47–56 hard to hear, either "what sex" or "butt sex"; 1:57–2:03 Hawaii, lucky there, sexy talk until he thanks me a lot; multi-listeners through both connections, all scatter when talker departs; 2:10–19 young, kissing style, sensuous, lots of girls, good body, work out (well-defined), great "cut up" stomach, 5'9", 165, 8 percent body fat, bone hard, likes long sessions, quickies OK; 2:20–27 no jackoff, problem is he likes sex, gets too wound up, b.j. standing up, doesn't eat out unclean crotch, bathe in oils to massage; 2:34–43 creeeak, silent!; 2:36–43 hello, sexy talk with listeners, let's all scream together?; 2:44 hello, click; 2:49–58 called back, love dog, use images later, big dick is a problem (nine inches), likes to listen; 2:59–3:08 fuck scene, big dick, relate to real fuck, needs wide-hipped, deep-cunted female, loves to hear about big cunts (hand fit the glove); 3:27–?? silent; 3:18–25 pretend to be wife being eaten by someone else since he won't

but then he does; 3:29–33 one talker, not much feedback, too silent; 3:34 someone still on??; 3:35–37 cock in hand, would gladly feed it to me; 3:??-28 silent or hang-up; 3:53–4:02 was male model for bachelorette party, six gals, 6'2", blond, 180, twenty-five- to thirty-year-old "audience," couple of hours, tie on bed for pics but stuck thermometer in his prick, didn't hurt at all (!?), (bride-to-be didn't play); 4:00 Sybil arrives, asks what's a gigolo? Caller said it wasn't a man who seduces women for their money or prestige...reassured her he was wrong.

The callers are not asking to butcher babies while dressed in a rubber teddy; they are not requesting girlish images; not very often are we asked to be submissive and, if so, we don't submit to pain or humiliation. We are asked to hold the men, to kiss them, to wrap our lips around their dicks, to lick their nipples, to finger their asses, to open ourselves, to show ourselves, to ask for what we want. They want variety on schedule, fit around other important activities like work, school, play. The wish is for something to happen to them, some sexual adventure, some bolt of erotic lightning, an encounter. They outright admit these ideas haunt them, tainting nonsexual times with their insistent imagery. Once vented, there is a quiet cycle until stray urges and building desires combine into that cloud of want which obscures their vision and muddies their dreams (depending on age and nature this cycle may be six to eighty-four hours in duration).

In an attempt to personalize the voice they hear, they ask about the operator's body. There is a fantasy blind between us, and lying takes place on both sides. In truth, as long as the description is of a healthy happy individual it will please the listener, any who have fetishistic desires such as big-boobed blondes will project that body onto the operator no matter how she describes herself. They like breasts and butts, crotches and thighs, smiles and whispers, and delighted sighs. In some cases, the caller pursues such detail that it is obvious he is actually listening to the description: how long is your hair, are your breasts round or oval, do you shave your legs, describe your nipples. Many disclaim an interest in the perfect female, they prefer the real ones, knowing that *Playboy*-style women are culled from thousands of applicants, seeking the photogenic, not necessarily the sexually talented, and he is more likely to encounter the more ordinary female with whom he can feel kinship.

"So, like I was saying, I need a woman who can share herself, not hold back, not make me hold back. I have so much energy."

"It's scary to show yourself to people. When girls are little, we're told not to trust anybody anywhere…then at twenty-one we're supposed to be able to differentiate between strangers… I don't know, it seems difficult from both sides."

"But, Jamie, you women get to do the easy part—it's us guys that have to do the calling and the asking and the paying."

"Yeah, she just spends money getting your attention in the first place! Then keeping it, against all natural odds."

"OK, OK, so what do we do about this? I mean, you and I hit it off just fine. Why can't I meet you?"

"You did, Joel, I'm your phone-friend."

"You know what I mean, I'd love a lady like you, I really would. I'd make you so happy."

"You already do! I'm honest with you, we have fun, you reconsider things I've said all week long. You have to accept that not all your friendships are physical, but they can add to the physical affairs you have."

"Jamie, every time I blast a woman I'll be thinking of you, and you damn well know it."

"Joel, I want you to think about me, especially if it helps you love that woman a little better. Lovemaking has its cycles: start slow, ease yourself in, then dip in deep, don't be afraid to use your ass—it ain't just for sitting on! Just remember to start slow and open her up for both your pleasure and hers; let her juice flow for a while, take your time, then rock those hips, honey, and wind that baby out, shift to your higher gears, you know?"

"I must sound stupid to you. I just didn't want to hurt anybody, but, God, I really want to *move* sometimes. You're the first woman who's ever convinced me she wasn't delirious when she was yelling, 'Harder, harder.'"

"Women are stronger than you think, doll, you can drop them with a fist to the face, sure, but they can take your 185 pounds pounding between their legs for hours, it's the anatomy…it feels good to take a man. Strength is sexy when you mix it with control."

"I better go, I'll talk to you next week, babe."

"I know you will. And I'll be here for you."

Click.

"On your knees, bitch."

"Yes, master."

"Raise that ass. You know what to do."

"My purple gown is stretched tight, you can see the mounds of flesh, big ass, heavy tits, I'm at your feet, your best bitch."

"I'm going to watch you fuck a friend of mine. He mentioned he was horny and I told him you'd gladly help him out, for my sake."

"I do what I'm told, master."

"He's watching you now. Tell me what you feel."

"I'm proud to be your slave, sir, glad you think I'm good enough to entertain your friend. I know he likes the sight of your woman, submissive, obedient. He can see my sexy body, and he knows you control it. You make me lift my gown and bare my flesh to him. It excites me that you are watching. Your friend likes what he sees."

"Use that big dildo."

"The plastic feels cool on my hot cunt. I tease my hollow with it, you both watch it disappear into my hole. Your friend is getting very excited by the sight of your slave-bitch, on her knees, you reach down and pull the gown off me, I'm naked, moving the dildo between my legs. I hear your friend open his zipper and I shudder. I can just imagine what he's thinking."

"Jamie, it's a big cock, the biggest you've ever seen."

"I can't see it, sir. I just feel a huge cockhead at my hole, bigger than the dildo, fleshy, and my cunt gushes with the thought of you making me take it. He's shoving it in but I'm still too tight; you tell him not to worry, your bitch will take it all."

"Get on the bed."

"On my back, knees up, big titties in that man's hands, and he's balling your bitch, master, he's using her…he's so big, but

I know you want me to have it, you want me to feel it moving in my body, and finally he's really balling me, I've got him! Your bitch is stealing that man's come right out of his proud prick."

"Take it, baby, take it out of him."

"Witchy-bitch magic...rob that man, absorb it, defuse it, control him, you watch him, master, he's surrendered to me...it is the woman who controls most men...even that big old cock weeps for me..."

"But you don't control me."

"Never you...you are the master."

"I...am...the...master..."

"I wait here for you."

"I...am...the...master..."

"You come when you want, where you want, it is yours to give away not mine to take. I wait, naked, your best bitch, the one who knows...."

"I....am...the...master!"

"Yes, yes, you are."

"Now. Yes, now. I am ready."

"I'm your slut, I've fucked many, many men, but I can't even remember them now. I think of you, your cock, your voice. I am yours, you control me, you make me wait, you give me away; always I am here for you, a loyal whore who understands a man like you, who can love you."

"Yes."

"Love you, I love you, I will always love you because I have always loved you."

"Love me."

"My man, my master, I am yours."

Click.

Some of the men become familiar. They are either memorably unique, like the booming-voiced black dude who always says hel-lo as if it were two words, or they quickly identify themselves. Miles, who likes boots; David, who wants to come down my throat. Some ask when they can reach me on the line again; others welcome me like an old friend when they discover by chance that I'm working when they happen to call. Others either don't remember me or pretend not to.

The regulars usually have a favorite scene or fantasy they replay again and again, always with the garter belt or the panties pulled down but not off...nipples between their teeth...fucking so hard their balls slap my crack...fingers in assholes...doggie style...my knees at my ears...some private trigger to the ultra-sexual images they replay for themselves.

It is illegal to sell sex, but it is legal to sell the *illusion* of sex. You can sell sex-oriented movies and cards and books and videos and music and dancers and strippers and various stimulatory attachments (both under, outer and inner wear), what you cannot sell is personal actual literal physical contact. We can provide illusions, we can imagine out loud the inevitable consequences of getting naked and rubbing up against each other, we can describe in the most graphic terms the subtle details of arousal and release. We cannot, by strict interpretation of the law, masturbate for/with the caller, but we can simulate the sounds of excitement. We cannot mislead them to believe there is a potential for contact; the fantasy wall is erected for our protection (and theirs, the scamming is much reduced when the transaction is rooted in the tele-wire network). We sell excitement.

The illusion of sex is valued by the caller in large part because he is accustomed to displaced arousal. He may be mounting his wife, but he's imagining a popular actress. He dates Ms. P and dreams of Mrs. V; he may never have sex with a certain woman who excites him but may consort with others who don't. Sexual projection is an effective means of stimulating a real response with an unreal expectation. His actual partner is unlikely to meta-morphose into his fantasy female (which is lucky for him because, in truth, few sex goddesses are satisfied with mortal males, so he's best served in a make-believe arena).

I think what surprised me most is the sheer number of devot-ed pussy-lickers there are out there. Now, maybe it is statistically disproportionate (e.g., more common) among men who will dial such a service (they are mouthy, after all)...but, even so, they want to dive down between my thighs and lick me until I'm screaming, dripping wet, pulsating. When I tell them I taste good, they sigh as if remembering the vintage of a favorite wine. If I mention the detail that I taste sweeter every time I come, they moan in agreement, visions of vaginas vivid in their minds.

I believe that many women miss the boat with their romances, never really understanding how to operate a man for their mutual advantage. In one sense, men need a lot of stimulation, collecting numerous images through their life; on the other hand, a single glimpse of a breast may haunt them, one word on the right lips will ring. Their view of sex is conditioned by the relentlessness of their own erections; unless suppressed by strain or depression, many men experience regular erections and have learned that even if they turn their minds from sex, their dicks will rise and throb, demanding stimulation and release. Yes, that pressure can be resisted, but sometimes it is psychosexually efficient to coax the frisky devil to cooperate with a bit of body massage. It's different: women get the itch, men get the ache.

Male pleasure is based on a tension-explosion cycle which is distinct from the female's cumulative sensations. A man is on a sliding board, climbing, climbing to the top for a glorious slide down; a woman is on a teeter-totter, up-down-up-down in an exhilarating shift of balance. No wonder there's confusion on the playground! The trick is to let the lady teeter-totter till she's dizzy, then let the man slide right into her...they'll both see stars.

"I'm back. It's me, Steve."

"Hi, buddy. What's happening in the video now?"

"The redhead is on her knees sucking the black dude while the white guy fingers her ass. She's got great tits, bouncy."

"That turn you on?"

"Oh, yeah, threesomes! It's my all-time fantasy."

"Pretend I look like the redhead, if you like. Imagine your hands on my body."

"Jamie, get on your back, OK?"

"OK, hold on, yeah, I'm on the bed, on my back. I'm naked."

"Lift your knees and spread them, wide, real wide, until it almost hurts, yes, spread 'em, I just want to look at your pussy. I stop the video at the cunt shots. I love women!"

Gift.Wrap Paris This Year.

Give gift subscriptions to Food & Wine for just $19.95. That's 44% off the newsstand price!

☐ **Yes!** Send Food & Wine gift subscriptions to the persons named below. My first gift subscription is $19.95 and each additional gift subscription is $17.95 each for one full year. Also, send a card in my name to announce my gift!

YOUR NAME _____

ADDRESS _____

CITY _____ STATE ____ ZIP ____

NAME _____

ADDRESS _____

CITY _____ STATE ____ ZIP ____

NAME _____

ADDRESS _____

CITY _____ STATE ____ ZIP ____

☐ PAYMENT ENCLOSED   ☐ BILL ME

Canadian orders add $8 plus 7% GST. If you need more room, attach a separate piece of paper.

Call our Holiday Hotline toll-free:
1-800-333-6569. ext. 243

Food&Wine

THE BEST OF PARIS

JJFC5

Food&Wine

"I've got a muscular pussy, pink-lipped, large and well-defined, with a thick patch of black pubic hair I keep trimmed."

"I could play with you for hours, like we could watch videos and I'd just stroke you."

"I get so wet, Steve, sticky-sweet and sexy. Run your finger down the slit, right into my secret hole, the one I show you…think of my hands on my thighs spreading wide for you so you can see it, feel it."

"I fast-forwarded to a come scene, Jamie, I've watched it a million times. She's masturbating on her back with her knees open, the camera is right there! You can see her whole body get rigid, she gets so close…I know what she's feeling!"

"Imagine me just like that with you as the camera. You are filming it for your imagination, you can see me open and inviting you closer, my cunt-hole is dripping I'm so excited, and my fingers are shoving my mound around, making my clit throb, my hips are lifting off the bed, you zoom in closer…"

"Ohhh, yeahhh, I zoom in closer…"

"You see it happen—you have captured it forever…"

"I watch it, close up, tight, you come in my face, right in my face, I can feel you come."

"Such a pretty pussy, she likes you."

"Ohh, I can't thank you enough, especially that zoom-thing, it was perfect."

"Darlin', you can direct me anytime. Remember me next time you're watching videos, OK?"

"You bet, Jamie, you bet I will. 'Bye, till next time."

Click.

"My name is Jamie. I'm right here waiting to talk to you. If you feel like talking, just say hi."

"Are you the only operator?"

"I'm on until seven. After that you could talk to Bridget."

"Is she older than you?"

"I don't know—you want something in particular?"

"I like a forty- to forty-five-year-old woman, I'm twenty-five."

"I'm thirty…probably too close in age, huh?"

"Well, do you have a business suit?"

"Listen to this: rose-red fitted skirt with matching jacket, sheer silk blouse, silver stockings, black heels, and nothing else. So elegant you know this woman does not work for her money."

"Yes, this could work. You'd invite me for drinks."

"I'd manage to press up against you when we are seated at the table. You'd sense my nipples, hard, under my blouse."

"You tell me you like young men."

"Young, yes, but a man…a man who pleases me, well-dressed and mannered, I could take you places."

"The opera."

"We'd hire a car. People in the lobby would stare. You are my young stud, the classic companion."

"Everybody knows…"

"It is so obvious: you are so young and I am so spoiled, we don't even have to touch each other, it is in the air around us."

"I would *never* let them see anything; they can imagine all they want, but our passion is our own."

"I can't wait to be alone with you. I want you, I don't have to say it, you read it in my eyes."

"We go to your penthouse. The minute we're alone you move into my arms, you are so beautiful, so mature…"

"You tremble, your desire is a flame in your belly, it has been burning for days, since I invited you to the opera."

"My time's almost up, I'm afraid we're about to get disconnected. Let me call you back, OK?"

"Have the maid show you in. I'll be waiting."

"Damn, you're good. Be right back."

Click.

SAMPLE 5-DAY SCHEDULE

	SONYA	SONYA	LIZ	HELEN	HONEY
MID-NIGHT	SONYA	SONYA	LIZ	HELEN	HONEY
1 AM	—	—	—	TAWNY	—
2 AM	HELEN	VICKI	—	—	—
3 AM	—	—	—	—	—
4 AM	—	—	JAMIE	—	HELEN
5 AM	—	—	—	LINDA	—
6 AM	DESIREE	JAMIE	—	—	—
7 AM	—	—	—	—	DESIREE
8 AM	CARLA	—	OPAL	OPAL	—
9 AM	—	HELEN	—	—	—
10 AM	—	—	GEORGIA	RITA	SONYA
11 AM	—	HONEY	—	—	—
NOON	HONEY	—	—	—	—
1 PM	—	—	OPAL	OPAL	MARY
2 PM	—	—	—	—	—
3 PM	—	SUSY	—	—	—
4 PM	JAMIE	—	DESIREE	VICKI	LIZ
5 PM	—	—	—	—	—
6 PM	—	RITA	—	—	—
7 PM	—	—	CHRIS	—	GEORGIA
8 PM	RITA	JILL	—	JILL	—
9 PM	—	—	—	—	JAMIE
10 PM	SONYA	—	HELEN	CARLA	—
11 PM	—	LIZ	—	—	—

The schedule never stabilizes. Operators shift all over the place, wanting time off, extra time, or trade time. Seven days a week, twenty-four hours a day…that's 168 hours divided among a dozen operators, the composition of which changes also. New voices help keep the regular callers interested, while the veteran operators keep me from going crazy.

The trick is to keep the ball in the air. The lady on the line really shouldn't leave until her replacement is there, ditto the replacement shouldn't dawdle as the previous operator may have serious plans to leave work on time. Dead-time is a bad thing, obviously; if you lose a caller the first time, he may never call back….

Short shifts keep the operators lively and provide variety on the line. Operators with long hours must break them up into four- and five-hour time slots. Even a two-hour break helps, and some operators like the short quick shifts; they can pick up eight of ten hours a week that way, a little spending money.

Imagine that you've been discussing sex for a few hours, talking about the way a lady can curl her hand "backward" around a penis so her palm is on the "inside" and her fingers play along the pulsing vein, a grip not natural for a man stroking himself; whispering to someone that he must lick your entire breast, the side as it swells from your ribs, that secret soft underside, the round smooth cleavage between the beauties, then press the jutting nipple inward with his strong flat tongue; telling some man that you want him to press that vibrator along the lips between your legs then just hold it there for the longest time; describing the sensation of being entered, ridden, riding. The better you do it, the more it affects you. If you really close your eyes and imagine sexual activities, sexual emotions, sexual positions, sexual successes, it is quite likely you'll be in a sexy mood.

"Yeah, well, I suppose you're right, I could just spend the money watching women I can't have instead of talking to one I can't meet…"

"So why not spend a little on each? Watch a video and tell me about it. You can be stimulated through your ears, baby."

"So I'm learning. You remind me of someone I used to know."

"Bring up those feelings, then, remember her."

"She was fantastic in bed, simply unbelievable; at the time we met I could count my conquests on the fingers of one hand. Damn, what a woman—named Marilyn. I'd call her on the phone and she'd tell me she was naked, ohh, how I'd howl for her."

"She probably loved it. I've always taken the time to send a little love to my guy if I can't see him in person—you know, just a reminder that somewhere someone wants him, specifically me!"

"Would you call me 'babe,' like she did?"

"Sure can, babe."

"And she'd always whisper, it sounded so sexy in the dark, I'd be stroking myself..."

"...is Jamie. If you feel like talking, just say hello..."
Click.

Callers with the "call waiting" feature on their phone have actually put me on hold, at a dollar a minute while answering an incoming call. I find that odd, don't you? Of course the clicks on their end are annoying, I'm sure. Besides, these are usually the chatty chums; they'll spend twenty dollars, fifty dollars on repeated calls. They are casual about the mounting charges as they gab.

Here's an odd thing. Once in a while, a caller with one of those phone lines that can "conference" multiple calls will connect to our service, then dial another live-line and let the operators meet head-on, each thinking they are on home turf, just to see what happens, most likely hoping that a cat fight results. I've learned to tell the other operator that since I can't dial and she can't dial, obviously somebody threw us together. Sometimes the guys prefer her to me or me to her and tell the other to hush and let the "hot" one talk, but it's usually so confusing that nothing much happens.

"...I have to dial back, Jamie. I don't want to be dropped right in the middle of my fantasy. Now, don't you go away."

"I'll be here, baby."
Click.

"Welcome back, baby."

"So, see, you're this department store clerk, OK?"

"I'll be selling wallets, ties, stuff like that."

"Oh, yeah, they always put the best ones there."

"When I reach into the display case to get the things you want to see, I bend very far forward and you can peek down my dress."

"But I'm afraid you'll catch me looking."

"I *do* catch you, but I just smile and bend even lower the next time, hold that pose, my round breasts tight against my soft dress."

"I invite you to lunch."

"Which is right away—"

"So we walk to the elevator—"

"But when it comes, I motion you to wait, and all the other people ride away. Then another elevator comes, and we have it all to ourselves—we're alone!"

"Oh, Jamie…Jamie…you make it so real!"

"I move up against you, put both my legs around one of yours, my breasts are soft against your chest, your cock is as hard as hard can be."

"You push the stop button—"

"Only stopping the elevator, baby—there's nothing stopping us. You're lifting my dress, my legs are so pretty. You fall to your knees, lay your head against my mound, caress my legs, circle my ankles with your hands, so slim and pretty, the high heels turn you on, so does my perfume."

"This is it, Jamie…this is it."

"I want you. I watched you walking around the store, I was so glad you came to my counter. You turn me on, you're so polite…but you fuck very well, you really do. You are a good fuck, the best fuck…in fact, baby, you're the greatest. That cock is so big, I was so surprised! I never took such a big cock, really, never. It feels so funny in there, so hot…am I tight enough, baby, wet enough? I want to please you, I want to turn you on. That's right, let it go, baby, let it go."

"Ohhh, Jamie…another dream come true!"

"Sleep like the sweet baby you are! Whew, anybody there want to talk a minute…that was too hot."

[new voice] "I was listening. Wow! You're good. Shit, I'm out of time. You be here next week, this time?"

"Real slow around 3:30…get you that personal attention you seem to crave…"

"It's a date. God, I'll be raw by then."

"Oil it up, lover, don't be a jerk. That skin is way too tender to withstand the palm of your hand for long…baby oil is fine…"

"Hey, yeah…right. I used to do that. Don't know why I stopped, hmmm."

"Well, now, you really will have something to think about this week, right?" *Click*. "Bye-bye, baby…bet's on you'll be back. Any takers? Am I alone out there? Come on, you wild men, talk to me…shake me up…say something, baby, this is Jamie, and I'm feeling fine."

Some days on the phone I'm really cocky, really steaming, really on a roll, almost a comic, definitely dramatic; it's to my advantage that the callers are often wide open when they dial us. They've decided to do it. The voice of the operator snakes into his ear. She calls him darling, she hisses and whispers, he sees something in his mind's eye, but is probably looking at his cock in his fist, his body in the mirror, a picture or movie, or he's in the dark. Sometimes they put this voice into a body they know, a neighbor, a girlfriend, a coworker. When I'm revved up like this, I really grab the call and run with it, smooth and even, snap tension with a laugh then ka-boom with the physical detail, the juiciness, the ripeness, the softness, the sweetness, the woman-ness and man-ness and sex-ness of it all.

They laugh easily, nervous and excited; some chuckle right along, but still they fondle their organs, poke at themselves. They primarily seek entertainment, actually, and as long as the time passes easily, they hang on. I do believe that these sorts of calls linger in their minds, causing them to re-create not only the call, but their own relaxation. And, surprisingly, they ejaculate in the midst of the call; then, after catching their breaths (I provide a courtesy verbal finale of compliments and satisfied sighs during which I can hear them settle down), they often ask technical questions or continue the banter.

Sex is not just the moments of genital connection. It is the dizzying choice presented by human variety, the scarcity of actual potential mates, the narrowing through time of the number of partners while the range of actions and feelings broadens. It is the sad irony of being denied personally that which is most abundant generally: sexual power. The amount of energy spent to repress it is evidence of its relentless surge.

Sometimes I commiserate over the ache between their legs, the need to let their cock work like a horse must gallop. Oh, sure, it can pull its weight slow and steady down the long road, but once in a while it needs an open field, some fresh air drawn deep in the lungs, a burn in the muscles...they want to *feel* their own strength, fill and empty their hearts with the steady pump of a healthy animal...then, fine, they'll get back to work.

I'll tell them my fantasies are of the same old thing, just lots of it. I say I'm one of those good-riding women, comfortable and strong, passionate, with a pretty pink smile and a long, strong tongue. My wide hips were built to catch and hold a man, the full breasts beckon. I ask if they've got the muscle to drive their dick in deep where I want it, can they take and hold a position, are they sure they can withstand a whole lot of balling, dig in and hold on? They respond with no lack of confidence: let me tell you, oh, yes, sure, can do, will do, yes, you got that right! In very many cases, just images of a woman bucking beneath them or bouncing astride their erect prick provides the flood of sensual memory necessary to trigger release; it's a kind of flip-toss during wrestling, the leverage of total body weight, the surprise of the rightness of it all.

Real-life humor is "in" (again) these days. This generation is tuned to it; we relish both the insight and the entertainment, a shared sense of the absurd or our position on the behavioral continuum, the opening of closed doors (which we slam with a laugh). The comic is the one who looked into Pandora's box and got away, lost a bit of the ordinary to gain a view of the weird which is then applied to the ordinary in others. Stand-up comics most often portray themselves as part of "us," but they're up there, aren't they, while we're down here. We *all* live, but they talk about it; some part of the act is in simply standing up and saying something (or, like Andy Kaufman, nothing, or something unfunny). It's the parent-as-nemesis, the dating horrors, marriage as hell on a budget—underneath it all a sense of community, of seeking mates and friends, peace in the home, respect on the streets, lush dreams.

So when I slide into my "let's talk" voice and do the old tête-à-tête with a single caller he feels that he can express himself in an offhand manner. They soon get around to saying their dick is (starting to get) (half) (already) (very) (really) (very) hard, more rare that they have (aching) (full) (heavy) balls. They want me to acknowledge overtly and specifically that they are sexual beings in a state of arousal and I am acting as a lightning rod for their erotic static.

I often substitute a personality I've known in the past that seems most like the caller so I can slide into a relaxed voice. If he's hesitant, I think of shy men I've known; if he's aggressive, I treat him as I have my bully boys. Sometimes their work or stage in life determines my actions: are they recently divorced, just back from military duty overseas, on a vacation? Have they had a few women, lots, or are they bored with it all and calling only to prove there's nothing new? I never talk down to any of them; there's no reason to flaunt my intelligence, though I certainly think it's fair to use it. It does create an unexpected challenge to certain "educated" types who fall victim to the presumption that a "bad" girl lacks alternatives owing to limits in internal/external assets.

If I sense the presence of an intellectual snob, I will notch up a few levels and, while never claiming to be smarter, let the sensation "something is wrong here" seep over the caller. (The bimbo thinks!) Wit is my best weapon because even simple remarks when placed adroitly indicate the maneuvering of a quick mind and bespeak the innate ability to process information effectively. If anything, these are my favorite calls, the ambush-style positioning, mine, in response to his presumption that he's way ahead of me from the first hello, as if he knows from the skeletal details, operator = bad = dumb. This attitude denies the bright woman her sexuality, diminishes the balance between body and mind, negates the fantasy element of experiencing contact with someone different than those to whom you more usually gravitate, refuses to stretch the imagination to find points of contact....

To their credit, some guys straighten right around with a blush of self-realization. In fact, it can turn the call into a real conversation about sexuality and its place in the world. At times I feel great knowing I'm busting down a stereotype for someone, helping them break a barrier. One of the obvious things is that they find this an erotic insight, qualifying hitherto dismissed females back into the fantasy arena, either seeing that a busy brain doesn't preclude a horny nature, or that the heart can soar above the mind.

And, of course, being capable of high-speed verbal maneuvering, I'm great with the hecklers and jerks.

My own style on the line emphasizes sexual movement and technique. I describe myself as full-bodied and strong, seeking a sturdy, reliable cock attached to a healthy, happy man. In terms of kissing, fondling and oral sex, I focus on the curves, the smoothness, the softness, the sweetness, senses of sight, touch, and scent. I claim that I am a private exhibitionist, would strut and stroke myself for an intimate audience, would bend right over and spread myself open for personal inspection, that I like Polaroid cameras and sexy trifles; skirts, thigh-high stockings (for Jamie, even a garter belt is "too much," she wants to be bare-assed), high heels. I do not claim that I've experienced every sexual variation known (or suspected), but I definitely act as if everything I've read is familiar to me and, remember, I've read hundreds of sexology books.

One complaint is that I don't moan enough—some of the guys really want to hear the panting and hissing of simulated orgasm—but I croon, and that's that. I figure that my style is rare enough and not a cop-out in any way. Some say I talk too fast, which is most likely true, but I laugh it off by saying that at a dollar a minute, I figured they wanted mass data—but I do slow it down. And one guy said I was scary, probably could never be satisfied by an ordinary man, based on my discussion of advanced sexual practices like group sex and water sports. I explained it wasn't as if you could substitute cake for bread and that special sex events were just that: out of the ordinary, distinctive, and not to be confused with the more usual expressions of love.

"This is Jamie…"
   "Is Mistress Maureen there?"
   "Maureen, gee, no, she retired a few weeks ago…"
   "Oh, no…how could she? Are you sure? I'm her slave. Lawrence. I called her every Thursday night. I thought maybe her hours just changed or something, and she couldn't warn me."
   "She's gone for now, but she may come back someday—you never know. In the meantime, maybe I could be of help. Want to tell me about it?"
   "No, thanks, I better not. We had something special, her and I. I can't believe she just quit without telling me."
   "Sorry, darling, it's a come-and-go business on both sides."
   "Oh, well, I don't know what to say."
   "Sorry to bear bad tidings. Good night, my friend."
   "Good night."

"…how about you, silent listener…you going to join in or take off?"
   "Ah, hello…my name is Marie."
   "Hello there, this is Jamie."
   "Could you do this with a woman?"
   "Talk you off…love to…you ever done this?"
   "No, but I've listened before."
   "Are you wearing anything, sweetheart?"
   "A gown—should I take it off?"
   "Lift it to expose yourself, so you can touch yourself. Do you like to stroke your breasts when you masturbate?"
   "Not usually, Jamie, do you?"
   "Oh, yeah, right hand between my legs, left at my breasts."
   "I'm rubbing my mound. Can I pretend you're watching me?"
   "I would, too, you pretty little bitch, teasing me like that, raising your gown so I can see your hairy cunt, look at your fingers digging between your legs. Go ahead, sweetheart, push

that clit for me, like I do myself, yes, come on, squeeze your thighs together, hold that hand tight against yourself. Come on, I can imagine you, would you let me watch you, pretty girl? Would you be Jamie's girl this morning?"

"I'm excited…"

"I know you are, baby girl, I know, I can hear it. It's like hearing myself, that sound…yes, pet, yes, love, rub it sweet and deep, right there under the hood, at that hot spot."

"Jamie, tell me what to do."

"Put your left hand on your breast—is the nipple hard?"

"No."

"Palm flat on it, in circles, lightly, is it rising, is it thickening for me, pretty bitch?"

"Call me names…"

"Come on, you little sweet piece, give me your titties, arch your back, show me, dirty woman. I would lick it, not suck it, not yet, just the tip of my tongue from the center, side to side, underneath, all the while my sweet bitch is jacking off, isn't she? She can't stop, can she?"

"I want to come for you, Jamie, I really want to."

"Come on, you fucking tease, don't play with me. I can imagine what you feel—can you imagine how I feel, to hear you moan like that, the sound of you…so delicate, haunting, feminine, so sexy, darling, so goddamned sexy."

"I want you to hear me…I'm hot down there."

"Yes, my darling, yes, finger it, put your finger in the nook, like men do, slip it in there, feel what they feel when they touch you. Do you like it when they spread you, bitch, do you like it when they touch you there? Does it make you wet?"

"Yes!"

"Do you let them lick it, dirty woman, do you let them get that close to you?"

"I want them to lick me."

"Gets you wet, doesn't it, lovely, doesn't it, darling, when those men shove your legs apart and touch that cunt? I know, I love it too, I wish I could watch you with somebody, see them do you right in front of me."

"Watch me! Yes…"

"You precious little fuck, come on, give it to Jamie now, she doesn't get many girls who sound as hot as you do, who come for me. This is between us, isn't it, come on, pretty baby, be mine this morning, be mine all day long, I'll think about you all day."

"I will, I will...I'm yours, Jamie."

"Spread those legs, you luscious cunt, and let me see, let me taste it, let me have it."

"Take it, you take it from me, I can't, I never can...I get so close..."

"You can. You will. For me, today, this time, it isn't for you, it's for me. I know, darling, I know how hard it is to go over the edge. It can be done. You can do it. Put your finger on the spot, feel for yourself, for the hot spot...there *is* a way, you can find the way, make it happen..."

"Oh, Jamie...Jamie..."

"Precious little pussy, come on, hairy-cunted bitch, sexy-titted woman, come on...Jamie's here, we're here together, come on...give it to me, baby, yes, ahh, yes, see, yes...do it for me, woman, like that, just like that, I can tell you've got it, you've got it this time, this time it's happening, spread it, open it, yes, for Jamie...this time it's for Jamie."

"Jamie...there! There...yes, right there..."

"Ohh, baby, ohh, precious bitch, you did good."

"I did it, I can't believe it, never...never before. That's wilder than fucking! Did you know that?"

"I've known that for some time...now imagine combining them, having a real fucking audience."

"You mean do it for a guy?"

"Why not? You don't think it'd turn you on to perform for him, and for him to watch?"

"Yes. I hadn't thought of those possibilities, but I think I need more practice on my own. So to speak. Oh, well, thank you, Jamie, for everything."

"You're welcome, honey. That was beautiful."

Click.

"Pardon me, hello? Jamie, I was listening in to that..."

"Gee, I wonder why I didn't notice you come on. Thanks for not interrupting, buddy. That was a pretty special call."

"Interrupt? I seriously doubt it. She sure sounded excited, and so did you!"

"Still am. How about you? Want to pretend we're sharing that lady?"

"Hell, no, I'd like to see the expert at work. I'll watch you— that OK?"

"How about this: I'm giving her a bath, she's floating belly down in the bathtub, I've got one hand underneath her, slipping under her body, the other on her ass parting the cheeks, sliding my finger into the crack..."

One night while monitoring an operator, I heard what was obviously a domestic dispute.

I listened in, wondering whether I should call 911 for them, but the operator clicked off the line. She called me within a minute to say she had trouble at home. I told her to take the night off; she said the cops were on their way. She said her ex-husband was threatening to pull her telephone for working our line and that she'd be in touch when she knew what was going on.

She didn't call the next day, so we filled her shift. That evening a man called, identified himself as her fiancé, and said he was to pick up the money we were going to give her. I said I'd talk to her, and he said she was in jail for attempted murder—his! He was just collecting her bail for her, including a loan from us she supposedly had been promised. I said I might have money for her, but I'd discuss that with her directly. He hung up.

The next day she *did* call. She was in jail and was grateful we hadn't fallen for his bullshit. She wanted her pay but couldn't cash a check, so my partner, M., agreed to bring the cash to the jail. He asked for directions to the women's section and she hesitated, then said, well, take it to the men's section. Then she explained hurriedly that she was a transsexual, had her hormone therapy but not the surgery. (Her voice was husky but her mannerisms and phrases were quite feminine.) She says she probably won't be back—she doesn't need more trouble than she's already got. It was too bad. She was especially good with callers looking for an older, homey-voiced woman and, not surprisingly, she had a strong sense of the male drive and crooned out a hard-driving litany of fuck-me sounds when the situation called for it.

I don't meet all the operators—a phone interview is usually successful, especially since if they can't open up with me, I know they'll never cut it on the line. I expect some hesitation while they figure out the boundaries, but once I explain the job, I want to hear them warm up, talk to me. Diffidence, shyness can be used to advantage: some operators warm slowly, yet the men sense their potential. I don't expect them to gush when triggered, but they shouldn't stumble over the word "cock," nor be awkward when talking about nipples, dildos, or lesbian love.

I know the transsexual angle would curdle some men, feeding into the male nightmare of being fooled by a cross-dresser into a quasi-homosexual act. Sometimes the she-male's style is so feminine that it is unreal, robotic—or else it's great, but she slips when excited or enthused. We would have dissuaded a sex-changed person from working on this particular sort of line had we known in advance. We'd use her on a specialty line, or one on which we could screen the calls and direct to her those who wouldn't panic. But that isn't how this line works, and now that we know more about it, we'd be less likely to encourage her return, which is too bad. This job is like towel attendant in the men's locker room. Sexual orientation may matter to the customer in that particular case, where such concern would be inappropriate in terms of who rang up his grocery purchases or mowed his lawn.

"So my ex-wife says she's going to come over tomorrow night. I think she wants to have sex."

"What do you want?"

"Sex, of course. But maybe not with her."

"You two usually have fun in bed together? Was that a good part of your relationship?"

"Well, in a way, yes. I mean, she's really built good and she knows what I like, but I got tired of paying for it."

"Excuse me?"

"It started as a game: ten dolars for head, twenty dollars for screwing, forty dollars for an ass-fuck...you know, I'd put the envelope on the dresser for her afterwards, or slip it into her bra."

"Sure, I can see that. Role playing, spice things up."

"But after a while she wouldn't do it unless I paid her, and then it got so I thought she did it only for the money...she said to me—get this—who cared *why* she did it as long as she let me have my way?"

"Ouch. Sounds like an attitude problem to me."

"You got it. Where was her desire? Didn't she want me or what, you know? I mean, it got so I'd check my wallet after dinner to see if I ought to bother getting excited."

"So, why's she calling now?"

"Maybe she's broke! Hey, you know, she kind of hinted around it would be like the old days, that's why I thought she might want to go to bed with me...shit...now what do I do?"

"Is she worth the ten dollars?"

"Well, yeah...maybe eight..."

"So...splurge...buy yourself a little of that...why not? On the other hand, maybe you ought to see her and not fuck her this time, but give her the money and tell her to deliver the merchandise when *she* feels like it...no more money till she delivers the pre-paid stuff...you know...make her work for it."

"Yeah, it never was the money that bugged me. I just wanted her to want me, or to have the decency to pretend she wanted me."

"You might be better off just not seeing her, you know?"

"I'd have to agree—"

Click.

"Hi again, I'm back. You know, since I've been talking to you these last couple weeks I've really admitted a lot about that marriage to myself...I'm saying, it hurt when I blurted out that I just wanted her to want me...I never realized it before. She made me feel unsexy."

"What makes you feel sexy?"

"Oh, you know, when a lady puts her arms around me, or kisses me when I don't expect it, a hand on my leg when I'm driving, maybe she'll lay out a sexy nightgown on the bed right after dinner so I can imagine her in it later…taking time to show me she thinks I'm something special."

"How about in bed—can she be aggressive with you? Grab at your dick, pull on your hair?"

"Are you kidding? Oh, yeah. My fantasy is a naked woman crawling all over me, her hands everywhere, she sits on my face, fucks my leg, gets on top, you know."

"Think of yourself laying back on your bed, hands behind your head, eyes closed, totally completely absolutely relaxed. I'm next to you on my knees making love to your erect penis, my lips are firm against its hardness, my tongue slithers around inside my mouth, teasing you, as I move my head up and down slowly so I go from the tip to the very base, drinking you in. Your hips move ever so slightly, tipping your cock deeper into my throat, and I stroke your thighs and belly as I devour your hard prick."

"I'm not going to be able to keep my hands behind my head much longer…"

"You reach out and one firm breast rolls into your hand, it is heavy and full, soft and smooth, and you bounce it gently as I eat you. You brush the nipple with the palm of your hand and it thickens, finally stands straight up, and you roll it between your fingers, pulling it, actually moving my breast by tugging the nipple. You run your hands to my sides, underneath the tit, down my smooth stomach to that patch of black hair."

"I'm so close, baby, talk to me…"

"I'm letting you thrust that cock up into my face…you flex your legs and lift your ass right off the bed, standing that cock up tall as can be. I'm sucking you, love, eating that dick, that cock, your cock in my face, love, yes, you feel yourself letting go, going over the edge, it's happening, let it happen, yes, love, let it happen."

"I can't stop coming…"

"Pump it out, baby, squeeze your ass, force it out, let it go, all that thick come pouring out of your cock, streaming out…yes, baby, let me have all of it."

"Ohhh, God, talk to me…"

"Jamie's here, love, taking you in, loving you, making it happen, your sweet-talking girl, loving our hot times, wanting to please you, thinking of that dick spilling all that juice, your balls empty and tired, your heart pounding in your ears, think of this wet cunt, your hand between my legs, letting me get off, help-ing me come, fingering my tight hole, pinching my swollen clit...making it happen, love, making love."

"Thanks, thanks a lot. And, you know, I just decided not to see the ex-wife. That's history."

"I can see what you mean. Best of luck, buddy."

"I'll call again, ohh, yeah, I will call again. Shit! Instead of pay-ing her, I'll pay you!"

"Do what works. You know we love talking to you."

Click.

When I'm getting ready to work on the line, I have various things to do: I select something soft and comfortable to wear, often panties and a form-fitting T-shirt or a loose long gown. If it's cool (late nights, for instance) I might wear a soft low-cut sweater; if it's warm outside I will work naked. (Nota bene: where does naked operator clip headset wire?) I wash my face and brush my teeth and comb my hair and put on lipstick. I want to feel prepared. I open a can of pop, set the diary and pencil near the phone, close or open the curtains depending on the time of day, spread my soft blanket over my chaise lounge and put the pillow just so on the high back. If I get chilly, I can pull the blan-ket around myself later. If I'm at my desk, I'm on a hard wood-en chair with my feet up on a footrest. I may or may not be turned to face my computer. If I work in bed, that means I'm reading out loud from an erotic novel on the break between calls.

The listening piece on the headsets we provide to the per-manent personnel is one-ear only so we can monitor house sounds in the free ear; the voice piece swivels all over, you have to position it so as not to catch the explosions of air, only the waves of sound. The headset is lightweight, very modern look-ing, and it leaves both hands free. I do find myself during peak traffic absently stroking my breasts or rocking the palm of my hand between my legs; this serves to heat up my voice and contributes to my feeling of wanton sensuality. I will become aroused by some callers, by their naked desire or the images they present to me, and I find I have to mop myself up periodically. I often sit where I can see a full-length mirror and excite myself visually, spreading my legs to see the dark shadow between them, lifting my arms to stretch my breasts, or standing and posing as I talk. I will sometimes bend over the dresser, brace my arms, and actually undulate my hips and ass as I describe intercourse. I notice the languid tone of my voice at these times especially excites some callers. Of course, whether you believe that or not doesn't matter to me because you can never know for sure. *Jamie always worked alone,* although there were many offers of operator assistance.

Immediately after a call I jot down the time (3:21–28) in my diary and key points (twenty-two, thick cock, b.j., ass-fuck) and things I want to remember ("you've done your job, thanks," "love muscle," or "Big Dick Dave"). I note being monitored by someone on the other access line (sometimes it is M. with business news, or a trainee; it could the bosses in Cal. checking up on us as local bosses) and also times people click on and won't talk or hang-up when they hear my voice/name. When it's busy it is hard to note details but I try, it makes for cryptic reading later (and forms the basis of this book).

9:02 Vivian says busy, has taped another TV show on phone sex if I want copy (yes); 9:09–11 silent; 9:12–16 slow to start, then grunts that I can do the talking; 9:17 hang-up; 10:17–20 hot juicy talk since we're both in bed, very warm; 10:33–43 very slow to greet, wants to be dominated, I do, I do...only his prick is important to me, take his ass w/ strap-on dildo; 10:45–48 am I black? will I be his Mean Queen? 10:48–49 silent; 10:49 hang-up; 11:03 silent; 11:06 hang-up, 11:18–23 will you fuck me, Jamie? Now can I fuck you in the ass? Thank you; 11:28-31 I masturbate while he's inside me, he feels slick & hot as I gush & clench around him; second caller asks when new operator on, "just curious" so I say at 1 P.M., he comes/goes and I continue; 11:39–48 gen'l sex monologue first six minutes, then he confesses to butt lust, anal virginity; 11:50–53 wife gangbanged buddies, too bad I wasn't there to share the load, he'd make her lick his come from my cunt, !!BINGO!! on making her watch HIM get fucked; 11:??–53 listens in, takes over, wants good head; 11:58–12:07 good-natured, several come/go's amidst this dude's fantasy of a resistant ass-fuck, tie 'em up so gal doesn't "blame" herself; 12:26 M., bad news, relief operator due at one o'clock was called to her "real" job, he is hunting sub now, I'm on "bonus" time; 1:00–09 earlier caller "just curious" about different operator, is back, I apologize for substitute problem and we do it again, I get his ass too, second caller listens three or four minutes in middle; 1:12–20 he's back, swears he'll come this time, I throw in extra girl, no go, then X-video of butt-fuck as he takes me...oh yes...you did want it, you luscious bitch; second caller listens in for two or three minutes mid-"stream"; 1:27–28 cock in hand, dildo in ass, idea of bath great but tongue-in-bung is trigger; 1:41–42 curious, first call, sex talk w/ me as aggressor; 2:00 Brenda arrives to substitute (time-and-a-half for same-day fill-in).

"...practically naked, waiting to talk to you...this is Jamie..."
   "Hi."
   "Hello there. What's on your mind tonight?"
   "I'm horny."
   "How horny?"
   "Super horny."
   "Oh, sugar, you sound a little young to me."
   "I'm nineteen."
   "No, no, I don't know...I'm guessing sixteen."
   "No way! I tell you, I'm nineteen. Graduated in '85. Barton."
   "What's your social security number?"
   "What?"
   "Grown-up people get jobs and learn their number, kiddo...or use it in college as ID. Not knowing it ain't proof you're under-age but it isn't a good sign. You know what I mean?"
   "I'm old enough to fuck."
   "Maybe so, but not to get me to talk dirty on the phone. Now, don't waste your money, you hear? You'll need it for the prom next year."
   "Bitch!"

"Real men don't whine. Bye-bye, baby, call in a couple years, it isn't *your* fault you're young, but it isn't mine either."

"Sorry...OK, OK. Well, good-bye."

"'Bye, hon, and relax. Your time will come."

Click.

"...let's a hear a hello in an adult voice this time, OK? I like talking to the big boys. A boy hasn't got what I'm looking for even if he has learned how to get a hard-on; I want someone with a man's body and a man's lust...a grown man can hear the potential in my voice and would speak right up."

"Hello."

"I knew someone was listening. Thanks for saying hello. How are you doing tonight, babe?"

"You were good with that kid—not rude, but firm."

"Smooth. I sense a man on the phone. Around here you learn to talk straight to everybody, just takes practice...those young studs are looking for outlets. I can sympathize but not collaborate."

"Some of us old dudes are looking just as hard. I never called before—the last thing I expected was a young lady arguing with what could be my own son!"

"How many kids?"

"The boy and two girls. He's the youngest, seventeen. Gee, I remember when I was seventeen; nothing like this phone line could have existed."

"Certainly not this openly, but don't you think men and women always used the phone for making arrangements, propositioning each other, love-talking the night away?"

"Yeah, but this! I don't even know what happens..."

"Lots of guys are already heated up, been watching videos or looking at pictures or just stroking themselves, thinking. Then they prop the phone between their head and the pillow and spend about six dollars fantasizing with one of us."

"And you don't mind?"

"We understand that we are a creative outlet, not a contact service. There is no meeting, only imaginary stimulation...if they masturbate or not isn't our business...they could just as easily "pay" a famous singer for masturbating to his/her music…or mail a check to the local TV station for their contribution to his jerking off…we sell conversation…so far it isn't illegal to bullshit on the phone, or commerce, as we know it, would stop."

"I get you…you aren't a prostitute."

"I'm like a radio personality: someone you think you know, but you wouldn't recognize if they stepped up to you—a voice and persona that links to you through your imagination."

"You have a sassy voice."

"You ought to hear some of the other operators—I mean, their voices just drip honey. My voice is very clear and low, it's OK, but do try to catch Panda or Jewel sometime, they would sound sexy reading a grocery list."

"I like your voice. What do you look like?"

"Healthy, 5'7", firm flesh, long, curly hair, green eyes."

"How old are you?"

"Thirty. I'm very stylish, I like to wear nice things and show off a little, low-cut blouses, short skirts, you know…"

"No, I don't…my wife is hardly on that wavelength."

"Fantasize about a long-legged woman in the front seat of your car, her high heels and stockings shimmer in the moonlight, her skirt is so short you can see the tops of her stockings and the garters holding them up. You can imagine the garter belt circling her waist."

"Beautiful, simply beautiful."

"Her breasts are covered in the thinnest silk, you can sense their curves and the bump of her nipple in the center. She puts the palms of her hands on her own thighs and parts her legs, releasing the faint scent of her pussy into the car."

"Ohh, lovely."

"Her nipples are dense now, you can sense them, you fondle her through her dress and your cock stiffens in your pants."

"I'm not that patient. I was throbbing when she got into the goddamn car! Pardon my French."

"You slide your other hand between her legs, her cunt is warm and wet. You trace her cunt-lips, slipping your fingertip up and down that juicy line between her legs. She raises up slightly so you can prod the hole but you can't get your finger inside, the angle is wrong. She lifts her legs, braces her feet on your dash-board and her pretty pussy is revealed, her plump thighs parted for you."

"I stick a finger in her hole. I feel her insides."

"That pussy wraps around your finger and clenches tight, your cock aches with the thought of fucking her."

"Ohh, Lord, I'll think of this…"

"She climaxes around your finger, you feel those waves of her excitement, feel the juice run down her crack, your cock is empty but you don't remember coming."

"It would have been when she lifted her legs. God, I even like saying it."

"So, how was this first call?"

"No wonder the kid was trying to sneak on the line. This was marvelous, simply fantastic. I'll call you again."

"If not me, there's always somebody waiting here for you."

"You I could talk to for hours, but I do have to say good night. Oh, what was your name again?"

"Jamie…moan it a few times for me this week, at critical moments…I like to think you'll think of me."

"Oh, my dear Jamie, I will, I truly will. Good night."
Click.

We call the service a party line because there can be multiple simultaneous connections with one operator, which implies a real gabby situation, but in fact usually one male is the focus and others listen to him interact with the operator. Usually this happens because one caller finds the operator alone and engages her attention; others simply join the call and do not speak up. This would obviously satisfy a voyeuristic wish to over(see)(hear) sexual interactions.

Sometimes they all hang up when the talking caller does, since it is logical if he is bringing himself to a peak, they can and will follow him over the edge. One or two might delay a half-minute; perhaps to see what I'll do once he's gone, perhaps to collect their wits.

Often a man will tell me to keep going, keep the heat on, start over at the dick-licking part, repeat what you said about kissing the clit…(rewind)…do you really do that, would you consider trying this other thing…how about me and this buddy of mine…you know a gal you can bring along…toys…if he gets me/keeps me going the others may stay, too.

At times the men will cooperate and surround the operator, as if they ringed her bed, cocks in hand, hopefully while she sported about with her hand, a dildo, or another person. These calls can be hilariously sexy; a sort of contact high reverberates and strengthens the connection. These are often late-night calls, like at 3:55 A.M., when all the good boys and girls are asleep, the drunks are passed out, and anyone who is awake is *wide* awake. It's the all-nighter syndrome, the decadence of not sleeping when everyone else is, then the luxury of sleeping when the day-sies are up; it's being out of cycle, off the path, and finding others like you. One of the best of these calls had all five guys agree to dial back so they'd be synchronized. (A spontaneous formation has people joining an ongoing call; the longer it's been going, the less group time is possible as each member of the party will fall away at his own ten-minute mark.)

The worst calls of all are when kids enter an ongoing stream of imagery, busting apart the sensation of adultness, privacy, eroticism, lust and hunger. They are cause for me to stop, halt, cease, desist and cut it out. I can sometimes over talk a rude man, or he is willing to pay only for a short burst of bullshit then disappear, during which I encourage the legit guys to hang on a second. But the kids kill calls, and I scatter the callers with apologies and promises to talk to them later.

I assess kids quickly. Are they truly curious, thus can be led to realize this is a mistake? Or are they hostile in intent, and then silence works as well as anything else? Sometimes I aggravate them by calling them teenie-weenie or ask if they are in a much lower grade in school than they probably are, or if their mommy is home to help them dial next time. Do they know how to spell "trouble"? Are they old enough to read a phone bill? I'll tell adult callers to dial back after the kid's in bed, 8:30 or so; I suggest the juniors join the Cub Scouts. I tell the snotty kids that I suppose they need to find out about sex on the phone as they'll never experience any in real life with this kind of personality problem. If they are persistently abusive to me, I'll insult their parents, outright say the parent must not have it together if their kid is messing around like this on the phone, and as they rise to defend the parent (bloodlines are thicker than phone lines), I ask how can they waste dear old dad's money like this, disappoint mom again, screw up something else? I'm judicious in my use of this scorn because it is sadly effective; after all, kids are kids, and they can't match wits with a true adult. At all costs I want them off the line. I want it to be an unpleasant experience, fraught with perils beyond hearing dirty words.

I tend to agree with the concept of context: in a balanced life, there is room for a little trauma; in an unhappy life, even minor incidents can scar. Any child harmed by hearing one or two minutes of this was so unstable s/he was an accident waiting to happen. Any child sneaking on the phone for hours is already dishonest and lacking a sense of accountability...the sadness is not in my service as it relates to adults, but in contemplating the lives of the kids who persistently call: the bleak hours of their boring days, the long days of their lonely week, so empty and unfulfilling, so isolated.

In point of fact you can overdose on this kind of talk. What is manageable as twenty minutes out of the 10,080 in an adult's week, as opposed to the effect of 242 minutes straight in anybody's life, is an obvious problem of dosage. Adults as well as minors can misuse it, attempting to treat it as a social outlet to satisfy their desire for human contact when indeed it is intended as a momentary focus of energies celebrating sexual contact.

I'm not kidding myself, my society is mismanaging its youth. But I confess to an isolationist policy on that for myself. I have no offspring and thus any interest, if any, in the future is speculative and altruistic. If I'd seeded the planet with versions of my own form I'd have an actual reason to worry about what happened to the world I expected to host them.

When people wind up to pitch shit at me about running a sex-telephone business, I literally hold up my hand and stop them. I tell them I will listen to their opinion if they listen to my facts first. Their objections are usually predictable: it's degrading to women (if anything, it's degrading to men to be so goddamned isolated they'll pay for a kind word); it promotes sexual perversion by letting maniacs talk about creepy sex (it's mostly average guys talking about ordinary sex); it panders to the baser human drives (deny "baser", admit "basic," however, so does boxing, many mainstream movies and much of network TV); it's an isolated phenomenon (sexual entertainment is a billion-dollar industry); and who would be an operator anyway (compassionate women who want to pay their rent). The fact we'll have thousands of callers a month surprises them, as does my speech on masturbation as a necessary and normal outlet deserving consideration by society. My main arguments relate to safe sex, fantasy outlets, privacy, and freedom of speech/association/religion. I can't sway the rabid, but I do have a way with the logical, the empirical, and the plain sensible. Perhaps if I had thought up the idea all alone, I'd take more heat but, come on, there are love lines all over. I find the question of demand—not only supply—is critical here.

People are still much too worried about using their control on other people's lives. Sexplicit phone conversations are as valid a pursuit as fashion or sports, surely, to which there are many magazines devoted. No doubt it ranks with nudism, swinging and celibacy as a sexual alternative, and it is—no more and no less—a product of our society. Our fascination with phones is part of it, the anonymity is punctuated by the individualism retained by each phone user. We learn to recognize people by the sound of their voices, their phrasing and pauses. We focus on the stimulus in our ear(s), often frowning with concentration or relaxing into a long listen. The phone is part of our life, for emergency help, for contact with loved ones, for business and personal arrangements, telemarketing, car phones, plane phones, cordless phones...you tell me why something as crucial in our lives as sex would be denied the benefits of the telephone.

The big outcry about children accessing these lines is purely mechanical, *for which a solution exists.* Basing access on major credit cards, for instance, is exclusionary, as all persons over eighteen who qualify for phone service and have the right to speak graphically about sexual issues do not qualify for these cards. Subscriber services (like HBO for telephones) stigmatize and segregate sex-based services. The solution is the "billing number" issued so that phone owners can, for instance, bill long-distance calls to their own phones when not at home... AT&T refers to this as the "Calling Card"...if 976 "CHAT" services were accessed via this existent unstigmatized, nonexclusionary system already associated with phone-billing activities, no one could incur these charges without that billing number. What's the big deal?

I know that much of it is in our squeamishness about sex. It is so much easier to pretend it is all Romeo and Juliet stuff, that each encounter is a spiritual bonanza, and that at any rate sexual energies are easily diverted to sports, housework, and religious treks if the appropriate partner (e.g., legally acquired spouse) is not available. For some reason, the raw vigor of our lust shames us. It might be that the veneration of the intellect corrupted our sense of the physical...we were so intent on developing our minds we forgot our bodies, which house the very minds we seek to revere.

Some people tell me that the most shocking aspect of this service is the good cheer in it all. Masturbation is too often thought of as an under-the-covers sort of thing, a shameful evacuation, much worse than shitting because you don't really "have to" do it. Autoeroticism is a natural instinct, in the same way that grooming and adornment are the products of a satisfied being with sufficient food, shelter and energy.

Men bear the onus of being the jerk-offs, beat-offs, fist-fuckers...part of that baffling division of the genders. Given the inequality of access to sex, it is no wonder that men find themselves alone when they don't want to be. A woman with such needs finds a partner more readily, or a variety of partners, or substitutes for such partners in the form of effective genital attachments—an interesting fact, don't you think, that there isn't a mitt or muff commonly utilized by men as a vaginal surrogate other than their own bare or oiled hand(s)? I don't know what that means, but it must mean something, given the ever-handy dildo. To argue that men "need" more sex than women is to beg the question. In point of fact, it is a human dilemma: we have neglected to understand and control one of our basic drives. (Given the rates of obesity, alcoholism, drug use, workaholism, and violent crime, we can't say we've tapped the human race's willpower in any meaningful form.)

"This is Jamie."

"Any guys on this line?"

"Not right now, lady, just me, I'm the operator. Can I help you?"

"I just want to talk to some guys."

"Well, this isn't exactly a chat line…and it isn't a contact line, either. You can't hustle the guys."

"Fuck you!"

"I'm bi, honey, but that's beyond even me. Now, cool down, mama, I'm just trying to explain how it works."

"I've talked to plenty of guys on this line."

"I hope you're nicer to them than you are to me. You're really in my face, and I don't know why."

"Fuck off!"

"Now I've got it. You're so desperately lonely you'll even hustle guys on a jack-off line. Try your luck at the bars, about closing time…even *you* might get lucky."

"You're a real bitch."

"No, baby, I'm a mirror…do you see yourself, love?"

"You're stupid and ugly."

"Don't know what to answer. Nobody looking at me ever said that—perhaps you could tell me the correct response?"

"I bet the guys hate you!"

"I'd take that bet, let's call your boyfriend, ask if he likes me…you do have at least one boyfriend, don't you? A sweet thing like you? So charming. So attractive…"

"Fuck you, fuck off."

"Honey, you're the one paying to stay here…why don't you hang up the phone? I'll laugh all the way to the bank about you, sweetie…desperate bitch…outclassed…outlasted…and paying to have it happen…delicious, darling, simply a giggle…"

"Oh, yeah? Oh, yeah???"

Click.

"...so deep, tight and wet, you're fighting to hold back, I'm trying to take it from you, twisting wildly, ass grinding...yes, Frank, now, let it go, make it happen...push it...push...ahhh, my pet, my darling, yes...it's so good...you made it happen this time...it can happen, see? Like the old days...oh, Frank, that was fun, wasn't it?"

"Young lady, you are remarkable. Whatever they pay you isn't enough."

"Gee, I always thought that way, too. But, then, if they double my pay, I'd suspect it should have been tripled, you know?"

"Good night, Jamie. And thank you again. You're something special, you know that?"

"So, I should call you a liar or what?"

"Stop with the jokes, already. Is nothing sacred to you?"

"Freedom of speech."

"*Stop*. I could talk to you day and night, then the other, well, it's been years. I tried to remember and couldn't...my arm is tired! But finally I feel in control."

"To tame the beast you must let it out of the cage...otherwise you are merely containing it...the art is to control it."

"I ought to record this stuff, everything you say makes sense."

"It wouldn't later, it's the flow...tripping lightly from idea to idea...no hang-ups along the way...you know, let it be, let it be."

Click.

The range in operator style is natural enough. Some are slow to warm but, once heated, retain that heat; others zap the caller from the first word and send him spinning off into the ozone when he hangs up, having relentlessly stimulated his imagination. The good ones have the ability to make quick changes in tempo and mood: seven minutes of heavy fuck talk, twenty minutes of silence, eight minutes of general chat, two minutes of annoying kid, ten minutes of a buggering, then four minutes of a harangue on bitchy women culminating in ten torrential minutes of love-sounds with a deep-voiced easy-talking man...a twenty-four-year-old country boy may call on the heels of a middle-aged business type followed by a jaded trucker who's heard it all. You just never know, and once you find out, you don't have a lot of time to adjust. These guys expect you to be right there, gaited to their pace. The sheer variety of the calls, however, is the job's saving grace.

It can be boring. Of course it can, so can being Queen after about 403 pageants. Alternatively, could you ever tire of seeing someone's eyes light up as you guided them to the Louvre? Every job has its days. The good days as a Sweet Talker are active, a steady stream of callers, some callbacks, enough time to lay back and contemplate a bit, no kids, no savior/saviorettes. The bad days are full of twelve-year-old boys yelling, "Oh, I want to fuck you," and teenage girls giggling at every dirty word, and people who will pay a dollar a minute to press their phone buttons in other people's ears. (And they think *we're* weird.)

It is tempting to actually meet some of the callers; they sound just right to the operator: the right age, size, use the right language, want the right things. Some operators admit the desire to the caller; others deny it to avoid leading them on. On this line, such a meeting would be cause for dismissal; even taking phone numbers is prohibited on the theory that it simply escalates the temptation to meet one man, then many men.

But like a waitress in a diner who may get to know a particular man by his repeated visits, so, too, an operator might get to know one particular individual patron whom she wishes to meet. We forbid it. If they do it and get away with it, well, they got away with it. But we don't give second chances: it's a flat-out risk on their part. They'll be inundated with invitations, it's part of the job, and they must learn to refuse gracefully.

The rule holds, for myself and the others. You have to keep that wall up, or the line would degenerate into a contact service, prey to hookers and hustlers, and losing its essential character as a fantasy outlet.

On occasion a man will become fascinated by an operator, calling her again and again, trying to pierce the fantasy persona to the woman beneath, but half-believing the fantastic details. He'll listen to her with other callers, wants to know when she'll be back on the line. I've had men tell me they are obsessed, wonder what I'm doing, where am I, what would it be like to hold me in their arms, feel that voice in their ear, touch me, please me. I don't encourage this sort of thing; we're intended to release tension not create an even greater sense of isolation or unattainability. I will allow a certain intellectual barrier to lower, describe to them what about them would appeal to me, what would drive me away, but always I stress that my own honesty forbids my jacking them along, can't meet, won't meet, no way, no time, no how.

Rarely, a man will do it in a healthy way: confine his calls to a datelike arrangement, usually during the latest hours of my Friday overnight shift. (If he's slavish, he'll call whenever he's told his time has come.) I suppose this would be the closest thing to an actual "stroke" or "reward" I get from the calls; most of the compliments I receive are for my matter-of-fact expression of overt sexuality, which has been denied to them by a repressive society, so I don't take it personally. But when a man connects with me by choice on a regular basis he is at some level responding to the uniqueness of my selected projection of personality...it isn't phone sex alone, it is *my* style of phone sex that pleases him, which pleases me.

"...now, darling, you gotta say hi if you're out there. With all the clicks, I don't know who's coming or going. It isn't like my phone rings and I pick it up, I'm just out here, on the line, waiting to talk to you...I'm not going to ask you hard questions like what's your credit-card number, I want to know how you're feeling, what you're doing, if there's anything special on your mind."

"...um, hello..."

"This is Jamie. How are you?"

"Fine. How are you?"

"I'm great."

"You are?"

"You bet."

"Oh."

"You ever called a service like this before?"

"Oh, no, never."

"Well, on this one you pay a dollar a minute on your phone bill, or you get ten minutes for ten dollars. Then the machine automatically drops the line, which gives others a chance to get on and keeps you from spending too much money without knowing it."

"I see."

"Often the men consider this an opportunity to talk about sexual topics they can't discuss in ordinary situations; they may want to talk about a fantasy, maybe experiencing sex with two women at the same time, which they have no reasonable hope of happening in real life anytime soon. They simply wish to discuss it, and for reasons of safety, they have determined their own ladylove is not the proper audience."

"Gee, you talk good. Do guys like that?"

"Do you?"

"Sure, I never had a smart lady like you take me seriously."

"Well, you can't say that ever again, I'm right here talking to you."

"I feel, I don't know, excited."

"It starts in your head, but it seeps down between your legs, right?"

"Well, yeah, I mean, I'm thinking you're so smart, but then you sound so sexy."

"I have a great big vocabulary of sex words, honey, that's all. It just takes some getting used to."

"Oh, I'd like to get used to it. It's kind of fun, you know, like, I don't know, something's happening."

"It turns you on, doesn't it, to think of me paying attention to you. You know it pleases me to hear your ideas and fulfill your fantasies."

"To think someone like you would care if I had a hard-on!"

"Care enough to help you get rid of it, and who could care more than that?"

"What could we do?"

"We could talk about it in your hand, thick and hard, heavy, you move it around, pull on it, come on, love, make it hard for us. That's right, stroke it for Jamie, it turns her on to know you have your cock out for her, that you're using her voice to stimulate yourself…think of her pretty mouth full of all those words, her lips laughing as you talk to her…"

"Yes, talk to me…"

"She's naked next to you, you reach out with your other hand, touch her breasts, so soft and feminine, alluring, the nipples pink and hard, rough against the back of your hand. All the while you stroke that hard cock…then you slide that other hand down my stomach to my crotch, just to the hair, and stop, feeling the warmth of my body, the soft curly nest of hair."

"I'm going too fast or something…I'm so close."

"That's my man, pumping hard, pushing himself to the limit…pull on it, baby, just like Jamie would…feel that come pushing to the top, the pressure right behind the head, you want to come, you know you do…do it for Jamie, baby, come on, ohh, yes, don't stop now, there's more there, baby, come on, empty it out, love, all of it, shoot it out, pump it out…yes, my friend, yes."

"Thank you."

Click.

After some discussion, we decided to avail ourselves of the Tele-Abuse services of the phone company. This unit will help you identify and eliminate abusive callers, but necessitates police involvement. After two hours of a crazy self-proclaimed prostitute soliciting business and ninety-four minutes of someone blasting a TV over the line, we came to the conclusion that we were a legitimate business with every right to use the services of these organizations to stop the abuse. We don't mean ten minutes of mad rambling or the occasional "whore, whore" chant of the religiously neurotic—that's part of the territory. What we won't tolerate is the deliberate disruption of our business by individuals sane enough to instigate and continue dialing the line.

You call the police, and they take the report over the phone. You tell them dates, times, details, and provide the real names of "witnesses to the crime," which is the operator and/or others who heard the call, like a monitor (unless they are using the monitor line). You explain what the business is, you tell them your name and address and business location and phone number and describe the incident over and over again. So far each officer has been curious and helpful, making sure they understand the situation.

They assign a case number, which is the magic key for the phone company.

The phone company. Big, giant phone company. Started a special Tele-Abuse unit to handle the weirdos and cheaters, probably both as a customer service and to protect themselves from rip-offs scamming free services. They need a legal reason to interfere in what is essentially a private transaction, and a police complaint is that reason. We keep a log of abusive calls: "12:08–18 beeped buttons and white male chanted: 'I'm going to shoot all the pussies.'"

"3:44-52 Whore-Ass/Horace wants anal rape scene including knife and gag with him as victim, invites callers to meet him at Sheraton downtown."

"3:13–24 TV (Ch. 5), 3:24–35 TV, 3:36-47 TV."

We can physically interfere with the abuse ourselves at the machine downtown, unplugging the callers as they dial in; even the monitor lines can be rerouted if that is the problem. But the trip downtown at 1:15 A.M. gets old fast, and there's no guarantee they will call again when you get down there, or won't call again after you leave, plus there is no sense of payback! So, in part, our reporting them is for the satisfaction of a natural enough wish to reciprocate in some fashion.

Often the shock of the phone bill scares them off, or the imperious demand from the phone company for a large deposit against future billings shocks them into new forms of antisocial behavior. No one persisted to the point we had to do anything beyond reporting it to the cops.

"…you're licking my breast, it is soft and smooth and warm. You press your face into the cleavage, my beautiful breasts almost smother you, the nipples puckered up for your kiss…"

"I would be so gentle."

"Your soft lips brush my nipple, delicately stimulating it to rise and blush, the entire breast seems firmer and rounder as you tongue the hard, knobby center, causing me to moan."

"I can touch them?"

"Fondle me, darling, caress my breasts, my bare breasts, all yours."

"Ohh, are they really good ones?"

"Oh, yes, men look at them all the time, try to sneak peeks down my blouse. I hardly ever wear a bra so my tits bounce when I walk, and the nipples show through my blouses."

"I'd like to see them, I mean the men looking at you, looking at your breasts, and I'd know they were envying me…"

"They know you get to put your hand inside my blouse and feel that soft skin. You unbutton me so you can lay your eyes on them, you get to suck my nipples, lick and nibble them until they ache with excitement."

"For me, would you wear a bra? I like them."

"Gladly, love, I have sexy push-up bras and dainty lace ones and even plain white cotton bras."

"The white cotton."

"My breasts fill the cups, swell slightly above the top, the band goes around my ribs and across my back, the straps flat on my shoulders."

"You let me unhook it, but I don't take it off you yet."

"The bra hangs loose around my breasts, you can put your hand in there and feel them, touch them…but not really see them."

"Touch them."

"…touch them, love, they're yours, your private playthings."

"Ohh, I'd come all over them then lick it off."

"I'd thrust them forward, let you splash all over them, your thick come pouring out of your cock and spilling on my big bare breasts, the soft skin glistening with your juice, quivering with excitement…yours."

"Yes, yes, thank you, ohh, this was the best yet. Thanks."
Click.

"I want to talk about my mother."

"Maybe, what about her?"

"I want to go to bed with her."

"Seriously?"

"Well, yeah, I think about it a lot."

"An older woman who looks like her—how about that?"

"No, it's her. She's foxy looking and, I don't know, I just think about doing it to her."

"Well, I can't encourage illegal activities, I can't pretend incest is a turn-on...but I'm curious...look, no offense, but you've been in her vagina once, right? In fact, you have had the distinction of being outward bound rather than just more of the incoming traffic..."

"Uh-huh, yeah, well, not in those words, but I see what you mean, like she's too special to mess with, right? But I still want to fuck her. If I knew it wouldn't cause any trouble, I'd do it."

"Is she single?"

"Yeah, since I was little."

"Makes more sense—you've been the man in her life. What about men she dates, are you jealous of them?"

"Nope. I don't want to *marry* her, I just want to get in her bed some morning and eat her pussy."

"Think she knows this?"

"I doubt it, I hope not...I don't know, maybe."

"She causing it?"

"No, I don't think so...maybe."

"Hmmm. Maybe you ought to think about it, I mean, I can talk about it like a general subject, but I just can't encourage it as a sexual outlet, you know, it just doesn't sit right with me. And I'm pretty open-minded. My guess is she just doesn't realize her baby is a man. But either way, it's a bad move for you to fixate on it. She has to deal with her problems, you've got your own set to contend with. I, for one, think that what you're feeling is wrong."

"Oh, OK, I think I understand. But I *am* serious—I didn't know who to talk to about it. She really turns me on. I can't stop wanting her."

"Quit saying that! That's how you become convinced of it. It might sound stupid, but try telling yourself it would endanger your mother/son relationship to be just another one of her men or her another one of your women, that you have the ultimate connection now, why risk that for another cunt/cock collision? Tell yourself it's a dumb idea. Then get out of that house and find yourself some other outlet. Maybe if you weren't so horny in general, she wouldn't look so good to you, right?"

"You know what you said, about her causing it, I think maybe she is...so, why am I the one feeling so guilty? She's the one who wears those clothes, and she leaves her bedroom door open in the morning...what does she expect, shit, I'm so horny, I'd fuck this phone if I thought I could fit in one of those tiny holes."

"Fantasize about me, then, a big-titted long-legged young woman, and think it over. Don't be a sucker, not even for your mom."

"I'm going to think about this, thanks, it was worth calling. I think I saw something I didn't see before. Hell, I don't even feel like jerking off now. Not about anybody. No offense."

"No problem, buddy. Thanks for calling."

Click.

The calls being used in this book are re-creations of actual live phone contacts between "Jamie" and various individuals. It would take an audio tape to capture the excitement, the breathy voices, the grateful sighs, the imperative whispers. Like all good operators, Jamie has a style all her own. I can talk about "her" as if she wasn't me because she isn't: she isn't burdened by reality. My voice and style precluded a cutesy name like Honey or Babe. Jamie is a tough-talking intelligent woman, quick to laugh, scornful only to the tele-abusers. When she croons to the men they respond with endearments and love-words, the interaction is very hard to capture in printed renderings of conversations. Often the men use her name, but that is because she uses it and responds to their using it; other operators may fail to realize how a name personalizes a voice. Her counseling-mode, as she calls it, is an important facet of her job to her; the men seek information and opinions. It is not to say they will follow her advice, but she's good at hooking them into a new thought or two, stimulating their thinking. These callers are as appreciative as the men who stimulate themselves with her voice more directly.

Humor helps. It defuses the abusive, encourages the shy. It takes the sting out of her opinions, sliding a point home with a laugh. She is complimented on her ease with sexual topics, an art she's earned through experience, using provocative language in a nonthreatening manner. Her aggression is healthy and challenges rather than overwhelms; she's not trying to dominate, but rather to share the power. Her performance is rated highly for its steady energy and attention to detail. She *works* the line.

"...I kiss the tip of your dick, lightly, these pretty pink lips incredibly soft, showering kisses all over your crotch, your cock, your balls, your thighs. Then I lick it, gently, up one side and down the other, gradually licking it harder and harder, wetting it, around your balls and that sensitive spot behind them, your sac is loose, feels full, as my mouth closes around it. I lift my head and pucker my lips around the head of your dick, the tongue touching the opening on top, teasing it, probing it, then racing around the rim of the head, and that hot place on the back of the head. I put my tongue flat against it as my lips ease down your shaft, slowly but surely to the base. I open my mouth wide, lift my head then close around your cock and slide back down. I do this over and over, close tight and slide down, tighter each time. My hand is caressing your balls, teasing the crack of your ass, as your dick fills my throat. My head is moving up and down, your hips lift to show your cock off to me, to make it long and tall...and as you become more excited I moan passionately, the sounds turn you on as much as the blowjob, and I feel your thighs tighten. My lips are clamped tight around you now, my tongue flickering inside my wet mouth, balls rocking in the palm of my hand. You call out my name, your dear darling Jamie, as your cock explodes in my face, the come filling my mouth, your sweet come running down my throat, and I suck as hard as I can to get every last drop, then ease off gently. You lay there, breathing hard, feeling good, feeling great."

"I'd pay you to come over here right now."

"Oh, darling, the company pays me to stay home on a regular basis. I'm so loyal I'd never dream of ripping them off."

"I came when you said you'd finger my ass. The rest of it was like a dream, I just listened."

"I thought I heard a scream back there."

"You ought to record this shit, I never heard anything like it. I mean, you just let it flow."

"Gee, thanks. It's fun—I envision the situation, then describe it. Almost a sin to get paid for something so easy."

"You didn't think I was calling you a prostitute, did you?"

"You mean when you offered to pay to fuck me? Oh, no, of course not...what you meant is you'd do anything it took to please me, right?"

"Yeah...including pay you! It's only money, after all. You're probably the hottest thing I'd ever get into bed with."

"And with me it doesn't take a bed! Car, kitchen table, back porch...wherever our bodies can go, we can come."

"I better go—it's almost time to go to work."

"Thanks for being so nice; flattery is a great aphrodisiac, I feel very sexy right now. And I have you to thank for that."

"Good-bye, Janey."

"Make that Jamie. J-a-m-i-e. I'd like you to remember me."

"Like I'm going to forget this, Jamie. 'Bye for now."

Click.

"...if you feel like talking, just say hi. Think of your voice like a trigger, a kid isn't strong enough to pull the trigger...can you?"

"Pussy! Bitch!" [young girls giggling]

"Flat-chested amateurs."

"Bitch, bitch!" [girls shrieking]

"Learn a new word, like *expensive*. Watch your mama read her phone bill and weep. Isn't it fun to make mommy miserable? And remember, it's a freebie for me, I don't even have to work for it...come on, girls, let's talk."

"You're ugly."

"Watch it! All God's children got feelings. What are you feeling right now, kind of stupid? Don't know what to say? It's because you're like a gun without ammunition, you can hit somebody over the head with it but you just can't shoot it, you're too young, not ready yet...am I talking too fast for you?"

"My pastor says girls like you go to hell."

"So do girls who steal, like you're stealing from my company by calling when you're too young. So do girls who try to hurt people's feelings by calling them ugly."

"You called me flat-chested."

"Was I lying? No. You called me ugly, are you lying? Yes. Can you see the difference? You're bad and I'm good in this situation. Think about that while you're waiting for that phone bill to arrive. Or ask your mom. Say 'Mom, I snuck behind your back and called a 976 number I knew I shouldn't call and didn't hang up even when I was told it was for grown-ups only and I said ugly words to a lady on the phone who was only trying to protect me from my own stupidity...'"

"We're going to hang up, so there!"

"So, 'bye."

Click.

Had to fire an operator for being boring, for describing herself as 5'3" and 195 pounds, for not knowing what a she-male was, for saying to one caller, "That really isn't normal, you know—why don't you find a nice girl?" She was defensive, said she was getting better, said the callers weren't all that exciting either, and it wasn't her fault she wasn't interested in sick sex like licking butts and kissing feet. I told her it was like an acting job; sometimes you were right for the part, and sometimes you were not.

Had to verbally warn an operator that calling the customers "boring fascist pricks" was prohibited and violated the spirit of our service, explaining they weren't here to entertain *her,* but the other way around, and that she couldn't apply her real personality to the job, nor broadcast her anti-male feelings on our time. She apologized and said she'd tighten up her act and lighten up her language. She's a good operator when she's good...unfortunately, erratic rather than erotic.

Had to contact an operator we terminated (for sleeping on job, taking men's numbers and abusing the monitor access number) about her calling in on the line and insulting the operators and/or callers. She was slow to return our calls, but we didn't give up.

Had to notify an operator that she'd been late seven shifts out of twelve, verbally warning her punctuality was becoming a job issue. She said it was her baby-sitter's fault for being late, I said it was her fault for not securing reliable baby-sitting as it would be considered my fault if I did not secure reliable operators. She said she'd try to be better about it, I reminded her that three more incidents and she would be terminated.

Informed a "trainee operator" of her raise in status and hourly rate to "operator," it will show on her next check having been made retroactive to the previous pay period, when she accumulated the requisite number of hours.

Informed operator who referred trainee above to us that her bonus for same would be on her next check. (Recruiting became a sideline for some of the veterans.)

"...all alone, feel like talking? That's what we're here for, just to talk. My name is Jamie, and I'm right here, waiting for you."

"Oh, Jamie, it's you! Is it really you?"

"It's me, baby. You got me now. Give me a clue, let me hear more of that voice, maybe I can guess."

"This is Ron, the guy with the arm...I mean, without the arm...you know, the motorcycle wreck."

"I remember. How are things working out?"

"Well, that's why I called, but you were never on when I called in...now you are. Gee, I missed you."

"The job, it worked out?"

"Are you kidding? I already got a promotion. Like you said, people are going to notice me now so I may as well make a good impression. I organized that job so I *could* do it one-handed! Oh, Jamie...I had to tell you."

"That's great, Ron, really great. But as I recall you weren't just worried about the job...there was a woman...Lauren?"

"Who? Oh, her. Yeah. Fuck her. Like I told you, she said my prosthesis gave her the creeps, but the empty pinned shirtsleeve was worse...so I told her her *mind* was crippled. Hope you don't mind I stole your line. No, I met someone new. We're dating, it's pretty serious."

"Got any practice on those one-armed push-ups?"

"No, that's just it. This girl, well, she's taking it slow. We really like each other, so I thought, well, it'd be better if I called you and got off rather than being frustrated and ruining my chance at something real with her."

"Now, that's good thinking, my friend. So, like last time...?"

"Yeah, let me get him out of my pants. I didn't know you'd be there…"

"Things like that getting any easier, Lefty?"

"Jamie…do you know you're the first person who had the courage to call me something like Lefty…you are one hell of a person…"

"And boy, can I suck cock!"

"I get so horny, but I'm so busy on the job, and seeing my girl-friend, well, I find I get off a lot easier these days, takes less stimulation. You said 'suck cock,' and I got hard as a rock."

"Tongue on tip. Hands on balls, lips on shaft, hair tickling belly, fingernails teasing the crack of your ass, warm breath, wet mouth, you moaning, my breasts against your side, your sweet Jamie making love to that pretty cock."

"I'm ready."

"I get on top, you thrust your dick inside, it fits so good, doesn't it, Ron, fills me up just right, and I lower myself until I'm flat on your body, laying belly to belly, thigh to thigh. Then we roll over, you're on top now, I'm on the bottom, your cock is still inside, deep inside, it feels so good to both of us, darling, so very good…then you brace your arm on the bed and lift your-self, slowly, raising your upper body off mine, changing the angle of your cock in my hole, making it even better, thrusting your cock even deeper…we're so close to coming, my love, so very close, and finally you lower yourself again, slowly, my breasts against your chest, our hips grinding as you shoot deep inside me."

"I could do it, I know it could…just like you say…yes, like you say, it could happen that way…"

"Oh, Ron, it will, it will because you'll make it happen…now, scoot, you rascal, your time is almost up."

"You know, I never thought I'd be happy again. And I am, oh, boy, am I ever. And the way you talk, shee-it, gives a man a rea-son to live."

"Good luck, Southpaw, and keep in touch."

"You can bet on that!"

Click.

"...I'm here another fifteen minutes tonight, might you be my final caller? The voice I remember most clearly as I snuggle into bed? Come on, talk to me, let me know what's going on."

"Hello. May I talk to a lady?"

"This is a lady, how may I help you?"

"My credit card number is 452..."

"*Stop*. I don't need that, this will be billed to your phone, one dollar per minute up to ten dollars."

"It will? On the bill that they send to my house? Oh, no, damn..."

Click.

Freedom of speech is a battle cry for movies, books and records... why not for conversations? Why can't two people arrange for a private exchange of air propelled through pursed lips? If he takes her to dinner and a movie, it's OK for her to "give" him sex, but if he gives her cash, it's prostitution...the age-old dilemma of defining the bartering of goods for feelings. It would appear that the legality of our service might hinge on the masturbation element; how specifically can an operator participate in the caller's fantasy? Is it OK if the callers pretend to be excited and we pretend to believe them? To moan or not to moan...We can't sell sex, we can sell the illusion of sex.

The prostitution angle is a tough one, as it is for many of the entertainment industries. Is Madonna in black underwear a musical statement, is Pia Zadora an actress or a walking sex toy? Do you call those teen-slasher movies drama or pandering? The major (logical) arguments against actual prostitution are disease, violence and blackmail. Sex workers and the people who hire them risk venereal disease. Either might be brutalized by the other for thrill or gain, and with the hypocritical anti-pro stance of our modern society, of course blackmailing customers is a lucrative sideline for some. The sensitive nature of sex adds a twist to the usual business transaction, burdening it with a sense of shame that creates vulnerability.

The phone is the safest form of personal contact. It provides distance and anonymity, is 100 percent safe in preventing the transmission of venereal disease, and it's impossible for either party to reach through the phone wires for any violent purpose. The men cannot be traced through our billing without police reports and much rigmarole; the phone company blinds them from us and us from them, reducing blackmail possibilities substantially. So the logical reasons for the most part are refuted...which leaves the moral/philosophical. Is it wrong for a person to take money to listen to the dreams and psychosexual emotions of another? Is it OK under controlled circumstances— e.g., licensed therapists—but not OK when done on an uncertified basis? If you feel better after talking to them, have they "done something to you," or have you done it to/for yourself?

Why is it wrong to compensate somebody for something you want? Why is the talent for dancing approved, but the talent for sex disdained? Can there be sanity in a society that muddles its messages about basic drives like food and sex? All I know is that I don't feel that I'm preying on the innocent or encouraging the psychotic. Mostly, I'm releasing the verbal inhibitions of men who desire pleasure to happen to them temporarily, on their terms, at their pace, for their purposes.

We are a social service at times, a peer-counseling concept where a person (usually male) may discuss his particular situation, ask for an opinion, test reactions, plan changes in strategy and/or methods for better results. Don't snicker about it—where else can you get this kind of opinion except a therapist, unless it is your friends, who may be no better at it than you? One buddy said that at our rate of one dollar per minute, we were just like a sixty-dollar-an-hour therapist—but I noted the distinction that our callers didn't have to commit for a full hour, they could use two minutes, or five, or twenty-two...by the minute, man! We also cut down on the preliminary chat by being a sexually open service. Within two or three minutes, a man might sketch his sexual history and current dilemma... Lady X expects this one particular activity, Madame S refuses to even consider that one...is it appropriate to decline Ms. P's oral sex or should he let her practice with his sensitive organ in the hopes she'll learn not to scrape it with her teeth? Mr. L is noticing that he's noticing men.

Like any good listener, many cues are taken from his choice of descriptions; it isn't our job to probe, but rather to react to the facts given. We aren't a reality-shock-therapy service, we exist to interact with the sexual entity presented to us. If they say they are single, we believe them; married, the same, divorced, bigamists, polygamists, cross-dressers, straight arrows, woman-worshipers, panty-freaks, nonmasturbators…in this fantasy universe, you are what you say you are, you've done what you say you've done, you're capable of what you claim, absolved of the unspoken.

Sometimes we really do just laugh it up. The callers tell me of their misadventures, past shenanigans, where and when they had good sex, bad sex, bisex, anal sex, why they like purple panties, tight sweaters, bare backs…who taught them, whom they taught. I have an easy manner, and often I break through a shy guy's caution and suspicion with a well-aimed jest, or merely by the unexpected frankness of my questions. "So, tell me, what's your best shot?" gets a chuckle. "Do you want to drive, or should I?" seems noncommittal. "You can ignore me until X o'clock; after that, you can call and ignore Delilah…"

"Around here your voice is your ID, if you're of age you're used to being carded…"

"Man, you sound just like the guy who wouldn't talk to me before; from here you look like him, too."

"It's bad enough I can't have you. Does that mean I can't hear you either?"

I'm more likely to surprise a guy with my insight if he's older; the young ones are triggered so easily that if you have the vocabulary down, you can do the job in your sleep. But when you get a grown-up adult caller, you often get the opportunity to discuss sexual ethics and the personal politics of love. The callers will discuss their own faults, admitting they fail to do some things, but lay quick claim to their virtues, their passion to please. Lots of divorced and de-mated men looking for answers….

And, boy, oh, boy, do they talk about the women with whom they associate. Sometimes they glow with praise: the women in their lives have gratified them, they've been enriched, their ideas enlarged, their bodies enhanced by coupling. Some men have been robbed, outright of their possessions, or insidiously of confidence, betrayed by their own judgment in the crucial area of love—scammed, conned, diminished. I listen to them and wish I could throttle any person who would do that to another. The selfish cruelty is such bald greed that it stinks like a rotten heart would when exposed to the air.

Some men are crude, uncouth, looking for a fight. (Alcohol is often a factor: disappointed cruisers home from the bars are the worst.) You can't win with them—passivity works best, or reminders of the premium they pay to sound off. Myself, I can usually outtalk a troublemaker, step up over him, stand on him if necessary, snow him with scorn until he sees I'm as serious as he is, and sometimes he'll make a truce because he's intrigued by the toughness.

"...all alone here, feeling like talking, so speak right up, let me know that you're out there, this is Jamie..."
Click.

"...don't be shy with me, come on, fellas, I'm the kind of person who'll stay up all night just in case you feel like talking. I'm stretched out on the couch, looking good, feeling fine. My name is Jamie, and I'm..."
Click.

Some people *will* talk about their feelings about the business. Some think it is the funniest thing they ever heard and they ask a million questions, volunteer to monitor the line, want to hear the juicy details; some become whimsical about how times have changed. It used to be that *Playboy* was considered hot-hot-hot, now you can dial up a fantasy on your home phone. Others want to know if the operators are paid well, do they ever meet the men, are they pretty, are they smart, are they for real? Many women are mesmerized by this phenomenon, men begging for love, men pleading for attention...some men shyly admit they've called such services, even our service, but quickly claim that they hang up if they hear my voice.

I have many funny stories: the man whose wife was sleeping next to him as he whispered; the caller who wanted the operator to pretend to be his aunt spanking him in front of his female cousin; men asking to be called "dumpling," "sweet feet," "shit-head" (as in, "love me, shithead, come on, shit head, please this pretty pussy, that's right, shithead"). They want you to be wearing garter belts, nightgowns, nothing, policewoman uniforms, tight panties, loose panties, damp panties, no panties. Do you have a dildo and/or vibrator, body oil, a mirror, rouge for your nipples, a razor to shave under your arms as the caller imagines the exquisite line of your lifted breast? Could you stand up, bend over, lift up, move this, shake that, pinch those, spread it, open it, look at it, touch it, describe it, describe it, describe it....

Do you suck cock, lick ass, fuck upside down? Have you ever done it in public, do you like it from the back, could you take it standing up, do your tits flatten out when you lie back, is your pussy hairy or what? Ever had two guys, three? Girls, do you like girls, what do you do, could I watch? Tell me about your hair, your breasts, your ass, your shoulders, your stomach, your crotch, your eyes, your interests. Could I fuck your white ass, put honey butter on your nipples, come on your leg and pretend it's an accident? Would you flash your tits at a passing bus, tie a man spread-eagle and sit on his face all afternoon, have you considered putting ice cubes up your butt? Did you know that men can't piss with a hard-on? Did you know men can piss with a hard-on?

"Then I spread the beautiful cheeks of your ass and gaze at your private secret place...ohh, Jamie, to have you there, so submissive, letting me kiss and caress that lovely ass."

"My plump thighs quiver with shame and anticipation, you know I'm a bad girl, I've let the other boys kiss me and touch me."

"But not there! Promise me, never there!"

"Oh, no, only you...only you pull down my panties, bare my pretty backside, put your hands on my ass, touch it, kiss it..."

"I want my tongue inside you, Jamie, the most intimate contact of all time, my face buried in that deep crack, the smell of your cunt so delicate, your ass is wet from your own juice, you're wet all over, and you taste so good. That little dark hole is so tight."

"I'm so ashamed, I want it so much, to be opened by you, to submit to your commands, especially this."

"My tongue is deep inside you, I can feel the heat of your cunt, the muscles in your legs shake with passion. You move back and forth against my tongue, showing me your pleasure."

"I can hear you stroking your cock, I know it turns you on to take me this way, I know what's going to happen…"

"You raise up, part those pretty cheeks for me, don't you, bad girl?"

"Ohh, please, I'm so ashamed…"

"Show me! Show me that teeny tiny hole, yes, my pretty, pull those cheeks far apart for me."

"You're getting ready, the sight of this woman, submissive to you, displaying her own ass to you for your pleasure, humiliated by her own passion and desire for you…"

"It's coming…"

"Ohhh, yes, cover my ass with your come, let it run down my crack. I can feel it drip down the backs of my thighs, I know how it must look, that smooth ass smeared with your juice. You don't let her clean it off, you look at her there, your best little bad girl."

"The best little bad girl…such a bad girl, I love you, Jamie."

"Good night, man. I love you, too."

Click.

"And I don't like Yvette either—she sounds like she should be laid out, as in funeral parlor, not laid as in sex."

"Look, man, you're way off base. Either be specific or let it go. Was she rude, did she not cooperate, what?"

"That bitch couldn't turn on a light bulb!"

"We need various types of operators because callers want all different kinds of things. Yvette is popular with other callers. She isn't here to please everybody, just to try."

"Mama, guys can call the morgue if they want a cadaver, now, I'm telling you…between Yvette and Sonya you have to wonder which one died longer ago."

"You get off on insulting women—is that it? So you think it's easy to pretend to be excited by a whiny voice in your ear, that every woman in the world is going to be able to pretend you are something to react to? Sonya is probably too tough for you; she might have thought you were an adolescent with a deep voice. As for Yvette, did it occur to you it was her first shift and she didn't have the experience to handle your brand of bullshit?"

"See, you have fire! What's the problem, darling? You're acting like a mother bear with her cubs. Are you the Head Mama, or what?"

"What I am is not interested in continuing this conversation. If I could issue a refund or something, I would. For sure this is going in my diary as a big X for dead-time, nothing happening, static..."

"So, fine, fine, I'm going, but let me tell you something. You're not even that good."

"Speaking of good, good-bye. Think of me when you pay that phone bill, you hear?"

Click.

The callers talk about the operators in general to the operator on duty, they list their favorites, note the ones who bored them, tattle on one to the other. It's perfectly natural that they have preferences, many of the comments are positive, even thoughtlessly so. (Telling Sara that Violet is the best is fine for Violet.) They may ask when their favorite will be on again. The operators are independent, don't know each other's schedules, but some are friends and do know when their buddy works next. As Head Mama with a copy of the weekly master schedule, I can suggest when a specific operator will probably be on again, but as fast as the schedule changes it is a bit risky to make promises. I never say it's a certainty, only that it appears likely.

The operators are instructed to play as a relay team (one may run at a time but as a team it's nonstop motion): no cattiness towards each other, a kind word for all. They are to report the complaints to us, not to the operator, as so many are just sour grapes that we look for patterns rather than isolated remarks. Every operator fails to satisfy a certain number of callers, so that is no cause for alarm. But do the complaints have substance, such as rudeness, leaving the line, personal distractions, lack of knowledge? Or is there a theme: can't relate to young men, can't relate to cross-dressers, can't relate in the morning but fine after noon?

Some of the most damaging information is given in (apparent) innocence by a caller: Harriet took my number, why don't you? Betty told me her name is Veronica—what's your real name? So I whistled into the phone and she woke up...isn't that funny? Penny's really hot, I could hear the bedsprings creaking and her boyfriend groaning—do you all fuck while you work? It must be tough for Georgia with all those kids running around—do you have any kids?

When we can arrange it, we monitor a suspect operator before dealing with any complaint since, obviously, if we can describe an actual incident verbatim it is much more effective than a complaint from a stranger passed on by an operator she probably doesn't know (and if it's a complaint passed on by a "friend-operator" we have to make sure we aren't stepping into the middle of some of their personal shit).

Liars are fired. There's too much trust involved in their doing this sort of work at home; we need basically honest people in our employ. They are on their honor to be on the line on time, to stay on the line, to work the line, and to preserve the fantasy aspect of the service. We spot-check as is our duty, but it isn't possible to listen in twenty-four hours a day; although, when necessary, we will monitor an operator's entire shift, of course. If we're that suspicious, we'd rather ease her off the peak hours and assess her value to us in general.

We monitor one of three ways: through the routine operator-access channels; by calling the 976 number and listening in, either of which connection can be detected by an operator unless we blend in with a caller crowd. The third and best way is to be down at the office, since there is a speaker box attached to the switching machine. The operator/callers cannot know we are listening, not when we start nor when we stop. One foolish operator's prime defense against an accusation of incredible rudeness was denial based on her "fact" that we couldn't have heard her do that as she knows she was alone with the caller at the time. But when we quoted details, she did an about-face and characterized it all as a misunderstanding. (She misunderstood herself right out of a job.)

I deliberately took part of the Halloween night shift. A few days beforehand I had some fun discussions with the callers about their costumes, and got plenty of reaction to my choice to appear as Elvira, Mistress of the Dark, TV horror show hostess. If you don't know of her, let me tell you she's a true vamp: she wears a tight black dress cut way down to beyond belief, revealing two round melon tits, which balances the thigh-high slit in her skirt. She's got a mass of black hair and black-lined eyes. She tells corny jokes. She bends forward frequently. I figured (correctly) that the guys would know her and used it to launch into fantasies of their hands up a skirt like that skirt, their faces buried in the cleavage like that displayed in her famous black dress, hands with long-nailed fingers like hers in their hair.

Ever angling to really meet a phone-sex operator they'd ask where I planned to be trick-or-treating. I was careful to say that I'd be attending private parties exclusively, no public appearances, so other ladies who chose to model themselves after Elvira weren't accosted in bars and on the street. It wasn't important that I ever really converted myself into anything, I only had to have the imagination to use the idea to focus their attention.

One man told me he'd talked his ladyfriend into making him a little girl's outfit to fit his 5'10" frame. He'd found the frilly dress and soft tights alarmingly disturbing to wear. That night after he got home alone, he had put the outfit back on then called the Sweet Talkers line, finally admitting to me he wasn't sure he was even going to mention his attire. I suggested he was wearing it not to excite a man's sexual attention, but to arouse tender feelings toward him from the female. He couldn't have agreed more. He felt he was searching for a vulnerable side of himself, in fact he could just as easily have been dressed as a little boy: he wanted to be presexual. I cannot eroticize children in any circumstance, but I certainly understand that it is so hard for men to get a grip on these feelings that they fall to the little-girl image when in fact what many want is simply to revert to an age of innocence when love wasn't mixed with sex at all. It was pure love, simple love, real love, lovely love. (This does not apply to pedophiles, who act against the defenseless.)

I find it simple to explain my stand on fantasy involving "innocent people" and "innocence," which is that anyone may reach for the innocence inside themselves, inside us all, but must not taint the innocence of an innocent being. One may be innocent by virtue of age, diminished capacity, traumatic circumstance, bodily, mental or emotional illness, cultural deprivation...the strong may choose to weaken themselves, but never to weaken the weak.

"...is Jamie, if you feel like talking..."

"Hi, uh, yeah, I have a question."

"Shoot."

"The ad I saw said Any Topic, Any Time. Is that right?"

"Anything legal. No drugs, no sex with kids or animals, no violence. Otherwise we can talk about anything."

"So, um, do you ever get kinky?"

"Kinky like tying you up or kinky like water sports?"

"Water sports—like that's doing the pee thing, right? I'm not sure that's quite right for me but I want something along that line."

"Well, some people include enemas in water sports; the pee thing would be considered golden showers. Myself, I figure enema people are anal. Right?"

"Um, I'm like that, anal, like you said. But I never thought of an enema."

"That turn you off?"

"Quite the opposite. Could we talk about it?"

"Sure thing. So, do you want to talk technical like the hows—some people do themselves as part of a masturbating ritual—or do you want to pretend we're giving you one?"

"Is this, like, too weird?"

"Sex is about getting naked and being vulnerable, admitting desire. Sometimes it takes an extreme act to express an extreme feeling."

"Well, this is pretty extreme for me, but hey, I'm game, so, what do I do if I want to pretend you're like my nurse and I need one?"

"You imagine yourself on a thick rug in a warm bathroom. This is no hospital, it's somewhere else. You are naked, you are on your hands and knees, chest low to the floor, your ass is raised to me. You know there is a disposable enema warming in water in the sink, and I'm there with you."

"I don't think I could do it."

"Some fantasies are not supposed to be lived yet; maybe they never will be. Don't fight me, you are going to be a good boy and do what I say, you hear? I'm in charge here."

"That would help, like if I was being made to do it."

"Raise that ass up, that's right, relax, don't be ashamed. I've seen a boy's butt before, and you have a nice one, it's very round and strong looking. Now let me complete my examination of you, I must check your penis, ahh, yes, it feels fine, growing nicely, whoops, is this a leak? There, drip all gone, and how are those testicles? Nice, very nice, you'll be fine, just fine, all we need to do is clean out your system for you, you understand, this will feel good. Now be a brave boy, see, that isn't so bad, it's just something smooth and slippery sliding into you."

"Maybe like you'd have to keep adjusting it."

"Don't wiggle around so much, now I'll have to start over. That's a good boy, yes, let's see if that's right, maybe it should be in a little deeper, no, I think this is just perfect."

"Perfect."

"Now this will feel warm inside, just a little trickle of warm water inside you, doesn't that feel good? Tilt forward more, so your head is way down and your ass is up…right, let me see what I'm doing. We're halfway there, darling. Relax for me, feel the fullness inside you, it's a warm feeling here. I'll rub your belly, take your mind off the fullness a minute, isn't that nice? Well, it's all inside you now, don't fight it, feel it."

"May I masturbate?"

"Not yet, but you were a good boy to ask first. Just for that, I'm going to give you a little more warm water inside."

"More?"

"Just a bit, don't resist me, submit, take this from me, surrender to me, relax, yes, I know what you can do."

"I'm afraid I can't hold it."

"Standing up will help—there, see? And what do I see, a big old cock, are you sure you're my sweet little boy? You look like a big bad boy to me, don't tell me all that hot water filled your dick too, ohh, dear, I'm going to have to do something about that. Now sit down there on the toilet, and see, you can wait, can't you, especially if I suck your hard prick. Think about your cock, ignore your belly, separate the two feelings, feel my tongue on your cock, you're in my face...slowly I substitute my hand for my mouth, I sit back, your cock is aimed at my beautiful breasts, you let go, let go of everything all at once, you seem to explode, everything happens at once...like that, baby, like that."

Click.

"...Jamie, my dear, you are in fine form tonight, that was exquisite and I'm straight as a board."

"To whom do I have the pleasure of speaking?"

"This is just one of your many fans, I listen in the background when you're on the line. You fascinate me."

"After something like that, I need a good old-fashioned fucking. All this exotica is fine, but I'm a simple female. I need to feel my man moving deep inside me."

"That man better be good to you."

"Oh, they are. If it isn't fun, I don't stick around for the slow-motion replay. My guys know this about me right away."

"Jamie, come on, give me a break. It's easier to pretend you have this bulldog boyfriend who has you on a leash than to think you're running out there loose."

"You know what's scarier? I control myself, don't need a leash except for decoration. I'm so tough I can afford to be soft."

"Like you always say, confidence counts. You sure do understand your own appeal."

"It drives me nuts to think of you guys listening to me, trying to make sense of what I say. I don't think it's quite fair. It's flattering but, I don't know, disconcerting."

"You know there are guys desperately in love with you probably."

"Yeah, for about 6 hours, until something new catches their fancy."

"Don't you worry?"

"Worry? Nah. I don't leave time for it. I figure the odds are on my side. Most people do more harm to themselves than to others."

"Sadly, true enough, I'm in a position to know."

"Oh, really?"

"Yes, actually I'm a therapist and one of my patients got caught up in calling these lines so I thought I better call in and see what I was up against...I had no idea it was anything this appealing, but he owes the phone company almost $1,000."

"Some percentage of the population abuses anything, I'm sorry your client expressed a problem this way."

"Adroit, Jamie, very good. My time is about up...back to the background for me. But I will say you're damn sane, lady."

Click.

Re: terminology. The use of "girl" instead of "woman" is used partly to establish the lighthearted playtime atmosphere on the line and to reach for the "bad boy" inside the caller; it was heartening that the callers would volunteer the term "woman" as a counterpart to "man" in discussions of relationships. "Bitch" means hot mama, sexual wanton, she-dog...the mercurial, mysterious seductress, man-eater, heartbreaker. The word retains its bite, so it is effective for jolting the imagination. Much of the fantasy language is fuck-oriented: "making love" is a romantic activity that is less likely with strangers on the phone. But many of the guys wished aloud for a partner to hold, to kiss, to hug, to dance with, to be with, to love. They actually choke up about it.

By the minute, man. We work by the minute. Each minute counts and the men approach this minute-by-minute opportunity in different ways. For their first call, they've probably decided to toss a couple of bucks into finding out what's going on, one eye on the clock, ear to the phone while they check it out. Now, some prize the open conversation above all and collect all the information they can, figuring to use the images later to please themselves. Some are stroking their cocks furiously when they dial the phone and want to come and go in several minutes.

There is the question-answer type: What color panties are you wearing? When did you first do it? How do you sound when you take it in the butt? Do you like the taste of semen? Ever do it with an opposite-color guy? Are your teeth straight?

There is the passive type. He has nothing special on his mind, nothing in particular attracts him, can't think of a topic about which to fantasize...so fine, I do one of my standard monologues for a minute or two to give him an idea of my style. Then I try again to steer myself to his special interest, but if he's old enough to listen and doesn't object, then I quit asking and just slide along a familiar conversational path, one that's proven effective in the past (or one I'm developing).

There are the callers who have a set idea of what they will and will not say or do before they ever dial. ("I'm going to fuck you, tell me how much you want it, say it feels real big, I'm fucking you now.")

"...name is Jamie, I'm your sweet talker tonight. If you feel like talking, just let me know you're out there..."

"Excuse me, but just what is this, anyway? I found the number on my phone bill. I know I never called it before."

"Well, ma'am, it's an adult conversation line. Do you live alone?"

"Just me and my son, but he's only fourteen."

"How much were the charges?"

"Three dollars."

"Well, I suspect he called in to check out what was what. Three dollars is only three minutes worth, and it's only the one call."

"He's too young to call these things!"

"I agree. But if he hasn't called back, you might figure he's smart enough to know that now and has given up calling."

"Oh, well, I'll keep my eye on him...good-bye."

Click.

"...is Jamie. Sure gets lonesome out here, come on, baby, your secret's safe with me...it's easy, just say Hello..."
Click.

Started a new operator at noon today with a two-hour shift, I'd hired her after three phone conversations and was expecting good things. She'd been referred by one of our operators so I knew she understood the nature of the job. Now we would see if she could do it. On my first monitoring of her performance, there was no one on the line, but she sounded inviting and provocative, which is the initial step to success. A bit later I dialed in again, and she had a caller panting over her big tits and tight twat. On my last check she was explaining to a caller that a cockring was worn to increase the sensation of pressure and to inhibit ejaculation; it wasn't supposed to hurt, exactly, although it might ache deliciously and increase the desire to finally release.... After her shift, I called to compliment her and raise her from the training rate to full salary after her first week instead of the usual three to four weeks. She's a natural operator, a real addition to the staff, and on top of that she's flexible about hours. Has she got any sisters?

Why do operators quit? Well, let's see, because her friend says this is wicked, because she got a real job, because she bought what she was working for in the first place, because she was in jail for attempted murder (aggravated domestic violence), because she finds the work depressing, because she thinks she should get a lot more per hour, because her child-assistance funds will be cut back if she earns money to ensure there is no net gain in her efforts, because she's had enough, because it underscores the fact she isn't getting any.

Some take a few days off and never return. Some just fade away. After the first rush of doing the job pales, they take more and more time off; we rely on them less and less. It's a natural part of the business.

Sometimes the pressure from family and friends about the nature of the work gets to them (or they tire of maneuvering so the nature of the work remains a mystery), and we're just as glad to lose such an operator because she displays a lack of self-definition. To choose not to work for us is one thing; to be pressured into not working for us is another. A number of operators could not easily qualify for traditional employment due to lack of training, or physical limitations (notably obesity), and/or small children at home. It is "nice" of the friends/family to be "concerned," but will they replace the lost wages?

"Jamie, be serious, I've called three times already—won't you meet me?"

"No, like I told you the first and second times you called. Besides I don't respond to guilt-therapy, so cut it out. You're barking up the wrong tree here, kiddo. We can fantasize about meeting, imagine what would happen if we did meet, pretend we'll meet again… Notice the verbs—none of them involves *really* doing anything."

"Yeah, I know, but I told you, I'm young, hung and handsome."

"Then you don't need to hustle ladies on the sex line, right?"

"But you're so special, you really know what you're talking about."

"Including the fact I know I won't meet you. So, please, don't badger me about it. I feel like I'm ripping you off, which isn't at all true."

"Well, OK, I guess I'll have to give up…but I really am hung and handsome…it's just hard to meet women who can cook like you do."

"We're out here, darlin', you can count on that."

"Well, OK, I guess I'll hang up now, but thanks for getting me off. I won't forget it."

"Thanks for calling."

Click.

"…is Jamie and I'm right here waiting to talk to you. Just speak right up."

"Hello."

"Hello."

"How are you today?"

"I'm fine. This is Jamie. Anything special on your mind?"

"Nope."

"Anything you'd like to talk about?"

"Sex."

"Straight, bi, or homosex; singly, in pairs or groups; with artificial devices or without, inside/outside, what?"

"Straight pair, no devices, outside."

"Me and you in a park just after dusk, there are people around but none too close, we step behind a bush and kiss."

"Your blouse is open."

"You can see the curves of my breasts and occasionally a flash of nipple, pink and puckered up for you. I run my hands all over your body, embracing you tightly."

"My cock is already hard, are you wet enough?"

"If you lift my skirt and bend me over I'll gush just thinking of us, exposed and vulnerable, but so horny we just don't care."

"You bend over, your backside is beautiful in the moonlight, it makes me want to ram up inside of your wet pussy."

"You slip into me, up to the hilt, and I cry out; you thrust forward and slam in deep."

"We're fucking and we hear people coming our way."

"We freeze, your cock deep inside me, and we try to be quiet and listen to hear where they are. I feel your dick throbbing inside me and I know you can hardly wait to start moving again. I clench the muscles of my cunt around your cock, but you can't react, can't cry out, can't even moan softly—the people are too close."

"Woman, you're driving me crazy."

"They are only a few yards a way when I start to rock my hips back and forth. Your cock responds by burying itself inside me, and I can feel your tension as I stimulate you."

"I'm afraid to even breathe too loudly, but I'm so excited I can hardly stand it. You are so fucking tight."

"I bend even deeper so you get farther in. Now I'm really moving, you gasp then fall silent, afraid the people might have heard you."

"Hoping they did, hoping they'd run over and catch me with my dick in your hole, see me fuck you, watch us do it."

"I concentrate on making you come, riding your cock like a

witch on a broomstick, flying all over the place, wild with lust and pleasure. Now you can't hold back, you screw like a wild man."

"Ohh, ohh."

"You look up, frantic, past the point of no return and you see a man watching us, a man dressed in blue with an official-looking hat…"

"Ohhhh."

"But it's too late to stop. You blast your come into me for the longest time. I shudder as it fills my pussy. The cop walks over to us as I disconnect myself and straighten up, smiling into his eyes. My blouse is still open, and my pretty breasts seem to hypnotize him. You watch, amazed, as he reaches out to fondle me. You hurriedly pack your cock away while he is distracted."

"He's very turned on by you, isn't he?"

"Well, he knows I'll fuck in the park, so, yeah, he's fantasizing about it. He's probably envying you for having such a passionate love-partner."

"Maybe he'd want to fuck you while you were still full of me."

"No maybe about it, baby, his dick is bulging in those uniform pants, his eyes are glazed, you know just what he feels."

"I watch as he lifts your skirt, your thighs are wet from our sex, and he falls to his knees to eat you out, suck me out of you."

"He smells my hot sexy pussy full of your come, his tongue is moving all around my box, from the clit to my asshole, and I'm as turned on by you watching me with him as you were when he watched you with me."

Click.

The operators I have met in person fit no mold. Some are lean, some are voluptuous; some are moms while others are childless (for now or for good); some are smart and others aren't; they live in apartments, houses, and trailers, alone or with others. Some have a natural style all their own; others copy mine from the training period or mimic the friend who referred them to the job. These operators take some time to establish a truly personal on-line identity (if they ever do). Many request a lot of background information on general sexual themes, we encourage them to rent sex videos and read sex manuals and practice, practice, practice. Some thought they were hot talkers until about two hours into their shift, when they ran out of steam or encountered an alien idea.

We don't coddle the operators about the nature of their performance. We never pretend this service is anything but what it is: a phone-fantasy concept which includes a thorough knowledge of sexual alternatives, sincerely discussed, re-creating love scenes for the caller. When an applicant displays serious interest in the job, we give her a ten-page manual which covers everything from taxes on her self-employment income to how to access the line, deal with abusive callers, and maintain an open mind. We follow up this manual with additional information as we are able to; I've reproduced one of our "theme bulletins" which are included in the payroll as often as I can produce them. (Production of the bulletin and payroll represent my administrative contribution to the organization, for which I am granted a monthly stipend. I am compensated for line time like any other operator, although at a slightly higher rate, which represents the incentive portion of my income. The more I perform, the more I earn, e.g., the more we save on actual payroll expenses.)

FANTASY TOY CHEST

DILDO is a solid penis-substitute either a smooth cylinder or a cock look-alike complete with head, in various sizes from tiny to extra large, to be used around and in the vagina and ass, between the breasts, and sometimes used orally. Can be used solo or put in the hands of a helper—like, when you fellate him, he can use a dildo on you, or two women might add it to their oral/manual stimulation. Some come! A chamber of warm water or other fluid can be released by squeezing for a flood of sensation (sensation of flood?). Some are worn over a penis to increase size.

DOUBLE DILDO is a dildo at either end of a flexible center for use by two people for mutual stimulation—for instance, two women on their backs, knees bent, their feet together, their heads apart, can feel each other's movements when they are connected by the double dildo.

STRAP-ON DILDO is worn by one partner and used literally as a cock, allowing the full force of the body's weight to maneuver the dildo. Best versions are actual step-in harnesses that allow complete control; some merely attach with a belt low around the hips.

STRAP-IN DILDO is worn for nonstop vaginal or anal stimulation, the strap prevents the dildo's ejection by the body's natural muscular resistance.

VIBRATOR is a motorized dildo, usually battery operated but some are electric. Soothing when applied to many parts of the body as a massage aid, particularly the entire pelvic region, or when utilized as a dildo. Popular masturbating aid for females. The "Wand" is a special vibrator with a long handle and a firm round head which works especially well for external stimulation of the female crotch.

ANAL DILDO is a small-scale dildo specifically intended for insertion into the asshole, often used before/during/after oral and vaginal sex; especially popular with the domination crowd.

PLEASURE BEADS/BALLS are plastic, like small-medium-large marbles, connected within a thin tube or along a string for insertion in the vagina or ass, they are often left in during intercourse and removed quickly at the point of climax for additional sensation. Sometimes they are inserted and removed very, very slowly over and over again.

BEN WA BALLS are deluxe pleasure beads, produced in various sizes from the small "marble" size to "Ping-Pong ball" size, to be worn inside the body either in conjunction with direct sexual stimulation or as nonstop excitement of its own. Inside the ball is a round weight which causes gentle vibrating sensation whenever the ball moves. Several balls are usually attached to a string which remains outside the body for easy removal of the balls. Balls might be left inside the vagina during intercourse to create sense of fullness if penis is small.

DILDO SUBSTITUTES should have smooth contours, not waxy such as a candle or waxed cucumber, washable, of a size calculated not to injure the body into which it is inserted.

To be continued...

The first bulletin was about Tele-Abuse, instructing the operators to record all the incidents including date, exact time, language used, etc., as they are serving as witnesses to a "crime". The second was on sexual domination of the caller by the operator which we selected because it seemed least familiar to most operators. Cocksucking was Bulletin #3, as it is the #1 topic on the line. Certain bulletins were informational; others concentrated on stylistic concerns. We elected not to provide scripts, to minimize the operators sounding too much alike. They were also encouraged to call me when not on the line to discuss specifics, and could listen in when I was working as part of the training process.

ORAL SEX/HEAD/FELLATIO/FRENCH/COCKSUCKING: MALE FANTASY #1

The art of describing oral sex is in the detail. You can stimulate the caller's erotic imagination with vivid descriptions of your entire body as you wrap your lips around his dick: don't just describe his cock in your face...where are your arms and legs, can he reach your breasts, are you kneeling next to him or is he standing next to a bed? Is he naked? Are you? Is someone watching? DETAIL.

Many women misunderstand the nature of oral sex and consider it a "lick quick" situation: gentle, romantic and of short duration...when in fact watching a man masturbate reveals his need for long-term intense stimulation...your mouth must grip his dick and move up and down on it from tip to base smoothly and with feeling; his balls and ass can be stroked with your hands, tickled with your long hair...done right, he should actually "fuck your face."

The nice thing about oral sex is it is very portable. You can do it in the kitchen, in the car, in the shower, or in bed. You should start each description with a choice of location, tell him you've met at a party where you dragged him into a closet and yanked down his pants, maybe he's just waking up to find your lips are already around his pretty cock…hard day at work? Mama's waiting at the door to welcome him home with a cool drink and a hot blowjob.

You can alter the sensation of oral sex by changing the temperature of your mouth: a sip of icy cold water or gulp of hot coffee does wonders. You can even hold small pieces of ice in your mouth as you go down on him, the contrast of your warm lips and tongue and the ice is a turn-on. Don't forget to mention to him that your mouth stays moist and you glide easily around his penis.

Use your hands. Stroke his thighs, cradle his balls, slide your hands palms-up under his ass so you can lift him closer to your mouth, rub his nipples, hold onto his hips…you can also close your fist around the base of his cock, combining a hand job with oral sex for maximum stimulation, your lips and tongue concentrating on the head and rim, your hand providing the power up and down the shaft. Many men like their ass included, too, your delicate hands parting his cheeks, a slim finger nudging at his asshole…or lick all the way back. DETAIL.

Use your tongue, not just the tip. Press your flat tongue on the backside of his dick and press firmly as you move down, until your tongue curls under his balls, flick it quickly in a circle over his throbbing cockhead, kiss his belly. Tell him you're sucking so hard your cheeks are sore and your lips tingle! DETAIL.

As he nears climax his cock will stiffen and his legs/belly will tighten, you should then increase pressure and/or speed. As he begins to ejaculate you continue, encouraging him to pump his come deep in your throat (can't taste it that way) or into your mouth or onto your face…or a combination…slowly disengage as most men are ultrasensitive after orgasm. Remember to kiss it good-bye!

Oh, hell…here's another one.

LADY-LADY LOVE

Have you noticed that the callers believe in the old Doublemint philosophy of love: double your pleasure, double your fun? If one girl is great, two girls are greater... If they're going to imagine the operator they can just as well imagine her bi-girlfriend too....

The sight of two women making love arouses most men; very often they say they'd be content just to watch! There is something ultraerotic to men about women pleasing each other, so you should be ready to provide a ladylove image for them...perhaps the woman is your opposite, she's white and you're black...she's short and round, you're tall and thin...or you could be twin-types. They may very well wish to provide the lady: their spouse or fantasy female. In any case, be ready to seduce the woman in much the way men have always seduced you...you kiss her sweet lips, you fondle her soft breasts, you pet her pussy, you make passionate love.

Women can make love orally, they can ride each other's thighs to stimulate their crotches, each can strap on a dildo and actually fuck her female partner, or may mutually masturbate to orgasm(s). One "episode" may last through multiple climaxes.

Involve a passive caller in the fantasy by telling him he's tied to a chair and forced to watch but not participate, or he's watching through the window as you and your girlfriend play around in the bed. For many men the very idea of peeking into the "secret world" of lesbian love is enough to raise their heart rate.

A caller who desires to experience two women may be less interested in what they do to each other and prefers they both work on him...one sucking his dick, one sitting on his face. Maybe one girl is on her back being eaten by the other girl who is being fucked from behind by the caller...when he kisses your lips he can taste the other girl's pussy juice...four breasts press against his body...hands and lips all over him. Use detail to arouse him.

Most callers will heat right up if you voluntarily throw in an extra girl; don't wait for them to ask. In this case, stress the attention paid to him: there are a few men in the world to whom lesbian sex is threatening (if women have so much fun together, they might not need guys!) or reassure them you two girls are just getting hot—it'll take a man to finish you off.

Men expect you to love eating pussy, describe with convincing detail her delicate scent, her teeny-tiny clit quivering under your tongue, the tightness of her cunt around your finger/tongue. Remember to tell them where your hands are: on her ass, pinching her nipples, parting her thighs…what's she doing to you?

Very often they want these images presented as real-life feelings, so be ready to tell them about your first girl, your last girl, your best girl, your next girl….

OK, OK…the ever-popular (of all the materials supplied to the TV show on which I appeared the following bulletin was the only item not returned with the packet):

SEXUAL DOMINATION OF CALLER BY OPERATOR

Operators are sometimes requested to establish CONTROL of a caller's sexuality…terms like "Bondage and Discipline" (B & D) might make you think of being tied and beaten… NO, NO, NO. Domination is a ritual power game using the victim's own sex drive as punishment & reward; your role is as Mistress or Queen, you are the source of torment and relief, you give and withhold his pleasure to entertain yourself.

You must sound confident and keep your poise. Your goal is to establish yourself as sexually desirable and physically in control. Obviously, the best way to subdue a man is to get him tied down—that's the bondage part. This is an important element of the man's surrender to you. Once he's in your physical control, you proceed to tease and taunt him with your desirability, disdaining his—this is the discipline part. He pleases you to be granted pleasure.

THE TIE DOWN: Any bed on a frame is suitable for bondage. One end of a rope is tied to each of the four legs, loops for wrists and ankles are already ready. The ropes are usually soft, often white, black or yellow. Most men want to be tied face-up so their cock is available and you can tease them visually; face-down is usually for anal erotic stimulation. LINGER ON THE DETAIL OF THEM HELPLESS, SPREAD-EAGLED FOR YOUR PLEASURE, UNABLE TO RESIST YOU, UNABLE TO ESCAPE YOU. HE IS ALL YOURS!!!

THE TEASE: Once surrendered physically, the man must be

dominated psychosexually. Each man has his own idea of this, but generally you can torment him by posing for him in a sexy outfit, gradually stripping before his eyes, mounting him on the bed but not letting him enter your vagina, lowering your cunt onto his face for oral sex, using his erection to shame him as proof he cannot resist you. You might suck his cock but only to tease him, not to please him! Some men may desire harsh language: He's a worthless shit who doesn't deserve you. Others want sensual, seductive sweet language: Are these soft breasts big enough, darling? Is my pussy sweet enough? Do you like it when I bend over like this for you, baby?

THE TENSION: The excitement for the caller is the loss of control since men are expected to direct most sexual activities. Your stimulation of his imagination and body is deliberately designed to be unbearable...he's just seconds away from coming and you quit the blowjob. His dick is thick with come but what do you care???? Again, you are the confident sexually irresistible female and he is the sex-hungry male whose cock betrays his excitement to anyone watching him...can he deny he's rock hard and dribbling for you? Would he dare try to lie to his Beautiful Bitch? Would he??? NO, ma'am, never!

THE FINALE: Having proven once and for all that you can and will control him, you then shift emphasis to his service to you; he might have to plead and beg, or promise to serve you faithfully. Your reward to him is allowing him to ejaculate. You have had him at the edge of orgasm all along and finally you will let him peak and climax, either by mounting & fucking him, or releasing one of his hands so he can masturbate for you, or untying him so he can fuck you like a man....

TWISTS AND VARIATIONS: Tie him to a chair, his arms behind his back. Bind him on his back with his knees bent tying his wrists to his ankles. Blindfold him. Gag him. Handcuff his arms over his head. Tie his ankles together. Put a cockring on his dick to prevent him coming too easily. Pull on his hair and pinch his nipples or squeeze his cock and balls. Emphasis is on stimulation, not pain. Force his head between your legs, grinding your cunt all over his face, yanking his hair when he displeases you...finger his ass or use an anal dildo...bring in witnesses/participants, a lady-friend perhaps who can help punish the bad boy, or a man to "force" him into eating cock. Say you'll take his picture while he's helpless so he can remember it later. Tell him you'll leave him tied there so he can think about his predicament while you change into something sexy...show X-videos and punish him if he gets a hard-on. Think of anything that will prolong his excitement and burn in his imagination. He wants to be out of control—you hold him in your power!

Remember, every caller will have different ideas. Don't presume they all want the same thing. Some want sexual humiliation, to be shamed for coming too quickly or not licking your asshole correctly. Others want to be tormented with regular sex—you're just an ordinary girl who happened to tie him up so he can't get to you.... Some want to be used bisexually. (Reduces potential guilt or homophobia if he can't escape, right?) As with all other sexual themes, this one will vary endlessly and you should be sensitive to the caller's reactions as you set the scene with him. The essential trick is to convince him you can and will USE him in a reversal of men's usual domination of women, thus making him the sexual object.

TURNAROUND ON THE THEME: The caller wants to tie *you* up. His ideas may be anything from the fantasy of burying his face between your spread legs and spending a morning there...to wanting to see you take a dildo in the cunt and ass simultaneously while he puts his cock into your mouth. Use detail: your arms stretched out, your legs open wide, your breasts bare. Emphasize that you can't resist or escape, he can do whatever he wants with little old vulnerable you for as long as he likes—force you into orgasm after orgasm, cover your tits with honey, lick whipped cream off your thighs.... Water sportsters will want you tied until you pee your panties, you poor helpless baby!

You don't have to submit to pain or humiliation, but please remember this is all RITUAL and FANTASY and you should be able to direct the action your way while still satisfying his imagination...

"Jamie, I can't call anymore. I can't afford it. I just wanted to say good-bye to you."

"Moderation in all things, right?"

"I've given up so damn much…cigarettes…drinking…then my wife left me. Fuck it, she was mean to me anyway."

"Let's not jack that bill up any higher if it's a problem right now. I appreciate your social grace in saying farewell. People these days are more into mannerisms than manners."

"Jamie, just between me and you, you're too smart to be doing this job…get out before it spoils that great brain of yours. Mannerisms—ain't it the truth?"

"Sorry, Jerry, you've got it backward. Having the brain makes the job."

"You remember me?"

"It's a great brain…you remember using that particular phrase with me before?"

"I use it all the time, I mean, on the rare occasion I meet a great brain that's what I'd call 'em."

"Got you. Wanna go around once, for old time's sake?"

"I better not. The first step is always the hardest…oh, well…here I go…"

Click.

"…is Jamie, it's hot outside…I'm hot inside…you hot, honey?"

"Garibaldi Plumbing?"

"Excuse me?"

"Garibaldi Plumbing, Gary Garibaldi…what in the hell is this?"

"It's a 976 number, Sweet Talkers, like the tape said…adult conversation."

"I wondered what that was. I didn't dial any 976 number…"

[!!DANGER!! This guy must have lucked into one of our "local" direct-dial access numbers. These are plain old phone numbers for operators and monitors. This one, evidently once in its history, belonged to Gary Garibaldi.]

"Phone company must have crossed wires—hopefully it won't cost you anything. You better check the number again, have you called it lately?"

"Nope, been working in Alaska…"

"Welcome back. Well, I gotta get to work. Get that new number, you hear me?"

"Yeah, I better cross this one out in my book. Sorry to bother you."

"No bother." [Just don't think too much about it, buddy…] *Click.*

People watching people have sex…people being watched; some people are wild for the idea. One variation, thanks to the phoney sex business, is couples calling in and incorporating the operator into their activities. The lady might speak first, maybe the man will; perhaps they use extension phones for a stereo effect. Often the man wants to be told what to do to her, where to touch her, how to get her hot, when to fuck her and for how long…. But sometimes the woman caller is acting as the operator's agent, performing when and as directed. Either way, most often the man instigates the call and certainly benefits most directly from it. The contact between the operator and the woman touches on that most favorite of male fantasies: two women attending to his sexual desires.

What is a woman thinking as the man she is touching hears another woman in his head, when his acts are dictated by the whims of a distant female? I can tell you: one wife didn't like it and insisted her husband disconnect immediately. Yet another urged her old man to listen to me explain how to eat pussy since she'd been trying for years to alter his technique to better suit her. By the end of that call I had her murmuring her thanks into the phone as he practiced what I had preached. (I guess he didn't say good-bye because a gentleman doesn't talk with his mouth full.)

Some of the couples have just met and in their experimentation wind up on the Sweet Talker line. In all these calls the man has definitely been the catalyst. It might be part bragging, part compensation for a missing element in the new arrangement, but for sure it is in some way an extension of the girl-girl-boy fantasy. Guys will set each other up: one might dial the number then hand the phone to his unsuspecting friend. Sometimes they'll say things like, "Hey, my buddy here just broke up with his lady, give him a pep talk…" or "Greg here thinks he's a sweet talker, why don't you check him out?…" Rarely are these overtly masturbatory, but they still represent a shared adventure of some sort.

"…late at night, I'm all alone, just waiting for your call, darling. This is Jamie."

"Ha, you couldn't know it was *me* calling."

"I could hope, couldn't I?"

"You bitches are all the same—you don't give a rip who calls, do you?"

"Sure. I like the polite callers."

"Very funny."

"Very true."

"So now I'm not polite enough, is that it?"

"This is Jamie, who is this? Got a nickname I can call you?"

"Call me Satan. Is this like, you know, the get-acquainted part, or what?"

"Satan…uh, look, you did say Satan, right…I can pretend to be hostile if that's your turn-on but I don't think it is."

"What turns me off is lies, like you're waiting for my call…you don't even know I exist."

"Sure I do. You're giving me a headache, so you must exist. I know you're a human male with an imagination, off-target though it may be, who wondered what would happen when he called. But why the paranoia?"

"Look, Janet, this isn't for me."

Click.

"…if you feel like talking, just say hi."

"Say something dirty."

"Do you mean dirty like the inside of a vacuum cleaner bag or sexy like a long-legged full-breasted beauty?"

"You know what I mean."

"I know what you said. You said 'dirty' which to me doesn't mean 'sexy.' Besides, you sound about 15 years old to me."

"Oh, yeah, well, fuck you."

"Babycakes, you're too busy fucking yourself up to fuck anybody else. Your attitude is shit, and your vocabulary is shittier. I think of you kids as teeny-weenies."

"So who cares what you think. You're probably a whore."

"No, a whore has a choice. I'm a sexual receptionist. I'm stuck with you until you hang up—see the difference?"

"You're probably ugly—that's why you do this job."

"You're spending your allowance mighty fast here, youngster, better rattle that piggy bank and see if you can afford to be stupid much longer."

"Oh, don't you worry—I don't pay the bills."

"I knew you were an adolescent. Save your money for Oxy-10, or does your mama buy that for you, too, when she drives you to the store?"

"I happen to have my learner's permit, so there."

"Which proves my point: you aren't even old enough to drive, so there!"

"Fuck, fuck, fuck you, bitch."

Click.

Home entertainment. An industry that works with audio/visual aids to provide the consumer with tailored options: a videocassette recorder can be used with Disney movies, taped TV, X-flicks, homemade videos, bootleg films, or simply as a huge digital clock in the bedroom to time your sex acts. Audio options are finally gaining in variety; it is easier to produce sexplicit verbal works for distribution given technology's revolution and customer demand.

As sexually graphic images become more familiar to us through TV/movie exposure, we seek language to match. Most porno flicks would be 200 percent hotter with proper dialogue, and not just the "baby, do it, do it, baby" litany. Hissing to a man that you want him, you need him and you are *taking him now* certainly doesn't involve an extensive vocabulary…call him handsome, sexy, hard, hot, manly, say he's driving it in, burying it, push it, shove it, fuck, screw, ball…. And, guys, you too could fill her ears with compliments and challenges. Ask if that's really all the wider she can spread those luscious legs, isn't there just a little more bounce in that hot ass of hers this mornin'? Talk to each other! Talk to yourselves. It's supposed to be fun.

The element of verbal shyness between people who are crushing their crotches together escapes me entirely. Half the time you don't have to say anything brilliant because the catch in your voice, the gasping, the low-throated chuckles electrify the listener. Some bedsprings even have an erotic creak to add to the sensation of rocking in and out of each other, or the headboard might add a backbeat from hitting the bedroom wall. Ears are sensory organs, too, and all these sounds spice up the messages being sent by your eyes, your skin, your innards and outtards.

Down and dirty...that bad-bad naughtiness. A woman who even *claims* she'll be that way is a turn-on to the man who is used to "nice" women, to "good" women. For many, sex is an act of extreme feeling, a divorce from their merged public identity (work, family, play) into the single purpose of their sexual self. Being physically naked may not be a big deal for men used to communal johns and showers, so simply dropping their pants may not create the sensation of vulnerability and exposure that they desire. Often language can catapult them to a new perspective. They are encouraged to use words most often kept silent, to verbalize and vocalize their sexuality.

Our live line contributes to the possibility that a man can talk about what is on his mind—the tape lines may as well be robots, audio-love dolls—while a live woman even when merely reciting sexual scenarios gives the *chance* of a change, of a response peculiar to his response, plus she can listen to him.

One guy apologized for being shy about what he really wanted because he'd literally never said it out loud. With some encouragement, he confessed to this outrageous fantasy: one time he'd like a woman to masturbate for him. He choked this out, as if he had asked to fuck a female rhino in front of young nuns.

There is a constriction of verbal expression for people even if they enjoy frequent sexual contacts. Callers will express surprised gratitude that for once they said what they meant about sex: that they hate women who fake it, that sloppy women seem mannish, that a stale crotch can turn them off to eating pussy for months.... It is fun for them to describe their bodies to me, I hear very real detail (well, I'm not shit-stopping ugly; I've got a very high round butt; my chest and upper arms are well-defined; I have great hair; I'm good-looking, I guess…a Rod Stewart/Al Pacino combination). If they'll start with that, I can usually get to real sexual details (they like curly vaginal lips, those little nipples that feel like hard raisins, a crinkly asshole, thighs plump enough to quiver, padded hips, bony babes, tight tits he can twist, a nice spine which he'll lick from nape to base).

Fantasies I've heard on the line: (1) He sees his boss at a club, she needs a lift home as she is just a wee bit inebriated, they make wild and passionate love because she seduces him, they never speak of it again but when he sees her at work he remembers the feel of her cunt-lips on his fingers; (2) I'm naked and bound on the bed and he ejaculates on my bare feet, then licks his come off the delicate arch, from between each pretty toe; (3) he's sucking on my earlobe while I jack him off; (4) he's bouncing up and down between my legs, hard and fast, jamming his dick into my pussy, and I'm begging, screaming, pleading for more; (5) I catch him going down on another man and I tell him if he wants to act like a female he can damn well take a cock into his body as I strap on my dildo and fill his ass with it; (6) I'm letting him clean me up after a gang bang; (7) I do it the regular way, him on top and me spread beneath him; (8) he's my neighbor and he listens to the sound of my lovemaking through our shared bedroom wall, he pretends he has a peephole and can see what makes me moan and cry out that way; (9) he dribbles cold oil on my hot asshole then fingers me until I'm rearing back on his hand and begging for something bigger, harder and full of man-juice; (10) I'm an adult virgin who's finally decided to give it up, he spends hours and hours introducing me to the pleasure of love.

"Hi, Georgia, this is Jamie. Are we alone?"

"Hi, girl. Yeah, it's been quiet. Too nice outside."

"I finally talked to that guy with the shoe-thing—you're right, he could make converts. I bought a pair of ankle-strap heels the next day!"

"Baby, that's the true truth…me, I started painting my toenails again…sometimes the guys do surprise me—how can you call this working?”

“As of a minute ago I’m working and you’re a volunteer…”

“Read you loud and clear. Catch you later, hon.”

“This is Jamie, fresh out of the shower, clean and sweet and wide awake…all the good boys and girls are outside playing…so why don’t you and I kick up some trouble?”

“Hi. I already talked to Georgia, she said another girl would be on at five.”

“And did she lie?”

“She’s good, but you know me—I like variety.”

“I’m a long-legged bitch with a big, beautiful ass—had any of that lately?”

“You brown sugar, Jamie?”

“Surprise, it’s that Motown sound in a white wrapper…lots of white folk be living in Dee-troit. It’s tough talk, that’s all. Any big deal to you, baby, you got a definite preference?”

“Nope, you’re all pink inside…I’m really into eating pussy, like I could do it all the time.”

“I’m sweet-tasting, spicy; I’d spread wide so you could get your whole face into my crotch, then I’d gently close my soft thighs around your head.”

“If you accidentally peed a little, I wouldn’t get mad.”

“Your tongue is sliding all over my crotch, you suck at my clit then flick it around my peehole as you head for my cunt. My hips are lifting off the bed and you know I’m out of control, you reach up and squeeze my tits while you rub your face all over me…my clit is throbbing, my cunt-lips quiver, I can’t seem to stop coming…I moan, then my body seems to relax entirely, my knees fall wide apart, you feel a hot trickle of piss escape, the piss mixes with the sweet juice of my cunt. I’m very ashamed, but I know it’s all your fault for torturing me with your tongue like that.”

“I know you’re embarrassed, honey, it’s OK, I’ll clean it up, see, I’m not mad. I understand, you were just so excited.”

“I’m afraid some got on my thigh…up high here.”

“Here, let me lick it off.”

“This never happened to me before, that I got so excited I let go like that—I peed right in your face while you were eating me.”

"Honey, you couldn't help it. It was just an accident."

"Please don't tell anyone, I'd be so ashamed."

"Did you say your name was Amy?"

"It's Jamie."

"Jamie...gee, that's a nice name."

"Thanks. What's your name?"

"Lloyd, but you can call me Gig—all my friends do."

"You sure get hot, Gig, you surrender to the feelings."

"You know, it is a kind of surrender, like being in a play or something, you aren't really yourself but you really are out there performing."

"What we talked about, has it happened to you?"

"Yes, accidentally. Haven't found a girl since who'd do it on purpose...or let me do it to her."

"It's certainly a recognized alternative, especially as people are more open about oral sex. Urine is sterile after all. From a biological standpoint, it's better than all the butt sex going on."

"Jamie, do you pee on guys—on purpose, I mean?"

"If the situation is right, sure, I understand the erotic link between cunts and piss. Men may just want to watch you do it or feel it splash their hand; others want to let it run over their lips but not into their mouths.... No matter what, it definitely is something I do only when requested, and I get very specific in advance to avoid an awkward situation. Some men can't accept accidents."

"Jamie...uh, would you let a guy pee on you?"

"If we arrange it, like he wants me to sit on the toilet and he pees over my cunt as I piss..."

"Oh, wow...I never thought of that."

"Or maybe I'll stand in the tub and let him spray me from my tits to my knees...watch it stream over my belly and down my legs, drip from my nipples...then he can wash me off...."

"I just came again without even touching it. Jamie, Jamie, Jamie. Wow."

"Gig, you keep looking; water sports aren't all that kinky, I hear about it all the time on the line...it's just one more variation you know."

"I've gotta go but thanks a million, Jamie. I'll call again."

Click.

"Let me finish, will you? I'm the one paying for the call."

"You may as well talk to the mirror about it, man, no way do I have to listen to this kind of shit."

"It's my fantasy, damn it, why won't you listen?"

"It's too much, that's all…electrodes? A foot-long dildo?"

"It's not like I want to hurt *you,* I want you to pretend to do it to *me.*"

"Look, this is a sweet-talking operation—you might need to call a more specialized service, for rougher trade."

"But I want a nice girl to do it to me…."

"Baby, I'd tie you up, slap your face, pinch your ass, twist your nipples…but that's just ritual around the sex. What you're describing is pain instead of sex… I don't go for that."

"It's my goddamned *fantasy.* I don't even have a fucking electrode, I just want to *talk* about it."

"How can I talk about it? I can't imagine it! I don't understand it—it doesn't turn me on, it turns me off. I'm sorry. I could issue you a refund on this call. Call our business number. If you send us a copy of that page of your phone bill…"

"You're making me feel like a fucking freak. I'm sure I'd send you my address…"

"Spanking is kinky, electrodes are freaky. I'll go on the record with that opinion—no problem. Now, please, don't waste any more money, we both feel bad enough."

"What other service could I call?"

"Buy a swinger magazine in any adult bookstore; the phone services are all listed. You'll find a willing partner, I'm not saying you're alone in the world with that thought, but for sure it doesn't belong on this line."

"Well, it's my fantasy, and I'll find someone who can handle it."

"Good luck. Good-bye."

Click.

Kinkier topics: (1) water sports (golden showers), enemas (brown showers); (2) bondage & discipline (B&D is ritual control and surrender, not SM [or sadomasochism] oriented to pain and degradation); and (3) men cross-dressing in women's clothes.

(1) Water sports/golden showers (eroticizing urination) involves a sterile fluid, thereby being "safer" in the microbiotic sense than any version of anal contact. It should be noted that this activity is usually conducted between fastidiously clean people who would be offended by the scent of a stale crotch or a musty-tasting cock. This is a form of intimacy for the man who is fascinated by the secret world of femininity and the woman who chooses to initiate her partner into caring for her freakier nature. What is more hidden than this for women? Even in lavatories reserved for their own sex they use individual stalls. The tinkle of piss, the whir of the tissue roll, the idea of her dabbing between her legs…some men would be content to observe from a distance, perhaps through an open door, as she seats herself on the toilet; others want to see up close, perhaps they sit on the edge of the tub, the dedicated kneel in front of her and do their watching unabashedly, hoping to be the one who wipes that delicate pussy with the soft white paper.

The close-up watchers may want to put their hand between her legs and feel the warmth stream over their fingers; some touch a fingertip to that tiniest hole and feel it open to let the fluid pass. If they go to this stage, they usually proceed to a true golden shower: while he's lying in the tub, the woman may squat over his lap or chest and urinate on him, splashing him with wet, hot pee while he masturbates and/or she does. The sweet scent of the urine makes him dizzy, the intimacy of this taboo contact even more potent.

The woman isn't always naked. Sometimes a pair of white cotton panties are worn at first so he can see the dainty crotch stain with yellow pee—he might save them for masturbating later. She might wear a pair of skintight jeans so he can watch the dark stain spread between her legs, or a miniskirt and he will see the stream as it reaches her legs high on the thighs.

They might pretend it was all an accident. The piss lickers are pussy gourmets: they are hypnotized by the size of her lips, the shape of her mound, the arrangement of her cunt. And in their ecstatic wish to drink in all of their partner they may arrange for one of several things to happen: with the bed well-padded with towels under her ass, thighs and back, he may eat her until she's quite excited. Then she signals him to back away an inch or two so she can piss. He then licks the traces of pee away, mixing it with the pussy's creamy lubricant creating a tangy sweet woman-juice. She might signal him she's going to let go and he'll let it run down his closed lips, over his chin, then lick her clean. She might not signal him at all (by prearrangement) and just flood his face with her urine. He may or may not fill his mouth with it, may or may not swallow it…some men want trickles and trickles of it; others expect her to empty her entire bladder by force.

Some men want to do the pissing, all over the female, spraying her tits and belly in the tub, or pissing between her legs while she sits on the toilet. Some want to piss while inserted in the cunt or ass, although it supposedly takes a true desire to piss through the hard-on that is required to fuck. Some want her to bend over and grab her ankles so her ass looks especially round and fully exposed so he can hose it down. Some want to stand above and behind her to piss over her shoulder so it cascades down her breasts, dripping from her nipples.

In some cases there is a disdainful element in the fantasy: he's such a dog he'll even lick her leavings, etc.; that she is the Queen who can do no wrong; that he is her Master and she must bend to his will—one will do anything for (or to) the other. At our service, surrender cannot approach degradation (although to many ears the difference is not perceived). In context it might be OK for him to anoint her gorgeous navel while not OK to piss in her eye. Specifically and by mutual unspoken agreement, so far none of the operators will take it in the face although they will surrender to his desire to take it that way himself.

The amateur operators, on the whole, shy away from this topic even when talking to me so I make them understand they can indicate they've never done it and don't understand it exactly, but should never act as if it is an unheard of interest. It is not as uncommon as the unaware might wish, were they to be made aware of it.

One reason it is popular, of course, is it is still a taboo act. Oral sex has moved into the mainstream of sexplicit conversation having finally made it into the agreed norms. (Certain religious definitions of sodomy included any sex act not capable of resulting in the conception of a legitimate child—ergo unmarried sex, oral sex, anal sex, masturbation, homosex, bestiality, and necrophilia were lumped into one category.)

Enemas, brown showers, fun shit...sexuality can express itself in a fetishistic interest in human excrement. In ritualizing the preparation for, observance of, and participation in the excretion of oneself and/or others the same emotions operative in urination sex come forward. Forbidden intimacy, supposedly private acts shared, debasement to the essential self, sacrifice and surrender, disdain—all of these can be triggered. Rather obviously, a fondness for the entire ass is often a prelude: becoming enamored of the roundness, and the dark crack bisecting the roundness, and then within that vertical line another roundness, a puckered tiny hole. Manual stimulation of the anus during foreplay and oral sex is mild; care should be taken to lubricate the asshole if it is to be probed by finger or toy. (Use a sex lube, please.) Anal/oral contact is most definitely an act that involves preparation—clean is sexy...vaginal fluids often flavor a woman's crack, to most asslickers' delight. A sex slave might be ordered to lick his mistress clean...another man's sexy babe tongues him all the way back.

One partner may shit for the other. Maybe she sucks his cock while she shits into the toilet. He might squat over a newspaper for her, then sniff his own pile in a ritual humiliation scenario. She may have her bowel movement in private, but he comes in to wipe her and flush the turds away. An enema often adds to the ceremony, obviously, but may also precede anal intercourse as a simple mechanical courtesy to empty the lower tract rather than as a sensual/sexual aspect (in which case it may be done solo, in advance). Enemas can also be given to oneself as part of a masturbation act; some people claim it's healthy to clean the system this way, but as in all things, good sense prevails (too much of a good thing is a bad thing). When shared, the idea is to expose oneself to another, experiencing the introduction of the thin nozzle-tube past the sphincter, the subtle but relentless filling of the "belly" with warm fluid, the aching and waiting as the need to evacuate intensifies, then the release: trickles and trickles, or jets and jets, first the water, then (if at all) the shit.

Actual coprophagia—eating shit—is so much more rare that in truth no caller on the line in my thousands of hours ever hinted at the idea. In point of fact, very few would go beyond sticking a finger in there; and those that would stopped at their tongue in a sweet clean hole. Seeing, smelling, feeling shit...I know it's out there, but it's *way* out there.... There is a difference between the border and the fringe.

Microbiologically speaking, human feces are dangerous. They contain many kinds of bacteria. Care must be taken to avoid introduction of even small traces of fecal matter into the vagina, whether it be on the finger, toy, tongue or penis, or as the result of a "mess" in her panties or his diapers, as the vagina's wet warmth acts as an incubator. Contamination could cause septic infections in small cuts on the hands, in or around the mouth and other places.

(2) Bondage & Discipline. B&D is a sexual art form, using ropes, chains, clips, clamps and other attachments to control the visual and physical presentation of a body, creating and maintaining postures that please the viewer or disturb the one viewed. Legs may be parted wide or bound, bent deep at the knees, to the chest. Arms may be tied to the ankles or high overhead on a handy hook in the ceiling. A woman's breasts may be bound by wrapping rope around her ribs, leaving only the nipples exposed. A man's cock may be bound by ropes around his hips and up between his legs (with just a little room to grow).

Bondage is not sadomasochism. Bondage is not for painful purposes. Bondage is not to scar or to mark. Bondage is an art form.

The discipline part is obviously much more easily sustained if the disciplinee cannot escape the discipliner, ergo the popularity of bondage/restraints. At its basic level, discipline is a mix of old-fashioned spanking and the classic pillory: the "bad one" has to bend over and take his/her licking. He or she may flinch, cry out, weep helplessly, but must stay bare-assed and vulnerable.

Spanking feels different if administered high on the rump or low at the fold of buttock and thigh. Fingertips can paddle a pussy. You can slap tits and faces. It is the sound of it, the sight and sting of it, and sometimes the warm flush on the skin from the contact...

But *why* are you being disciplined, my pretty? Were we looking at other men on the beach? Did we get caught kissing our gal pal in the basement? Did we or did we not go out without a bra in contravention of the accepted policy to harness those magnificent breasts when in public? Did we come too soon/too late/not enough? Are we going to admit we deserve it or not?

It doesn't stop (or even always start) with spanking; there is the "humiliation" aspect, the being pilloried for an audience of one, the exposure of private parts, sometimes with inanimate objects inserted to distend them. A vibrator might be turned on and tied in (crisscross ropes between legs so it cannot escape), or while spread-eagle on his back a man's lips and nipples colored red, or a cockring snapped around his cock and balls.

You might be left tied on the bed, your orifices stuffed full, blindfolded, gagged and *most likely ignored*. Your torment is not knowing when or if your discipliner even bothers to cast a glance your way...yet for all you know, he or she stands at the doorway stricken silent by your beauty even when it has temporarily been made grotesque....

There she is, naked, on her belly, pillow beneath her forcing her ass to curve invitingly, legs parted, when her discipliner brings a man in the room. All she'll ever know about him is that he saw her like that. He fucked her with a long, thin dick, and he moans deep in his throat when he comes.

He's kissing her breasts, one then the other, kissing the curve underneath and the soft warm cleavage and the jutting tips, kissing her breasts, one then the other, while another woman he dearly wishes to fuck but will never even get to touch fills his ass with an enema. She makes him hold and hold and hold it while the two women masturbate side by side standing in front of him. He shits when they come; they continue to climax as his cock explodes. He is left to clean up while the two women retreat to the bedroom, without him. If he cleans up very, very fast, he may get over to hear them through the closed and locked bed-room door before they come to inspect his work and decide on further punishment or reward.

Discipline is peculiar to the people in the scene, although their own oddities may be well rehearsed. She may wear a dog collar to the dinner table as a signal she has been naughty. He may come in the house with that special attaché case he keeps for the soft ropes and the rubber paddle. On their way to dinner, she may order the cab to a seedy hotel. He knows what this means… through long hours of training, he's learned to ejaculate when her flat palm slaps his thigh.

Sometimes using forbidden language and gestures heats the blood, which can then be transferred to more traditional sex— just a few minutes of her over his knee while he calls her a big-assed floozy may flip his switch from respectable mate to ravaging lover; it may be in simply admitting she likes something up between her legs in that juicy hole, yes, damn it, yes, she likes it, that she finds her catalyst from tired to tigress.

Surrender. That's what it's all about. Demanding it, allowing it.

(3) Cross-dressing. Clothes are designed to enhance the body, to cover/reveal it, to support it, to draw attention to it, to protect it from prying eyes, blowing winds, the shining sun and scratchy furniture. Clothes are gender-fied to an obsessive degree in this culture: real men don't wear skirts, feminine women wear dresses…men don't wear hats with veils, women wear the lace.

Once you polarize people, it makes some people giddy to dash up to the opposite pole. If you separate the school play-ground by either gender or grade, raiding the restricted zone becomes a game. Ditto the underwear issue: spend a lifetime being told these panties are for others, not you, this silk is for them, not you, this lace is not yours, it's theirs…in that atmos-phere donning a pair of lacy silk panties is an act of rebellion and submission both.

The yin/yang, concave/convex, female/male opposites cre-ate the perfect tug-of-war inside ourselves. Our roles are very well defined by external forces, but may be unruly internally when it comes down to what gets your blood pumping. Some fetishes are easily explained: his first woman wore a red bra and he'll never ever forget the sight of her boobs filling it...the twistier the road to get there, the less likely you are to retrace the route.

In the X-dress crowd there are the dabblers, the macho men who find the whole thing disorienting, and it is in this surrender that the passion is found. It is visible proof of an emotional fact that they would and could do anything in a sexual sense with this partner, even indulge a kooky idea like getting all dolled up if it ties directly into a thorough fucking. Games are games, and fucking is fucking; one may lead to the other.

There are the serious cross-dressers who have every intention of passing in public as a woman, with the makeup, the heels, the handbag and stockings and perfume and undergarments and fashionable clothes. In these men the sexual link is muted or nonexistent, in the sense they aren't doing this to express themselves sexually, but to release an aspect of their being. They are not necessarily opting to be female substitutes to other males; if anything, they wish to be accepted as a "sister" to most people, reserving her love for one man as many women do.

Transsexuals are people who believe they have the mind and personality of one sex trapped in a body of the opposite sex—hormonal hell. Sometimes they are truly borderline in appearance: the man may be slight with very little body hair and small hands and feet; the woman may have slim hips or tiny breasts, a powerful deep voice, the hair heavy on her limbs, in the beard area, and along the crack of the ass. There may have been a disruption in their imprinting the usual gender roles. Perhaps a doting grandmother treated him like her sweet darling. Her dad, in the grief of young widowerhood might de-emphasize anything reminiscent of his dead wife in his daughter until she extinguishes her femininity. But in other cases the fact is there is no obvious external trigger.

Women slip into the opposite role more easily because traditionally it made more sense for a female to "aspire" to the superior male role than for a male to "demean" himself with female notions. Every slave may naturally long for a day as the master, but which masters would want to be caught sneaking into slave's clothes?

For some it isn't any big deal at all. They might just so happen to sleep in a flannel nightgown because it keeps them warm and snug but does not constrict the genitals...but even so, in case of fire they would ditch the gown and escape naked into the night rather than appear publicly, no matter how comfortable and safe, in the "wrong" attire.

Women's apparel is sensuous, tactile in nature. This is a case where texture matters, slippery/smooth fabrics are considered feminine, indulgent, and some men make no bones about wanting that same pampered feeling against their skin, in their mirror.

"Pretend you're about sixteen, in a tight, short cheerleader's outfit, I'll be watching you practice...."

"Pretend you're in jail explaining this fantasy to your fellow inmates...."

"They'd love it...it'd turn them on...."

"Ah, yes, but who would be there to satisfy them then? Shall we talk about that, Mr. Tight-For-Now-Asshole?"

Click.

"...sweet-talking Jamie, here in your ear for as long as you like...now, listen up, I can't just hope you're old enough to be on an adult conversation line, I have to know it, which means you have to tell me. So come on, can you count up to eighteen? Were you born before 1970? Think it over. In the meantime, I'll quiet down so you can concentrate. Take off your shoes if it'll help you count..."

Click.

One bit of luck has been some free publicity; a newspaper article picked up through Associated Press by other local papers, the guest appearance on a local television show. In each case we did not seek the attention, did not position ourselves to be noticed, took no action to get such results. It has always been that way with us: we manage to be in the right place at the right time.

The newspaper article came about when a freelance writer

caught me on the phone and got talking with me. In a rare breach of truly personal revelation, I said I was writing a book about the business. He said he would like to do a newspaper feature on "a day in the life of a phone-sex operator" to go along with a similar article on exotic dancers he had written. We discussed it off the live-line, exchanged some data, but the article never came to fruition and I figured he was a dead end, or a hustler with a good line. Then he called and said the paper had assigned a female staff reporter and photographer to do the story. Even so, a month passed before it appeared.

The article generated a lot of calls and as it passed through other local papers in shortened form under more appealing head-line, it continued to feed us new business. Ironically, we are forbidden to advertise in the papers which carried the story—not even a classified ad with no fanfare—so it seemed poetic justice that even a mere acknowledgment of our existence brought us business, belying their theory that it is an offensively terrible enterprise in which no decent person has an interest. Their readership responded to us with their dollars, whether the twenty-five-cent newspapers care to believe that or not.

My appearance on the TV show followed about three weeks later. The show on phone sex had been planned in advance, but they were having trouble arranging for a pro-phone-sex personality, had even considered importing talent from New York for the purpose, since the antis were ever-ready with a spokes-mob. The show's producer called our line for background information and was told by the operator that he really needed to connect with me, which he did by contacting M. at the business phone, taking the opportunity of interviewing him in the process.

Other phone-sex businesses called the TV show after hearing the topic announced in advance and probably weren't too happy to learn that we were getting more free publicity but, as I said, we hadn't maneuvered either case of media attention. We do represent a temperate element in the business, a straight service not trying to cross-market sexy videos by claiming that stars work on our line, or acting as an outcall service for prostitution.

Met the Head-Mama of a competing phone fantasy business at a local bar (turns out we have a mutual friend) and it would have been a typical cat fight if I hadn't sidestepped her snide openings (she said she made $600/week, I smiled and said I remembered back when I started making that kind of money). You know, her girls were hotter and all that. Nothing much was said after I refused her bait, but I did realize one problem is that the intra-industry animosity draws off energy from fighting the outsiders. A vigorous competitor stimulates business activity in general, like rival gas stations across the street from each other. Our services are distinctive enough that it isn't head-to-head. If the energy spent on harassing competition were spent on advertising and promotion of the service itself, the competitor might be truly beaten.

The swinger contact magazines and adult bookstores have been quite helpful: we represent advertising revenue and stimulate the adult-entertainment industry. Sure, we all compete for the consumer's dollars, but the relationship is much more balanced. I always recommend magazines and stores by name on the line when callers are seeking general information, it helps us all.

Another thing I realized is the sense of secrecy and shame this other woman held toward her job. She was livid that I used her "real" name when in fact I'd heard her use it herself—how would I know it if she didn't tell me?—and harangued me about having a husband and kid she had to protect. I never felt that I had to apologize about my involvement with this business. When I'm on the line, I project a feeling of acceptance and honest interest. The hostility and suspicion in this woman has got to seep into her calls, into her relations with the operators. This business is so susceptible to negative nuances that I cringed at her fulfillment of the stereotypical hostile whore adjusted for phone-fantasy mode.

Six or eight weeks later, during a phone interview with a prospective operator, I learned that the bitchy manageress of our competition who was oh-so-snotty to me one night was demoted from boss back to operator, pay rates were cut all around...the applicant said I could expect more of their former operators to apply for work...can't say I didn't smile (more than once).

That particular service has the operators sign a "noncompetition" agreement which prohibits them from getting a job with another service while employed by them and for *months* after terminating their service, a concept I don't think is fair at this level of employment. High-tech research, pivotal management positions, complex creative relationships, yes. Teachers, waiters and phone-sex operators, no. I maybe can understand the exclusive service while employed if they are guaranteed adequate income, but no single operator should be able to fold their business by leaving. Of course the operators shouldn't steal customers when they quit in order to start a private business or abuse what they learned about that company's operation while on the payroll. A contract to that effect might be helpful to ensure that both sides understand the legitimate rules. What seems wrong is attempting to restrict the operator's employment opportunities when her relationship to that particular service has ended.

Some of the operators are intimidated by the contract, which means it serves its purpose of psyching out the unsophisticated. It is doubtful that the company would actually allow a lawsuit to result, with the big risk of the legal-discovery process revealing too much about their methods in general. But that's no comfort to an operator who doesn't understand the mechanics of legal actions or who couldn't afford to retain a lawyer to defend her. That's why I think the agreement is wrong: it works on the presumption the signer doesn't understand the law and will not pursue her rights to enter and exit an employment relationship with reasonable notice and good faith.

If I find out that a prospective operator is from the competition, I tell her I've never seen the contract and cannot say whether or not it binds her but she is welcome here as a freelance subcontractor with no obligation except to work the hours promised and use her Sweet Talker identity for us alone. Some say they would march into court to prove their right to work for whom they want, if necessary. In all this time, we have heard of no action being taken on the contract breach by our operators who have come from that company. We never raided that company's operator pool, but it seems natural enough that having done this work before they'd apply to do it again, and that we would hire experienced people.

There are companies that make each operator pretend to be multiple personalities (as if the men can't recognize that Sasha/Bridget/Joy all have the same odd lisp), encourage the operators to claim that they are in a sex video which just so happens to be available through the company, pay the operators on commission so they have to hustle the guys into calling back for them specifically. Each phone-fantasy enterprise has its own tone.

"Tell me how you'd eat a pussy."

"Very well, my friend. I would part her pretty thighs and kiss her gently from her belly to her ass, just kiss her lightly and thoroughly up and down her still-dry snatch. I'd use my fingers to part her lips as I kissed more firmly, darting my tongue out to tease her. As I peeled her lips back, I'd catch the delicate scent of her excitement, and it would inspire me to tongue her firmly, pressing it flat against her clit, then flicking it down to her vagina. I'd stick it right inside her, drawing out her sweet juice, causing her to lift her hips for me. My hands would slip under her ass and part her cheeks, I'd raise her slightly so I could lick farther back—are you imagining watching this? Seeing my face buried between her legs? My ass is up in the air, legs parted, you could step up behind me and fuck me while I ate her, jam your cock in as she climaxes for me, see my long-nailed fingers on her pretty little tits…"

"Don't stop now."

"I'm grinding my ass against your belly as I finger and lick my girlfriend's cunt, she's wriggling all over the bed because I've got my finger up her ass. I'm stroking her breasts until the nipples are dark and hard, she's holding my head tight against her pussy, and all the while you're just stroking your cock with my pussy, filling me up with it. I'm hot and wet and very tight…"

"Now you can stop."

Click.

"…is Jamie, a good woman in a great mood. It's too damn cold outside to have any fun—let's all crawl under blankets and get cozy. I'm naked under mine, how about you?"

"Hey, Jamie, it's Lefty!"

"Lefty! Long time no hear. Does that mean you found yourself a live one?"

"Sure fucking did. We might even live together in a few months if everything works out. She's got a lease on her place, which is too small, and I don't like this place so...fuck it, let's talk about you. How are you, Jamie? Anything new?"

"Same old story. Pitching shit and catching hell."

"You were right about the one-armed push-ups, worked like a charm. We have another way, too: I sit on a chair and she straddles my lap...she's real willing to practice. But it was important to me that I do it the regular way, you know, me on top...now I know I can, it doesn't seem so important."

"You any better at jerking off left-handed?"

"It's different, I swear, my cock is pulling to the left now, after all these years of being a rightie. But I can't play with my ass like I used to."

"Not like you used to, maybe, but you could stimulate yourself first, insert a dildo then lay flat on it and bounce around a bit..."

"A dildo? No...not me. I felt weird just using a finger."

"Now you have a fake forearm, a waxwork hand, a metal hook...one little plastic finger-sized dildo just might complete the set."

"Damn, you're honest. OK, OK. Do they work?"

"What's to work? I doubt your sweet ass is so tight you'll collapse the thing!"

"I take it you have one."

"Several, different sizes and shapes. Some vibrate, which might enhance your situation."

"OK, OK, I'll try it."

"Besides, you can let your girlfriend use it on you, too."

"Maybe. I'd have to try it myself first."

"Well, call me when you do, I'll tell you exactly what to do, OK?"

"How long are you on the line?"

"Another two hours."

"I'll be back..."

"Bad boy going shopping, eh? Drive carefully...you *do* drive now, right?"

"Yeah, had to sell the stick and buy an automatic. That accident really changed my life! But, you know, I *like* not shifting gears. It makes driving a lot less work, so I'm not complaining, I just hope my hard-on doesn't get in the way of the steering wheel."

"Hurry safely, baby...we'll do you up right."

"I'm flying, Jamie. This is one time I won't linger over the magazines at the back of the store!"

Click.

"...feel like talking, just say hi. I can't see your driver's license from here, so your voice will have to do it. You have to be 18 to turn me on! Now, baby, Jamie's getting lonesome out here...speak up now or forever hold your piece..."

Click.

The idea of two women having sex fascinates many callers. If they don't ask for it themselves, they rarely refuse it when offered... some want to hear what the girls do to each other, some care only what the two will do to him....

Lesbian love excludes men; we avoid the term. Bisex includes men; we always reassure them that fun is fun, but cocks have their place(s). It can be daunting to a man who has actually seen women making love to each other—the two come and come and come and come, kissing and caressing for hours. The sheer romance of it may seem to diminish men's efforts in this regard. The skillful operator de-emphasizes anything hurtful to the caller while concentrating on his fantasy.

The passive caller wants to watch, either secretly as if from the window or tied to a chair so he is prevented from involving himself, or up close, eyes to thighs. He wants them to notice him, ignore him, tease him, refuse him, satisfy him and/or call more girls over that he can/can't have. He is part of the "drama"; he is the captive audience.

The aggressive caller wants them all over him, one licking his ass while the other rides his face, the two of them sucking his cock, four tits for him to fondle. One girl has to hold the other open. One girl has to eat pussy while she gets balled. One girl has to dildo-bang the other while he masturbates. One girl has to wait her turn.

Many married men imagine the operator swinging into the conjugal bed, seducing his bi-passive wife slowly, sweetly, as he watches, and helps if requested. Finally the operator is eating the wife while the husband gets his cock into some new flesh…his wife's joy and his own mingle in his mind…how can she object to his experience when she's cruising Cloud 9? Yet there isn't any cock (spell it c-h-a-l-l-e-n-g-e) for him to contend with; it's only another harmless pussycat, no roving dog….

"What color panties are you wearing?"

"Actually I'm not wearing any."

"Ooooh…."

Click.

"…so I told him I had this girlfriend who came to town unexpectedly, I'd have to cancel our date, and he said bring her along, we'd all see a movie or something…. Well, one thing led to another and there we were, the three of us, feeling no pain, back at my one-bedroom apartment. She was going to sleep on the couch, but I have this huge king-sized bed. I said I always slept on the right side, she said she just had to sleep on the left side of a bed, so he got stuck in the middle."

"Hell, I'd sleep on a rug at the foot of the bed if you were in it with another girl…."

"Aren't you the sweetest thing? Just for that we'd invite you up to join us. We'd each reach out and stroke one thigh, our other hands on our own tits. You'd be going crazy but trying to act cool. When we kept brushing up against your cock, though, you'd have to let out one little tiny moan, yeah, just like that one. We turn to you and press our bodies up against you on either side…"

"All that skin…"

"We'd both be kissing your face and neck and shoulders and belly and groin and dick, you'd feel my big firm tit in one hand and her tiny hard-nippled tit in the other…my mouth would close around your cock and swallow it as she moved up on the bed and lowered her crotch onto your smiling face, she tastes so good. I know, I said she was my girlfriend, didn't I?"

"Oh, wow, could I fuck you while I ate her? It's like my dream, my all-time dream."

"My knees slide around your hips, my cunt tickles your dick, my girlfriend is riding your tongue as I guide your cock into my hole...I can put my arms around my girlfriend and pinch her nipples while you eat her. You can feel how that excites her, she's sopping wet. I'm churning on your dick, faster and faster, squeezing that muscle between my legs, bouncing up and down in your lap."

"I'm so close..."

"Your ass is tight, you flex your legs to shove your dick higher into me, your hands are clenched as you concentrate on putting your tongue in her hole as far as your dick is in my hole, I'm masturbating while I ride you. You can feel my cunt ripple as we fuck, coaxing the come to the head of your cock."

"That's it, that's it..."

"You let it go, that thick come pumps up the length of your dick, surging out of your balls then creaming out the top into my juicy hole. She realizes you've come and she comes all over your face. You drink her in, we all fall back on the bed, sticky but happy...."

"Ohh, girl...you're just too hot to be true."

"Can't play good tennis alone, baby...my God, the way you breathe, it's really sexy. Gasp-gasp, then those silences. I knew you were concentrating, I could hear your hand slapping up and down. You beat meat!"

"I will call again—this was incredible. Like a talking dream, girl. You sound very beautiful."

"You be cool, now, you hear?"

"Will do. *Adios.*"

"*Hasta* whenever, *amigo.*"

Click.

A good operator is in control, she sets the pace and determines the direction of the phone caller's fantasies. His suggestions are just that: suggestions...she hears what's underneath that first-level (speakable) fantasy, so if he says he wants his cock sucked, she tries to guess whether that includes his balls being squeezed, his asshole being stimulated, his nipples pinched. For some men, cunnilingus means the tip of his tongue at the top of her mound near the clit only, others want their tongue up your vagina, some ignore the hooded area completely. It isn't always what they want to do but how they want to do it that marks the success or failure of the call: to some men tits are to be touched gently, others want to crush them. Power-fucking is an alien concept to the caller who wants to rock gently between your legs. The trick is to nudge the caller in a direction and listen closely for his response. If your hands stroking his ass elicit a sigh, you can slip closer to finger-fucking his ass; if he is silent, you switch your hands to a neutral location. When men want a bisex fantasy, it usually means they'll suck cock and/or let a man eat them (no hugging or kissing, please), but it can mean he wants to be bum-fucked while the operator watches. Guessing wrong can kill a call.

The big surprise? Men want their butts played with. An overwhelming majority will gasp if you volunteer that detail during the re-creation of a sex act...just grabbing it while he screws is a turn-on. If you detail that you'll pry his cheeks apart to expose his asshole, he'll more often than not say "yes, oh yes," and once you put a finger in it, he is going to climax rapidly. In part it is the novelty, I'm sure, since many women do not think to do this. (Neither do many men). The stimulation itself is a turn-on, the intimacy, the forbidden-ness, the tantalizing insertion of a finger or a lubricated dildo into the tiny, tight hole; the idea that the particular partner is doing it is another source of pleasure. Men must remember to use one hand for the ass exclusively and the other for the vagina exclusively and to wash them both thoroughly. Men don't have a warm, moist incubator between their legs, so the chance of bacterial contamination is much less, although anal intercourse creates a similar risk to them via the urinary tract (and to the woman if he switches from ass to cunt without first pissing, then washing his dick). These kinds of details are important in the flesh, of course, and less so on the phone—but it sometimes helps a call if you talk frankly about the mechanics of the intimacy. The men then know you are taking them seriously and also sense the voice of experience.

Some of the most evocative talk is the raw stuff, the times when a man feels free to say what's really on his mind. He doesn't want a sweet cunt, he wants a juicy smooshy cooze. Those statuesque breasts had better jiggle and sway. He wants to shove his hand all the way up inside. He wants to be smothered in pussy, drowning in it, soaked in it, his stick/rod/wand is bursting, itching to be soothed by the smooth fluids of the female. Can he shoot all over my breasts, my belly, my face and hair, up high on the mound, over the bent ass, into the split crack...when? soon? now?

Certain of my phrases get very definite response—if I say he can "cream deep inside" or "spill yourself" or "empty it, all of it" or that "he's full of fuck" at just the right moment, it is as good as over...he will ejaculate with a gusto that spells *bingo*. Some men are amazed that they can be operated so easily by a stranger, but I laugh it off, telling them I'm every woman they've ever known, so of course I'm strangely familiar.

They mostly want to push, shove, jam, slam, slide, swoosh, glide, cram and thrust/drive/force their dicks into, way into, all the way into, totally into some(one)(where)(thing). They apparently like that I use different verbs like ball, bang, hump, dick, screw, ride, etc., for the fuck talk, but I do say I'm a fuckin' female, that I like a powerfuck, that I fuck a man as hard as he fucks me, that I'll let him fuck my face, that he can fuck my ass, that he can fuck my hole, that he can fuck the deep cleavage between my round full breasts, that he can fuck and fuck and fuck until his ass hurts, until his thighs tremble, that if he doesn't scream he doesn't mean it, that he'd better give me everything, even that hidden inch that they'll pull out when they *really* get going. (This is a really popular concept: they'll all brag that, yeah, they got plenty, if only their partner can coax it out of them.)

Not surprisingly, the oral lovers are most verbal about their interest. They want to lick and nibble between your lean thighs, tongue the tiny holes between your legs (all three), mouth not just the nipple but the entire tip of the tit, put suck marks up and down your throat. I tell them I'll masturbate right into their face, climax around their tongue, ooze the sweetest fluid of all for them around the hard vibrating dildo they thrust into me, shake my fanny until they are nuts with lust, spread that pussy wide open with my fingers so they can bury their face between my legs—he's belly down and face forward, me on my back, soles of my feet flat on the bed, knees bent high for maximum bounce in the butt, easy tilt of the pelvis and heaving of the chest.

Fuck positions? On my back with my knees around my ears; on my belly with my ass raised; on my knees with straight arms braced against the wall; on his lap, face forward, tits against his chest; standing up holding my ankles; in the arms of another man; leaning over the bed with my face between the legs of his lady friend; in the backseat of the car; on a picnic table in the park after hours; him on his side with me on my back, legs over his waist; me on top of him thigh to thigh so he can slide me side to side; on top facing away so he can watch it; on my shoulders hauled up by my ankles; on my back with straight legs pressed against my chest by his body weight; on all fours in front of the mirror; with a dildo in my ass, with my fingers on my clit, crushing my tits in my hands, plucking my nipples in front of his eyes, running my hands through my long, curly hair, raising my arms so he can see the curve of my breast and my shaved/hairy armpit; upside-down from a bondage frame; standing up bent into his lap while the biggest, hugest, hardest, fullest dick of all time piles into me and shoves my mouth deeper onto his throbbing cock; on the waterbed with him on top, me flat on my back with legs twined around his, undulating....

More fantasies from callers: (1) let's pretend we're in an adult movie theater, getting it on in the center seats, while all around us people watch us instead of the movie; (2) you be soaking in the bath when I come home from work, and I'll get so excited I'll ruin my good blue suit plunging my hands into the water to get at you; (3) I'm a general contractor who's come to knock a wall out in your bedroom so it connects to the bath, and all the while I do the work you are very reserved but on the last day you seduce me in the big beautiful room; (4) you tell me you went out shopping, but when I eat you out, I taste sperm; (5) we're strangers, we dance once, when I dance with you again I realize you've taken off your bra, the third dance and I can't feel panties under your skirt; (6) you seduce my wife in the backseat of the car while I drive around; (7) we're watching an X-rated movie you had made specially for my birthday—you're the star; (8) I lie on the floor and you squat over me…I can see and smell you, but I can't even lick it until you say so; (9) I'm the first man up your ass; (10) I'm giving a lecture, and you're in the front row, flashing your pussy at me, I can see your nipples under your sheer blouse, but you leave before the lecture is over, and when I go to the men's room you are naked in a stall waiting for me, standing on the toilet, and I eat you right then and there.

"Jamie, now be honest, I have a small dick. I mean it is nowhere near six inches, like average…"

"Remember, it takes a lot of fives and a lot of sevens to make a six average, so relax a bit."

"I'm four, Jamie…four!"

"Thick or thin?"

"Oh, it's fat enough, just short."

"Most of the stimulation of fucking is at the vaginal opening, so a thick cock of any length is good for that. After that it's only the eights and nines that really make a dent in a girl."

"I give good head to make up for it."

"I hope even if you had a ten-incher you'd learn to give head. Sex is not spelled p-e-n-i-s, and you're really missing the boat if you think it is. Grinding against her mound to stimulate her clit is as important to getting her off as the love-sounds you make when she pleases you."

"I wish more women felt the way you do."

"More women do than you know, evidently; very, very rarely have I met a woman who was hung up on dick size. Honestly. Females are less measurement oriented than males in that area."

"Well, I don't know. It's hard to believe, all the magazines and videos…"

"Yeah, you need a fast car, a condo, and lots of money to have sex. You need a perfect body, no brains and always have sex in an orgy situation...that's what the videos and mags tell you."

"OK, another point for you."

"Why are you so insistent that I'm wrong? Are you used to using the excuse that you have a little dick to explain your problems with women? Let me tell you, those hung dudes call and tell me they can't find a woman who can fit them in, they can't find a lady who can swallow all of it, they can't have anal sex, they never do really bang between a lady's legs...you have any of *those* problems? No, you have a perfect cock for oral sex, excellent for sitting on and riding, maybe a bit thick for butt-sex."

"Come on, those guys really do call and say that?"

"You bet, buddy. The grass is always greener...."

"OK, OK...you win."

"Remember, short and stiff is better than long and limp!"

"Now, that's something I will remember. Thanks. Sorry it wasn't the sexiest call in the world."

"It was real, wasn't it, and that's what sex is all about; if you fuck with even an ounce more confidence, this call was well worth the money."

"You bet it was. 'Bye for now."

Click.

"...so, my pretty boy, tell me what you're wearing..."

"Black stockings, black shoes, black garter belt. It looks great."

"I bet it does, with those long legs of yours. You have a bra on?"

"I don't wear any fucking bra, damn you..."

Click.

"Content neutral" is the phrase used by phone companies when explaining their record of not judging phone users. In order to gain their monopolistic hold on telephones in this country, they had to service every little town, every "bad" neighborhood, each and every financially qualified individual, without regard to their purpose as long as it was legal—legal being a judicial question, one to be resolved only by court-ordered search warrant. This meant gun companies and antigun lobbies could have phones; right-to-lifers and pro-choicers; Gentile, Jew, agnostic, atheist; liquor distributors and temperance leagues...phone companies were charged with providing phones, not moral guidance. Now they have segregated sex-related businesses as being "not in keeping with the corporate philosophies" of the companies, as if *these* are their first sex-related profits. Don't they sell phone services to adult bookstores and theaters, to erotic toy stores, to fantasy magazines, to singles bars, to escort services? Many murderers have had phones—do *they* contribute to corporate goodwill?

We cannot sell sex: that is illegal, and phone service can be denied legitimately (see, however, reference to legalities). *We can sell the illusion of sex,* which is legal and for which phone service should not be denied.

Phone sex and the public outcry over the phone companies' involvement in it isn't a simple issue, in large part because of the monopoly that exists in phone service. If some outraged citizens claim the companies "invade" their privacy by having these numbers available (although the individual may freely choose to never dial them), others can rightly claim "denial" if the numbers are not available to be dialed if and when desired. A monopoly cuts both ways. The real problem is the *content* of phone conversations, and that is protected by law, like your closet or the trunk of your car. The court must be petitioned in each and every instance, must be given probable cause for the breach of privacy, meaning reasonable suspicion of criminal involvement, and specific unlawful evidence must be sought. Knowing this, the phone company as a policy was "content neutral" meaning that it did not judge the quality or character of what was said in the call unless and until ordered to reveal specific information by and to the court. They bill charges for gun companies and liquor distributors and bible makers and motels that rent rooms by the hour and for every other type of business. People use the phone to make money to varyingly direct degrees: some sell by phone, some merely make contact by phone and sell in person.

The changes in early 1988 that segregated sexplicit phone services from any and all other types of businesses is an abuse of the "lobbying" concept, wherein a vocal minority silences an opposing minority, while the majority doesn't understand the battle. These moralists are forcing the phone companies to abandon a long-held responsibility to service the entire country, not just the popular cities, not just at peak hours, not just when it was profitable, or popular, or universal. To burden them with judging the nature of an installation (which cannot be done without monitoring, which cannot be done without breaching the privacy of everyone's phone) is displacing the responsibility for moral judgment.

It is fundamental to believe that we are a nation of individuals and that our private lives are exactly that. If we pay our taxes, do our duty within contemporary local moral boundaries, we have the right to expect privacy as to the rest of our time. Any infringement diminishes the power of the right for everyone else because restricting a person from expressing personal opinion—be it how often he masturbates or when he prays—is beyond the scope of any government sanction, and the phone companies are a monopolistic extension of our public utility concept.

The fight over phone fantasy is fanned by the hell-and-damnation crowd, inspired by their visions of a lust-free world. They have effectively but inappropriately pressured the phone companies into applying subjective judging criteria to a properly fiscal transaction.

To protect the little towns, the high-risk neighborhoods, the low-profit phone users, it was a cornerstone of the telecommunications structure to service each and every corner of the country, not only geographically (but of course that was crucial—it would not have been sufficient to have phones in popular places, they had to wire up all the towns), not judge whether the phone was for right-to-lifers or pro-choice people, no special services for gentiles only. What do gun companies, alcohol distributors, tobacco growers, child-care centers, hospitals, strip joints, churches, gay-rights groups, pit-bull breeders, nightclubs, Democrats, Republicans, Socialists, Communists and Independents have in common? They can all have phones.

Segregating sex-oriented phone services erodes the long-held policy of neutrality necessary to ensure that "profit" alone was not the judgment, for although phone-fantasy cash flow is high, it is disproportionately costly in terms of defending against the Morality Gestapo. The phone company is specifically stating they will not allow users who do not conform to the "corporate image," although how that criteria could be judged is anybody's guess. First the sex businesses, then who? Are gun lobbyists next? How about the Mormons—do they bug anybody at the home office? And those Dianetics people—sounds cultish to the CEO. Who says homos need phones? What are the demographics on long-term marketing to the hospice crowd? Sorry, no speaking Spanish on American phones!

"...this is Jamie, I know you're out there, next time put the Siamese outside...I'm sorry, I shouldn't tease...we're all alone on the line. The longer you wait, the harder it is to speak up...I'm just checking your ID..."

"I'm old enough."

"Any special topic? ...I guess not...today I'm in the mood to show off...I think of you in bed, naked, masturbating, bored, just yanking it around, the bedroom door swings open, I'm standing there in black heels, black stockings, black garter belt, black bra, black mask... My pale skin shines in the light from the hallway, but your room is dim and you can't believe what you're seeing. I move to the end of the bed and stand there, tough, sexy, curvaceous, and your hand stops moving on your cock. I turn around, show myself off, bend over and wiggle my hips, strut around, my firm breasts swell over the top of the bra, the cleavage is deep and full. I stand next to you and you reach up and feel my cunt. It's hot and dry. My thighs feel cool above the silky stockings. You can sense the strong muscles in my legs and ass as I rub my crotch against your hand. I get moist right near the hole and you catch the scent of my pussy, delicate and haunting. You push your face against my fleshy bare mound. I spread my legs wider, and you move over so you're face-up, your forehead at my ass, your chin at my clit. I lower myself slightly so you can just touch me with your tongue, and I control the pressure by lifting and lowering myself onto your waiting face. I come a little, seep more juice, the taste is stronger and sweeter, you can't get enough of it. You come on your belly and don't even notice as I continue to let you fuck me with your face."

"Are you reading this?"

"Shit, no, but I ought to be writing it…now, come on, sweetheart, don't tell me this doesn't arouse you."

"It got me off about 3 sentences into it. You're way too smooth, though, it sounds rehearsed. I thought you'd mostly moan and groan, I like that."

"Gee, why didn't you stop me—I can groan with the best of them. Some guys like the nonstop patter; most girls can gasp like they mean it. We each have our own style, and if the guy seems verbal, there's a lot more back-and-forth. I thought you just wanted to listen."

"Well, mix a few in, you know, moans, take a breath, let the details sink in. Don't get me wrong, you're good, you're great, you really had me thinking right with you…"

"Got you—sounds like good advice. Thanks for the tip."

"But you sure do sweet-talk, it was a pleasure, believe me. I got the evidence here on the sheets to prove it."

"I'll take that as a compliment."

"Good night."

"Good night."

Click.

"…in fact, Jamie, I wrote you a letter. I want to send it to you, OK?"

"Not OK, sorry; we can't accept fan mail. But I'm really flattered. I guess that means I'm getting to you."

"I don't mean to send it to *you*, I mean I'd send it to your company and they could give it to you. Really, it's just my way of saying thank you."

"Oh, go on. You probably jerked off after you wrote it, right…more likely right in the middle…"

"So? That doesn't mean I didn't mean what I wrote."

"It means you're a smart man who used a pen and paper to focus his energy for his own pleasure, like some men might grab the baby oil and slick up their dick. It is a compliment to me, and

I really am flattered. But we don't publish the company's address—too many cranks out there."

"Well, if I can't, I can't...but I could write to the magazine where I got your ad. Maybe they'd forward it."

"We told them to destroy all such correspondence. They aren't the P.O., you know...."

"I give up, but I'm going to keep on writing the letters. I guess you're right, they turn me on..."

"Great. I approve. Collecting your thoughts is an important part of good fantasy. Have fun, you hear me?"

"Bye, Jamie and you're missing one hot letter, let me tell you."

"That I don't doubt a bit. Now, scoot along, you're almost at your limit."

" 'Bye, Jamie, it was really fun talkin'—"
Click.

I've had men tell me they've "had me" before, they've "already done me, thanks," or [once] "yuck, not you again." One guy told me he thought there was only me and one other woman covering the whole clock since he'd run into each of us a few times and missed everyone else.

I do get slammed for being too smooth, too quick to slide into a ready-made fantasy, not enough moaning, talking too fast, and being unbelievable. I understand I'm verbally quicker on most subjects than many people, and definitely out front on the sex talk, and also that my style is distinct from the "simulator" operator who relies on gasps and giggles to feed the fantasy element. If I can, I recover the call, or I will outright tell a caller when the shift will change, if that's what he wants. Some men tell me to "pretend" I'm coming but I tell them that's one thing I never learned to fake.

Men tell me I couldn't possibly be real—how can I argue? "Jamie" isn't real, but I am. "Jamie" is patterned on my reality as much as a character could be since I am writer/producer/actress. If I were to interpret someone else's writing, or write a role for someone other than myself, then "Jamie" would be a blend of personalities. She's by me and for me; she exists as different aspects of one person blended into one strong projection.

I'm not ordinary, but I fall within the range of "normal," in the sense of averaging human potential, so there is low-normal and medium-normal and high-normal. An average penis is six inches long; you could be normal at 5.1 or 7.6.

Ordinary means without distinguishing characteristics, so if all raccoons have circles around their eyes, that trait, which would be distinctive in a dog, is ordinary in a raccoon. For a single female who was sexually active through the late 1970s and the 1980s, it is not unusual for me to accept the idea of gender equality while insisting on chivalrous attentions; in a business meeting, gender is mute, while on a date it is a matter of some interest. Many women my age experienced sex with multiple partners and found it satisfying for then, if not for always. Others were, as is normal, married to (one of) their first lover(s) and remained primarily faithful. Both fall within the range.

The one characteristic I put into Jamie most deliberately is her wish to *move*, to *feel*, to *get it* and *have it* and *do it*, since the one characteristic mourned by men is women's passivity in sex. At first, they appreciate permission to do, but as they mature they want to be done to. They seek in the female a matching hunger and desire; it excites them tremendously when a woman reaches for them, maneuvers them into sex, calls them forth.

The pressure on men to imagine new ways and new things and new settings can ruin what should be a mutual opportunity to express feeling. Men I've spoken to will accept boldness in a woman, although there is a line between being gracefully aggressive and being overwhelmingly greedy. Just as they don't like being thought of as forever in charge, neither do they express any fondness for being a walking dildo. (OK, OK, the slave calls *do* wish for that function but they're abdicating gender-defined presumption of sexual authority by doing so.)

The operators' schedules had to be shifted around; our instincts plus corporate advice indicated a need for shorter shifts, more voices. Several operators were holding more hours than was wise; they were uneven in performance, sometimes dull and hard to get started, other times shrill from exhaustion. Also, it is easier to fill in when we have more operators who need the hours rather than running on fewer who are maxed out. In the future all new-hires will be told there is a twenty-hour maximum standard rotation with five hours fill-in per week if available, average fifteen to eighteen hours is preferred. In point of fact, we don't want anyone with a full-time gotta-be-here attitude; we want the money to be a welcome addition to an existing income and the time given gladly in three- and four-hour bursts. We want the operators to sound like gifted amateurs, not tired old pros. We also reserve the right to bounce them around the clock a bit, asking them to sacrifice a few hours on a Saturday afternoon once a month or hopping on for a mid-morning shift…variety, variety, variety.

The veterans kicked. We'd been easing them back from thirty-five hours to thirty as it was, partly because we finally had more operators to work with. It's all part of the growth of the business, and they will have to understand that to preserve the very existence of the business, they might have to sacrifice some personal convenience. None of the operators is so peculiarly talented that she could not be replaced, but surely we'd miss them and hope they'd reconsider once the lost income was truly missed. We've made it clear the schedules were never set in concrete; everything about this business is an experiment.

This change made scheduling harder, of course, but it paid off in increased caller satisfaction so it was well worth the extra bit of work. The old way we just wrote in the regulars and then filled as we could: now we make a tentative schedule, confirm and adjust it all around. The operators got used to that soon enough because we work it that way; those who didn't cooperate lost hours. We know that they have to look out for themselves, but we have to watch out for all of them and for ourselves, too.

"So, Paul, do you eat pussy?"
"No."
"Oh, OK, you're a straight fuck, then?"
"Hard fuck. I like it hard and fast and for a long time."
"I love the feel of it slipping inside me."

"I slam."

"Hope you have the ass and thighs to drive that thing around, it takes a lot of muscle to powerfuck like you're describing."

"I ride a bicycle ten miles a day."

"Yep, that would do it. So, what should I do?"

"Can you take a lot of cock?"

"A small cock for a long time, or a long cock quickly?"

"A huge dick for a long, long time?"

"If you can keep me wet…how big?"

"It's nine and a half and thick, and it's hard to get off."

"Large cocks sometimes are. You got a big old body attached to that thing?"

"No, that's the kick. I'm 5'5", thin, with a monster cock."

"Gee, I bet that looks hot—you know, when a guy is 6'2", a big cock like that just looks like it's in proportion—yours must jut out like a big surprise. But don't you worry, my cunt is built just right for a man like you. I'm muscular and tight, so you'd have to ease it in…no slamming yet…and help me open up to fit you inside."

"I had a girl like that once. I thought I'd never get in, and she was the best yet."

"We muscular women are like that, we can be stretched slowly to fit just about anything. We'd start with you on top, holding yourself high up on straight arms, my legs parted, knees up so I can keep you back a bit."

"Are your titties bare? I want them to jiggle when I fuck you."

"Here they are! Shake me up, lover!"

"I'm putting it in slow, like you said, but I really just want to get up inside you."

"Baby, with a cock like that, you better learn some patience. If you want a long ride, you can't bruise the sweet thing getting inside now, can you? Oh, no, ease it in then pull it out, let my juice flow a bit, then ease in deeper."

"You're driving me crazy."

"That's nothing, baby, wait until you get it all the way in."

"I can't wait, the head is big and once it's inside, I really can't resist shoving harder."

"I know, darling, all that hot cock, wants to bury itself, doesn't it, wants me to open wide and take that throbbing cock, yes, love, shove it on in, that's it, all the way, yes, baby, I want it from you, take it from you."

"Those tits moving yet?"

"They're all over the place, you're moving so fast, just quivering and bouncing as you cram that cock into my hole."

"Big tits, I love 'em, like if I'm behind you I watch them swaying while I ball you."

"We can do it in front of the mirror so you can see everything."

"Would you call me 'darling' again, I liked that."

"Darling, you fill me up, that beautiful cock feels so good inside me, I want you, dear heart, want you to take me and make me yours, want to feel you fill me up inside, oh, darling, fuck me, fuck me harder."

"I'm fucking you, darling, I'm fucking you hard, and you like it, don't you, darling, don't you? Call me Paul..."

"I love it, Paul, I love you inside me, ohh, darling, let me have it, I've waited for a big boy like you, those strong legs driving that dick up deep, it's *so* fucking big, darling, so fucking, fucking big. Come on, Paul, give it to Jamie...slam it, fuck."

"Ohh, darling..."

"Jamie's here, darling, she's here to take that big old dick and squeeze him dry, coax the come right to the head..."

"Ohhhh, dear heart..."

"Sweetest man, you aren't such a bad ass, are you, no, Paul, I didn't think so, you're my darling, my baby, my love."

"Yessss, I'm your love."

"Let it go, Paul, let it go..."

Click.

"...like talking, just say hello. If you feel like listening, you still have to say hi so I know you're out there. Now, we don't want to burn the ears off some little kid whose mama is too busy making dinner to watch him/her/them..."

"I just want to listen."

"Well, you're over eighteen."

"Way over. So…talk."

"Pick a topic or take the Talk du Jour."

"The daily special, please."

"Today we feature a naked woman asleep on a bed, soundly, deeply, totally asleep. She's so peaceful and quiet you want to sit next to her and just look to your eyes' content."

"I like this."

"You reach out and touch her skin—it's warm and smooth. You run your hands over her hips, down her legs, afraid you'll wake her if you move too fast, but this is a fantasy and she won't wake up…you lean down and press your lips to her tender bosom and as your hand works slowly between her thighs, she turns on her back, her legs fall apart and you can't believe it—her pussy's shaved."

"I've never seen a real one shaved, just movies."

"It's less romantic in real life, stubble and all that. But this fantasy woman is shaved smooth and hairless, her lips are clearly visible and the faintest hint of moisture glistens on her cunt-lips."

"I'm amazed at how real you make it sound."

"Amazed is nice, aroused is better."

"I'm amazed at how arousing it is."

"You put one finger along her slit, so smooth, so delicate and suck her nipple into your mouth, filling your mouth with the ripe fullness of her breast. You're fingering her cunt as her nipples harden into points. You feel her pussy pulsing around your finger, and your cock aches to get inside her."

"I never fucked a sleeping woman, sure have thought about it. You're all so beautiful when you're asleep."

"She's a fantasy fuck, she'll stay deeply asleep as you move inside her; there is no resistance, no shyness, she is waiting for you to use her any way you like."

"I'd come on her stomach, that's what I'd do."

"You pull your cock out and stroke it, it's slippery from her juice, her peaceful body naked beneath you, you gasp and moan as you cream all over her."

"What a fantasy. Thanks, this was fun."

"We aim to please, thanks for calling."

Click.

When you work the line, you are exposed to the emotions of others. You hear the loneliness, the bragging, the kindness. If you've never listened for hours and hours on end, you barely get a sense of it; it is the cumulative effect of all those emotions working on you. The passion is only part of it, though it is a major part. The reaching out is the most distinctive sensation, the way the men yearn for contact. The majority of callers quickly accept that you won't meet them and continue the call anyway. Many don't even ask. What happens is a strange chemistry of strangers being open with each other. What barrier exists between two voices? There is physical safety; there is social anonymity; there is erotic intrigue. The caller can disconnect at his whim or call back. He can admit to things without fear they'll be flung back in his face at a less appropriate time; he can ask questions and know no one will ask why that is on his mind now.

The objection that phone-y sex is impersonal lacks foundation without defining personal. Personal: of, relating to, or affecting a person; done in person without the intervention of another; carried on between individuals directly...if the hinge is the phone as inanimate device, then is a love letter impersonal because paper is used? If the issue is that the individuals are not previously known to each other, then what is a first date? If the objection is that they won't meet in the flesh, what is the value of a long-distance call to an old friend?

No act can be defined without establishing scene, motive and reactions. Slapping someone's face could be the best thing you could do if he or she has just slid into hysterics. Kissing someone's lips might be for the first exciting time or the last sad farewell. A person's private actions are taken in context of his or her life and the society in which he or she is living that life. In certain Middle Eastern countries, it is offensive to eat with the hand that is reserved for bodily cleansing, since the other is preserved "untainted" for contact with food. In some cities there are no X-movie outlets; in others there are dozens. Numbers of churches, clothing stores and fruit stands vary. In some places it is considered déclassé to drive an American car; in others it is considered unpatriotic not to do so.

Times change. What was in goes out and transforms a little later into the newest thing again. There are phases in society. This phase is characterized by verbal freedom, by saying anything that comes into your mind, talk shows on TV, free-for-all encounter sessions, opinion polls, interview-on-the-street journalism. We are breaking the restraint on imagination in order, hopefully, to free our race from self-imposed limits. Lacking the essential changeability so irrepressibly present in the human animal, major institutions like church and family are failing us. The brain is a stunning quick-change artist and, as such, demands expression. When rage explodes, we sputter and yowl; when sorrow hits, we weep and moan. The impact of humor and pathos draws us together, binds us, creates a link between our lonely brains and the lonely brains of other people.

The point? In the late 1980s it is safer and more fun to use the ever-present telephone for fantasy interaction than to risk being smashed by a drunk driver on your way to a bar to be ignored and rejected. It is an outgrowth of our understanding that sex can be procreative or recreative, with emphasis on planning the first and pacing the second. Men are discovering that the women's movement has changed the expectations in and out of the boudoir, granting higher marks for honesty and self-containment, ridding both sides of inaccurate presumptions (he's always horny, she never is). Amidst this revolution, phone sex is just one element.

"…you can't escape me now, you bad boy, you're tied spread on that bed, helpless, naked in front of me, mine to control. I see that cock of yours jumping around, you like the sight of me in a leather bra, don't you, the nipples jutting through the rips in the leather. Now stick out your tongue and lick my dangling breast as I slide my knees around your hips…don't move, you fucker, don't lift that cock up, you haven't earned the right to fuck me yet, did I ask for that dick, did I say lift it to me?"

"I'm sorry, Mistress, I'm sorry."

"Ohh, no, it's too easy for you to pretend to be sorry. You men are all alike—I want you to really regret being so impetuous…I just knew you couldn't be controlled so easily…now close your eyes, I'm blindfolding you."

"Ohh, Mistress...I'm so sorry."

"You hear the bedroom door open. Who is it? Who fucking is it? I don't say a word, I'm still on top of you, my cunt just inches away from your cock. You feel another hand brush against you as it reaches for my pussy, you can feel me moving in response to the stimulation, I'm being masturbated right above you, so close and yet you'll never get it, will you, you little fuck?"

"I'm sorry, Mistress."

"You'll never get it, not unless you learn to behave. You hold your breath, listening. Who is it who sees you this way? Who is staring at your tied hands, your spread legs?"

"Is it a man?"

"The other hand of this person is on your cock, the leather glove feels sexy to you, it handles your cock well, holding it upright so you can barely feel the heat of my cunt above it; but each time you near climax, the hand strangles your cock, kills the urge to come, stops you, then starts again. I come right above your cock and roll off you, go to this person, kiss them, you can hear me moaning as they strip me and touch me all over. Your cock is aching...you want to be part of the fun, but you aren't a good-enough boy, are you? This person strokes your cock again, forces you to ejaculate all over yourself. You can feel the come pooling on your belly, but you're still hard, aren't you?"

"Oh, tell me...who is it?"

"Suddenly I'm next to you again, pulling your hair so your head is back, your throat exposed to my kisses, and I suck your neck, leaving marks, deep red marks of my love on you. You feel the other person join us on the bed, from the sounds you hear you know I'm being mounted...I work his dick up inside me, in my pussy! He's in my cunt, you bad, bad boy. He's in my sweet hole, taking what you've waited for. The blindfold is removed and you see a strong mean-looking man piling his thick dick into me...he gets what you want."

"Is he...I mean...did you make him...?"

"He puts his face near yours, looks right in your eyes, tells you he used to be like you, stupid and untrained, unable to control himself. But now, with my help, he's capable of anything, can do anything, can surrender. You see that muscular body in a slip, his cock huge and hard as it pleases me, the smell of my perfume on him, I suck the lipstick off his lips…he gets to fuck the Mistress, take the Mistress…why? Because he earned it, because he goddamn fucking surrendered."

"I would, I do, I am surrendering…"

"Watch me, you fucker, watch me get it from another man—not you, you aren't worthy. You're tied in the bed like a puppy who can't be trusted, you only get to watch a real man make love to me. What's he doing to your Mistress, how is she treating him?"

"He's fucking you in front of me, right next to me, looking at me helpless on the bed. He gets to touch you and hold you."

"You're jealous but you know you were wrong, you tried to sneak into my cunt and that didn't work, did it, you fuck?"

"No, Mistress, I'm sorry."

"You can't steal from me, you shit, you can only accept what I give when I give, which I'll do if you earn it."

"I'll earn it, I swear I will, I'll do anything."

"Next time you call, have your legs tied together. You hear me? And don't lie to me—I know when you're lying to me."

"I'll do it, I swear I'll do it."

"Now hang-up and don't touch that cock, let it ache, you hear, the only way you can get off is to *think* it off. Don't touch it! Call Thursday at ten."

"But I have to—"

"You have to call, you hear? At ten. Sharp. And be tied up."
Click.

"I kiss your sweet lips, suck them, use my tongue to pry them apart, lick your mouth, kiss your throat and shoulders, right on down your belly, soft nibbling kisses. I lick your nipples then breathe softly on them…doesn't that feel good, my dear, isn't it nice to lay back and be made love to for a change? Yes, dear, I know you like it. Sweet Jamie is all over you, her smooth skin brushes against you, round and firm flesh, whisper soft…ohh, dear, you are getting awfully big, aren't you, that dick of yours is all swollen, I bet it aches, doesn't it, baby? See, mama knows, she'll take care of you, see how softly she touches it, caresses your

cock? Her slim fingers hold you gently, firmly, and you gasp—
like that—as she applies the first pressure, down against the
head, strokes it slowly then faster, harder and harder, yes, it
feels good, doesn't it, dear, doesn't it, darling? I thought so.
Now, sweet love, tell me what you want...come on, say it."

"Make love to me, Jamie!"

"Do you want to put that throbbing cock inside me, David?"

"Yes, oh yes..."

"Say it, lover, say it to me..."

"Love me, please, I need it so much. I need it."

"Yes, love, I'll love you. I'll slide right onto that pretty prick,
no, no, no...not so fast, ease it in there, darling, let me feel every
delicious inch of it. Yesss, slide it in...so good, David, it's so
good."

"Take me deep, all the way, love me all the way, Jamie."

"Yes! You're in, you can feel the wetness, the closeness of my
cunt, that sweet woman feeling, my body close to yours, our
lips kissing, your arms around me, holding me tight."

"Fuck me, sweetheart, fuck me all night long."

"My hips twitch above you, sending shivers up your spine,
the feelings explode in your head, you cling to me as we make
love, pressed together, intimately, lovingly...."

"I come in you, deep inside you. I fill you up, don't I?"

"Yes, oh, yes, you make me happy, you fill me up."

"Ohh, baby, it felt so good, to hear you talking to me. When
can I call you again?"

"I'll be back on Thursday, dinnertime, 4 to 7 P.M. Now, don't
wear that dick out beating him off, you hear? Save some for
me."

"Don't you worry—by Thursday I'll be bursting."

"Thanks for calling again, David. This is such a sweet time for
me; so many guys lack your finesse."

"Until Thursday...sweet dreams, lovely lady. You really add
something to my fantasies."

"It's that dash of reality, you know I'm real as real can be."

"Too real, I feel like I could reach out and touch you.
Sometimes I want to kiss the phone!"

"Whoa, buddy...don't you dare slobber on an electrical device.

Who'd cheer me up on Thursday if you fry your lips and can't talk?"

"OK, OK, I'll restrain myself. Good-bye."

"Good-bye."

Click.

People will ask me if, in my own actual love life, I talk like this to my lovers. What do you think?

Only one caller has admitted to having a "love doll," a life-size plastic surrogate love-object, and I didn't hear that until after I'd worked over 1,000 hours on the line. He said it was no good on top—no pressure—but was OK to lay on top of and hump into...it wasn't as if he *talked* to it, after all.

Phone sex is a phenomenon of the 1980s. It started at the beginning of the decade, came of age around 1985, was in full flower by 1987, and by 1988 showed its first signs of (imposed) restraint. It is part free speech, part freedom of assembly, part freedom of philosophic and/or religious expression. It has attracted horrendous media attention as out-of-control children use the lines to call attention to their fundamental boredom and lack of constructive activities for which, of course, the phone-sex industry, as a whole, is blamed. Luckily, the hot-talk business has the same range of participants as any other activity—some good, some bad, most ordinary.

I appeared on television about it, first time for me, on camera for an entire hour-long show.... There is a green room for waiting guests. In the first segment, I was all alone on-stage facing a curious audience, listening to a bleeped tape of a simulated performance, establishing myself as "Jamie," the name I use when I work the line. The talk show was a local Phil Donahue-esque forum of small audience, paternal host and bipolar guests, showing the pro and con, miserable and worse, triumphant and beyond. They paired me with a lawyer from a decency league which serves as ideological soldiers of fortune, dashing to the scene of any and all "pornography" controversies to shoot off their legal fireworks, in any case, on their predecided side. I much prefer a guardian of process to a lawyer-with-a-cause-on-salary, dollars/hour zeal. The lawyer placed me in the "bright but misguided" category. I didn't waste my limited airtime trying to convince him, I talked to the audience. On the whole, they were genuinely curious about what in the heck was going on. People want to be given "evidence", which they'll weigh—they like information. I trust the average individual to figure out that phone sex is not the scourge on humanity as portrayed by moralizing busybodies. (An affirmative use of energy—running a shelter or quilting for charity—does not satisfy zealots. The clue is the destructive nature of their quest, they want to *ruin* something, not save something.)

Constitutional issues seem obscure to me when whitewashed in modern debates of taste and decorum; the founding documents of our country were written by people who were familiar with sex and intoxicants and literature, yet none of these was singled out in their wisdom and foresight. These minds came from a society rich in specific repressions—they fought instead for conceptual freedoms to think, to speak, to associate, to believe. The Constitution was written to support unpopular views since the majority protects itself by its very inertia; and the additional Bill of Rights developed over the tumultuous first years of this country stressed individual liberty; amendments thereto supported freedom for all.

Of course these kind souls of the morality Gestapo pick up children as battering rams against adults with whom they disagree as if a society geared to its weakest members can satisfy the needs of its strongest. Children are a cherished resource in a functioning society, and common sense dictates that they remain unpolluted. However, phone sex is but one tiny temptation in a complicated world. We must focus on the underlying loneliness any child suffers if phone sex represents "contact" and "entertainment" in his world.

The host of the TV show stayed as neutral as possible in such a black/white confrontation. I stayed firmly in the position of invited pariah, knowing in advance that my very appearance disturbed a portion of the audience, confident my actual existence validated the respect of some others. My opponent wasn't rabid, and the show proceeded along the usual lines of "oh, yes, no one wants to hurt the kids," and "why can't adults discuss what they want to discuss?" Some people are against sexual expression in books, films, music, or life; others wonder why time is spent on a nonissue like this when hunger and war plague our planet.

I was disappointed that this theme dominated the TV show, it is one aspect of the tele-sex industry but it is not the only one. There are legitimate adult callers who are willing to pay for something, that "something" rarely defined, frequently (erroneously) presumed to be a simple litany of scatological phrases. I had hoped to focus more attention on the reality of the business, who calls and when, what we talk about, why they call again and again, or never again. It is my belief that there are some people who want inside info on this phenomenon upon which to base their opinions. As manager/operator of such a service, I have that information.

I'm not suggesting that there aren't grotesquely crude phone sex-vendors; there are also corrupt church administrations, which doesn't damn all religion, and there are crooked coaches who don't put an end to professional sports. Stereotyping at any level reduces understanding of a topic. Dismissing people as props to ideas rather than accepting them as the creators of links for ideas is to miss the essential humanness in us all, the basic drive in any enterprise, the goal of any act. The only group "worthy" of any such stereotyping is the do-goodniks who presume to intrude on *my* life for *their* comfort. Like it or not, this is a "live-and-let-live" society and they infringe on the rights of others with their presumption of moral judgment. To seek to inform is one thing; to seek to infringe is another. Lobbying is *OK*, harassment is *not OK*.

You know I'm inexperienced about this TV stuff because I forgot to even mention that I'd just completed this book, even though I had two openings of a sort; once when I laid claim to a literary heritage, and again when such lofty aims were doubted. But then, you don't shoot every gun in the artillery at the first sighting of hostility.

Any reaction to the TV show delivered to me directly has been all positive—forceful, unabashed, tolerant, classy, right on.

I'm pretty tough so I doubt that the critics are going to seek out a face-to-face confirmation, but surely I've got the old gals in the Rosary Society clicking their beads. My decision to speak out is as natural as can be—if I won't, who would? Either what I'm doing is right and can be acknowledged, or it is wrong and should be stopped. My goal on TV was to give as much practical information about the service as I could slip between the cluck-clucks and tsk-tsks.

I figure that Americans vote with their dollars more often than they vote with their ballots and, in our economy, some citizens are actually diverting personal income to the support and development of phone-sex activities—even under guidelines with restrictions and stigmatization, people call and pay for those calls. If it were a small brand of depraved maniacs, the issue would *still* be freedom of speech; but with the numbers involved, it means more than just a test case in court. It is a statement of values and priorities, of need and want, of searching for contact, for anonymity, for control. If phone sex is a billion-dollar industry, we're getting a strong signal of need/desire for it, aren't we? The sad fact is that more people will take action to complain in letters and calls to editors of advertising publications and to legislators than the many, many callers who, perhaps rightfully, presume that they have made their statement by literally supporting the service.

The sheer sanity of the line is refreshing, even when taken out of context most fantasies involve the connection of human beings, perhaps symbolized by certain articles of clothing or portions of anatomy, but essentially men express a desire to please women, to witness women's joy and release. The routine ejection of sperm can either be a bland chore or an expression of self, depending on the man and circumstances.

Those individuals who claim that we depersonalize sex miss the essence of our service: a voice in telephone-land is not a "real" person, ergo does not demand the same rights as a real female which by negation of a duty bespeaks it, e.g., men know that in actuality things are more complicated than the ten-minute interaction with an operator (which is why they value it, in the sense that a vacation is not intended to replace "actual" life, but to enhance it). I'm not going to lie; I've heard some less-than-politically-correct statements fly by, but often it was just as well that I be reminded that men still harbor mixed emotions toward their complements.

Women don't speak up if they even call in, which I can't know if they don't speak up. I can state with considerable assurance that they represent less than 5 percent of our interactive business, no matter how many might listen in. Now, some men claim they have women with them when they call in; however, in only a small portion of those claims is any evidence (female voice), other than what might be sound tracks from come scenes in sex flicks, offered as proof. Others may never say that in fact there is another person present. I talk to men, I hear men groan and laugh and sigh, I suffer the bestial children...but rarely do I speak to a woman.

For several months after the TV show, positive comments trickled in. When I crossed paths with acquaintances or former business associates, they would do one of two things: they'd say they saw me on TV, or they'd call me "Jamie." Now, the Jamie-name is not confined strictly to use on the phone, so it isn't as if I've never heard it except through my headset, but it will still jar me into paying more attention, especially on the lips of business contacts.

The people who say something about my TV appearance say something positive: I handled myself with poise and grace, I held the audience's attention, I was witty, I was tough...many are women, so we do a bit of girlish giggling over my double life. On the whole, the men don't leer (the better they know me the less likely the leer). Especially the people who just slip a "Jamie" into an otherwise businessy conversation tell me they think the whole thing is hilarious and refreshing, offbeat, outrageously like me.

The grapevine is working fine: those who didn't catch the show will say they heard I was poised/brazen, witty/flippant, good/bad—you get the idea, eyes-of-the-beholder stuff. For the TV generation, being a guest on a talk show is an honor accorded to "interesting" people, "provocative" people, spokes-people. So seeing someone you know in one context fielding audience reaction to something as topical as phone fantasy is stunning; most wondered where I'd been this last year. I was on sexological sabbatical from a career in computers.

Over and over again on the talk show, the audience informed me that I was doing it only for the money. I didn't see fit to explain that I made many times the money per hour as a high-tech consultant and that indeed I expected compensation but wasn't seeking riches. In fact, most operators *do* do it for the money, and my peculiar position doesn't diminish that fact. It *is* a job. If we had to work with volunteers, the whole business would change; we want the operators to have a rational, measurable reason to engage in these conversations. In the sense that nurses, crane operators, accountants (work-for-hire-people) do it for the money, so do we, but of all the things each of us might hire out to do, we happen to do what we do.

Why don't women call? At first thought it is obvious: a woman need not pay a premium price to speak to a man in sexual terms; randomly dialing numbers on her phone would connect her to a willing listener quickly enough. A man on a similar quest would probably meet the police. Why the access situation is that way is a psycho/sociological happenstance; but, yes, when a woman seeks to connect with a man, her chances are much greater of succeeding—providing, however, that we may emphasize *a* man, not *the* man here.

People respond to stimuli; sensory organs exist for the purpose of gathering clues, they are biomechanical devices evolved over time. The filter on this information—the mind—files this information following a unique system not even consciously known to it without deep analysis (if then). One person sees red and thinks of Christmas bows, a favorite dress, vibrant sunsets; another thinks of a twisted truck, blood, roses on a coffin. What does red mean?

Sex is not merely a cultural force, it is a life force, an innate drive, present in our beings as surely as in any cat that ever moaned in heat, in every peacock that showed his feathers, in every pollen-laden flower that flaunted its pistils at a carousing bee. In our American culture in this day and age, our roles are being reshaped even as we live them.

Gender roles continue to be a focus. Suffragettes shifted attention to society's loss of potential by excluding women from the process and, in the usual rush to compensate, there has been a tendency to penalize living men for the sins of their forefathers and reward living women for the suffering of their foremothers. As in any case of prejudicial policy, the institutional imbalance must be corrected, but, in fact, culturally, we still have not fused the strongest elements in our race: emotions.

From birth, gender is determined by a physical reality of chemicals, equipment, and "nature," which if not altered into the rare transsexual being, proceeds through life to define body structure, sexual cycles, and individual potential. Society piles on the heavy baggage of expectation, which from the vantage point of an infant in a pink/blue blanket is cumbersome indeed. From their booties to their toys to their names to their family position, gender is often used as sole determinant. If the only factor is gender, then the decision is flawed; toys, clothes, rooms, roles should consider temperament, ability, interest, stage of development, all of which are more complex than the presence or absence of certain hormonal and/or genital configurations.

Aggression, nurturing, conquest, surrender, pride, intuition are all human traits, present in varying degrees in each of us based on genetics, developed in each of us to varying degrees often based on gender; female aggression is suppressed, male nurturing is de-emphasized. Out of this shaping come creatures who, at least in the 1980s, aren't sure just what they should be, do, feel.

Predefined roles might lend comfort at times. Who can blame the individual for lacks in the system? The stereotypical housewife is "saved" from a life in the mines; the traditional breadwinner husband is "denied" the role of prime parent, so need not test himself there. Small comfort.

Men who call me on the phones express this confusion with more and less success; some just dismiss women as unfeeling and disrespectful of men's needs, others blame men for being unlovable dogs. I think that men are exactly what they are raised to be in this world: as confused as the women with whom they are supposed to connect.

"...listen to what? You call that *beeping*? I know people who can play music on their phone buttons, you don't even have a theme song...why don't you just sit on the thing? Yes, I said, cram it up your ass. You obviously don't know how to use it correctly."
Click.

"...one down, one to go...don't think I didn't hear you click on the line, dearie, so, tell me, what's wrong with you...if the cat's got your tongue you're no use to me...I figure it's been five minutes since you connected, and not one word. I know you have nice phone equipment because you must have this on broadcast, I don't hear a breath or a hand on the receiver.... Since you have so much, much money, why don't you get a roll of quarters before you call next time...drop a quarter every fifteen seconds...that's what you're doing, you know, spilling money on the floor. But don't you worry—the phone company is just waiting to sweep that up... Shit, why not just send them a charitable donation? We all know they never have enough. You're paying for nothing anyway. If you hoped to overhear something hot, too bad, your karma must be bad...this is the quietest it's been all night...guys can probably smell a creep on the line and are waiting until you leave and the air clears...are you the same worthless jerk who didn't say anything before? You sound just like him! But don't you worry—I'm not mad, just curious. When I see a pasty-faced, unkempt zero, I'll think of you...legitimate callers speak up, and kids don't have this much patience...."
"This one does..."
"Did, dopey, *did*."
"Shit..."
Click.

It's a funny business, the men are revved up and ready to race when they hit the Sweet Talker line, some confess they have even said hello to the greeting tape, keyed to the first sound of femininity. Then they usually freeze when they hit the open airwaves and listen in, sometimes to an ongoing conversation, which may or may not be hot, or to the operator seeking his consent to proceed. *Click.* You hear them leave, you never know why...turned off? inhibited? wrong operator? wrong topic? wants group? wants solo? just curious?

First interaction is sometimes quite businesslike. They ask how it works, I tell them. Sometimes they click off without a word, sometimes they say, "No, thanks, not for me" or "I'll call again, now that I know how it works." Some want to know when to call to overhear others on the line. Some are startled at the liveness of the operator; they hem and haw at first.

I've read hundreds of sexology books, keep current on the latest psychological concepts regarding sexual alternatives like cross-dressing. (If you don't start as a kid, it's unlikely you're a TV—it is an imperative thing; dabblers late in life are merely experimenting with fabrics.) I have words for sexual imagery. I don't doubt that the information I provide some callers adds as much to their sexuality as the sexplicit language. This is not a nonstop orgasmic exchange; when kids call in, they are just as likely to hear a discussion of pacing, stamina and endurance, control...that isn't "hot" to a teen who doesn't understand sex.

Sometimes I tell a kid who's trying to sneak on the line that he is like unripe fruit. It would make me sick to eat him—he's just not ready, must be left on the tree or he will never ripen into his potential; that he must not resist the cycles of growth or he will stunt himself. Whether or not he understands me, he gets the idea that he is not going to get more of the senseless raised-voice "discipline" of an angry mom out of me, he is going to get sound advice with little entertainment value.

I will tell a kid that my talking to him is like wasting rocket fuel in a go-cart. I tell a kid he's too puny to go to jail over. I'm on a shark hunt, and he's a pesky minnow. He's Little League while I want the majors. I say his brain isn't big enough yet.

Every once in a while you get a mature kid, probably seventeen or so, has a good head on his shoulders, is curious. If I'm alone on the line, he'll often speak up finally, admit he is underage, for which honest admission I tell him he is well on his way to growing up. We talk about things in general and I explain the cops will shut down the business if kids persist in calling, and to preserve the fun for the majority, the minority (age pun intended) have to resist the temptation to call. I might discuss sex in general, remind him to wrap it when he uses it, to take his time in picking partners, to enjoy shopping around, get into kissing, necking, mutual masturbation; fucking isn't everything. I like these calls, I'm refreshed by them.

I spend a lot of my time giving advice to all ages of caller. Often, after a steamy scene, the man will stay on the line and when he can talk again he'll ask questions like if I really did stuff like that or where could he find a cockring? We talk about AIDS and herpes and getting caught by significant others. Sometimes we get pretty heavy, and I don't hold back. I say what I think.

The guys aren't faking. Any person who has been the object of a man's sexual desire knows there is a richness in the voice, a pace to the breathing, an air of supercharged power punctuated by holding-the-breath silences as the body strives for the ultimate tension. The sounds of longing, challenge, fear of failure (either his to perform or the partner's failure to inspire performance) are not diluted by the phone, although the gleam in the eye, the swelling chest, the aggressive/submissive postures are lost. If anything might be traumatic to the underage listener, it is the raw and powerful gasps and groans of a person in climax. It doesn't exactly fit the image of sex as spiritual experience—sounding more like a cross between the 100-yd. dash and a punk opera, with some sobs and hysterical laughter thrown in for good measure.

I do marvel at some men's concern for the operator's feelings. They ask me what will turn me on? Am I tired of talking about sex, would I prefer just to talk? Do I mind repeating that thing about a guy in the bathtub? Would it be OK if we discussed anal stuff? Did I say yes, did I mean I would do that for him?

Frankly, here's a woman on this phone he'll never see, to whom he pays premium price to "have" for a moment, who is advertised as his sexual fantasy, and he's worried about her happiness! There may be a lot of jerks visible in the press, con men and creepo-types, but there is no lack of the true gentle-man.

On the flip side, of course, some men do take the opportunity to talk tough, to call a woman a bitch, a slut, a whore. They take the chance to make accusations of wanton man-eating and insatiable fucking, indulge in the rare and provocative right to drop the "please" and "thank-you" stuff and get to the "fuck and stuff it" stuff.

I hate the snotty ones, I think of them as the "oh, yeah?" boys. They doubt everything, twist it to the negative, destroy the mood of sensual appreciation. Being quick-witted and having the advantage of being confident in the role of manager/operator I am much more aggressively negative with these yahoos than the other operators. In the interest of irony I don't shoo them away unless they are costing me money by sending away legitimate callers; the more they pay, the better I feel!

Much of it is childishly abusive, a "nyaa nyaa, you're a whore" kind of remark that is so off the mark it has no sting. We aren't offended as much as we're annoyed. I tell them, "Gee, with an attitude like that, you probably do know whores best—the good women ignore bugs like you," or "Not very creative, cretin, I've been called worse names by an outraged nun!" or "Spore? You called me a spore? Oh, you said more? What? Say it again, didn't catch it...buck mew, what...Food buy???"

When I'm in the mood, I'll let them sting a couple of times. Then I'll turn and chase them clear off the phone. "You bet I'm a bitch, baby, I'm the bitchingest bitch that ever bitched about low-life scum like you, I'm that sassy-assed slut who makes you wet your pants when you think of me in bed. You want to get in line with the real men, but you're chickenshit. All this experience has taught me to smell a turd like you when you ooze into the room. You're so goddamn fascinated with bad girls, you probably wish you *were* a slut—that's why you use the word so much, isn't it? You wish you could make somebody notice your sexuality for a change. Well, I've got bad news for you, cock-breath, it isn't going to happen on this planet, better luck on your home world, you twisted empty dick, you are what you are and I'm here to tell you that ain't much at all. Do you happen to know if your dad is a priest? You sure are quick with the moral judgments. Or did you learn this language between your mother's knees?"

The snappier the put-down, the longer they stay ($$$$$&$!). It doesn't matter if this feeds into their belief of woman-as-cunt since that particular variety of warp takes major deprogramming and/or brain remodeling to straighten out. It isn't to stop their thinking in those terms but to cause them to pay for their ignorance that I deliver an entertaining put-down, in fact I've been complimented on this sort of rap from callers who connected mid-tirade and thought I handled the swine well.

Some even apologize ("Gee, I lost my head." I say, "Well, gee, then I'll just have to give you some.").

If you don't bail out at the point of climax, you may be treated to the beautiful finales some of the men share with the operator. The younger man often reverts to a simple boyish appreciation: "Gee, that felt so nice, you sound so pretty..." while the mature man wishes to be precise: "Stupend—, no, beyond that, exquisite! Yes, extremely well done." It isn't only thanks, but thanksgiving.

"I'm in a hurry. What color panties are you wearing?"

"None. I'm wearing thin cotton pants, dark blue, sheer enough to feel my pussy-lips through them."

"Are you wearing a bra?"

"No, a sky-blue sweater hugging my full breasts. I can see the nipples thick under the soft fabric."

"Did you say your name was Janey?"

"Jamie...mmm...Jamie."

"Jamie, I'm going to drive to work thinking of you in those pants and sweater, wishing I could touch you."

"Honey, you do that. I'll touch myself while you think about me. Imagine, somewhere a woman has your cock in mind..."

"Oh, what a thought... 'Bye for now."

Click.

"...you're lying, you girls are all the same, done everything, like everything..."

"Baby, hang up the phone, OK? This service isn't for you, you don't have any imagination...."

"I'll stay on as long as I like. Why don't you tell me some more lies, bitch?"

"Haven't told any yet, so I can't tell more."

"Quit fucking me over, cunt, talk to me."

"You're a sad and lonely individual. You have few friends. Women don't like you because you're paranoid and suspicious of them. You spend a lot of your time wondering why people don't like you instead of admitting it's because you don't like them much."

"Save the penny analysis for some other sucker. I'm not buying it."

"Sure you are, you're buying it by the minute, man, that's a dollar a minute, sixty dollars an hour, like a budget shrink, except I'll volunteer my honest opinion rather than blaming your mother for everything. You're bitter and foul, selfish, unkind, and you can think about that when you pay your phone bill...."

"I happen to have a lot of friends."

"Then call one of them to listen to your shit—we aren't interested. But we'll take your money, sure, you bet; in fact, when you get disconnected call right back, OK? Let's run that phone bill up a bit. It'll be my pleasure. We can talk about your maladjustment to reality, your disordered personality, your sexual inadequacy reflected in your presumption that sex is bad...it probably *is* when you're involved."

"Cut it out—I don't have to take this kind of shit from a bitch like you."

"Dumb fuck, you asked for it, you're paying for it. Don't tell me you don't have to take it. You'll take anything I say or you'll hang up—that's your only choice...it's pretty simple—even you should understand the principle. You called us, you set the tone, you're nasty, so this call is nasty."

"I'll never call again—you can bet on that."

"Running out of pennies, friend?"

Click.

Bondage/Discipline. I must be good at it because these guys

really fall hard when I assume the Dominatrix role. Of course, I do have a strong voice and an aggressive style, so it fits quickly into their fantasy pattern of a tough-talking bitch using them as she pleases. Most want to be controlled, forced to hold their come, serve me first, bathe me, dress me, rouge my nipples... I am surprised at the longing in their voices. More than any type of caller these men will make extravagant offers to meet me for real; they find the dominance in my character hard to replicate in real life.

If the guy says I'm supposed to order him around, my first instinct is to resist his order for being ordered; a guy like this I'd maneuver into a physical restraint so he'd have no choice about obeying my whims. If another wants to be tied down, I order him to prepare the bedchamber first, see? I make the choices. To succeed in actually satisfying them, you have to be on top, stay ahead, control the scene in order to control them.

Guys say they want me dressed in black lingerie, I describe myself in a torn dark leather vest and skintight leather cutoffs, thigh-high boots. Their grunts and groans indicate a direct hit on the essence of domination. I am in control of myself first and most of all. They are incidental to my pleasure; any old sex slave would do.

I tell them I'm wearing ben-wa balls, you know, the vaginal stimulators worn inside to churn things up and create sensation when you move (like if he inserts them, then takes me dancing). I tell them they will take the string that links the balls together between their teeth and tug gently until the first ball is straining at the opening, then push that slick ball back in with their tongues; they will stimulate me like this until I am dripping with desire. I tell them I've strapped a small dildo to their thigh and I'm going to lower my ass onto it, they will feel me climax very near to their unwanted dick. I tell them I will take my biggest vibrator with the newest batteries and shove it inside myself, then lie on their belly and grind against them as I get off. They seem to like the idea of my doing what I want while they serve as an appendage, to be used if and as I see fit.

The guys that want to be slapped usually respond to my basic wrassling approach. I say I'm shoving him around, rubbing up against his body, bumping my ass into his crotch, slapping at his face and pulling his hair. We tumble onto the bed and I crawl all over him, treating his body like a big toy, teasing him with my beautiful breasts or shocking him with my physical strength. I pin him down and kiss him deeply, put my knee between his legs (carefully) so he can clasp my thighs between his, I taunt him with my hard nipples and when he raises his head to suck them, I lean back and laugh at him. I tell him he's going to have to beg me, plead with me, or I'll never let him have me...but if he does beg he can have it all, everything he's worked so hard for.

These calls sometimes fizzle; they are paradoxically delicate fantasies, vivid desires like a leather-dressed tough-talking dream-woman hit too close to home, especially for the new boys. Once in a while I regret choices I've made: I can sense the gloom at the other end of the line; another woman has failed to keep control.

I suggest ways to help draw this out of his woman: I tell him to soft-pedal the humiliation/pain aspects and start out with her as Ultimate Sex Queen and him as the unworthy servant to her beauty. He can break the ice by offering to bathe her, oil her body and, as he does so, to berate his own excitement, to treat his erection as traitorous, much too rude and insistent, too quickly aroused. He can introduce a cockring or the idea of tying it down by wrapping soft rope around his torso....

Mostly I emphasize that he must lead her to understand that he is not weak or unmanly, but rather that he wishes to surrender his manliness to her, to make a mockery of his aggression, to force himself to accept that a hard dick is nothing; she alone knows this and can use it to control him—it is a private submissiveness, one not disclosed in public as you might admit you like oral sex, oh, no, this is secret dream stuff.

And, ladies, please! Open your hearts to the dreams of your lovers. It isn't necessary to dominate a worm; the power and glory come from taming the wild beast, forcing a strong man down, holding a horny man back, slapping the face of a proud man for licking you wrong. Taunt him, tease him, call him names, pull his head back with his hair and suck on his throat, deny him your body unless he makes certain concessions, make him work for your pleasure.

"...feel like talking, just say hi. My name is Jamie..."

"Hi, this is Clint."

"Hi, this is Jamie. Did you say your name was Kent?"

"No, Clint, like Eastwood."

"Gotcha. So, Clint, what are you doing up at 4 in the morning?"

"Worked late, went out to eat, saw this girl...I don't know, something about her made me horny."

"Was it her looks or her actions?"

"Both. She wasn't really pretty, but she had the look about her—you know, I guess you'd call it stylish. She was with an older couple, like her aunt and uncle or something. They were planning a trip, had a map out, were laughing together. I wanted to join them, to belong with them."

"If she'd been alone, would you have approached her?"

"If she was alone, I probably wouldn't have seen her laughing and so relaxed, and that's what attracted me. She wasn't putting on a show for anybody, just being herself."

"What usually catches your eye about a woman?"

"Her smile. The way she moves, her style. Her tits."

"If a long-legged full-breasted woman came on to you at a party, how would you react?"

"Quickly, I hope. I'd try to figure out what she wanted and how to please her, fetch her a drink, light her cigarette although I prefer nonsmokers, you know, show her that I'm interested."

"Could she haul you off to the john for some head?"

"Could she? *Would* she—that's the question. Talk about a fantasy situation...have you ever done that?"

"I know sex can be thrilling if it's handled right. I'd have to say that, yeah, I'd do that, but it would have to be the right situation and definitely the right man."

"What turns you on about a man?"

"His smile. His confidence. His ass and thighs, I like a meaty man. I like to climb all over my guy."

"I'm massive, Jamie...6'1", 250, no fat...thick arms, big legs...would you like some of that?"

"Clint, I can hear that voice rumbling out of a big old chest, figured you weren't a small man...otherwise I'd never admit my personal preference for you hunks...but I'm not a little girl, I'm 5'7", 136 pounds, strong and fit, no way I could flip you or anything but I'd sure put some push into my fucking."

"Oh, damn, the way you say things. I'd love to be pushing up inside you right now."

"Now, listen, Clint, stretch those big old bones out, get comfortable, look at your body, the pure sensuality of all that flesh and muscle and those thick, hard bones...think of me looking at you through the window as you stroke your cock. I'd get turned on watching you please yourself. Now close your eyes, big boy, clear your mind and listen...."

"Guess what—I came when we started talking. I'm ready to go again!"

"Yeah...my kind of man, gets hot, stays hot. Now close those eyes and imagine me, long legs in black stockings, a garter belt around my waist emphasizing my wide hips and round ass, my breasts in a black bra, shoved together so the cleavage is deep and you see the high round mounds of tits...I'm standing next to your bed watching you handle your cock, pulling on it, making it hard, I watch for the longest time. You stare at me as you masturbate, drink in the sight of me...when you are good and ready, I slide up around your hips and sit on your cock, the stockings silky against your legs, my pussy hot from watching..."

"Jesus."

"...you, you turn me on, Clint, all that skin for me to kiss, that big body all mine. I feel so small on top of you, so fragile, but it's just an illusion. I'm tough, you can let go..."

"Wow!"

"...shove it deep, when you're firmly inside we can roll over so I'm on my back, legs up in the air, you hold my slim ankles in those huge hands and spread me wide, look right at me, Clint, at this throbbing cunt, hot from your fucking..."

"Yes, please...don't stop talking, I'm so close."

"...me so hard before. I unhook the bra, my tits tumble out, so round and full...you lean down and kiss them, suck the nipples, and you can feel my reaction between my legs, hot, smooth cunt to slide into, firm breasts jiggling as you ride me...."

"Jamie, here it comes..."

"My darling love, big old boy, strong man, tough guy, ohh, yes, let it go, pump it out for me…"

"Damn, goddamn!"

"…now, all of it, Clint, yes, Clint, my sweet, Jamie wants to hear you, come on, share it with me, give it…"

"Baby, oh, baby, so much…"

"…up to me, squeeze hard, force it, don't fail me now, yes, that last thrust forward, the last cream from your cock…yes, big boy, you're so fine…."

"You're wonderful, I feel wonderful…I could sleep for a week, thank you."

"You're welcome."

Click.

"…is Jamie, if you…"

"What do you look like?"

"Long-legged, large-breasted, with a big smile."

"What are you wearing?"

"Wine-red tights, a blue sweater…soft against my body, shows my shape."

"Touch yourself while you talk to me."

"Honey, I don't have to be invited to enjoy myself, I can't keep my hands off myself, and you wouldn't be able to resist me either. These curves cry out to be caressed; my breasts swell from my ribs, my hips and ass are smooth curves."

"Do you suck cock?"

"Yes. Do you eat cunt?"

"Yes. Take it in the ass?"

"Sometimes, if it's the right time…you butt-fuck much?"

"When I can, babe, when I can…."

Click.

The operator-hour cutback continues. Bitch, moan, threaten and whine. Some go so far as to harass the new operators on the line, which I explain, as I fire them, is exactly why I need new operators; immaturity and selfishness turn off the callers. What is most amazing to me is they will call complaining in their ugliest voices and not long after need a favor and turn on the honey. I'm cold-blooded enough to mention the difference in tone and suggest they even it out in the future, a little more sugar with the bad news, a little less when they want something.

One operator who objected strenuously to a cutback in hours became enraged when I suggested that her habit of leaving the line to answer her personal calls, her repeated absences due to a series of odd unverifiable emergencies, and her overall negative attitude indicated that she wasn't all that interested in the work in the first place. She ranted like a banshee that I was trying to fire her. I told her I didn't have to *try* to fire her, I could do it in a minute. What I was trying to do was get the good quality hours she did have in her onto the line and drop the bullshit time. She latched onto the compliment and did an about-face, which didn't surprise me. She is unstable, unhappy and immensely talented when she cares to be.

If any experience in my life will stand out as fulfilling the stereotype of woman-as-cats, this will do it. They report each other's failings with glee and deny outright any of their own. In the middle of a general conversation, they'll slip out the claws and swipe like lightning, then preen innocently. My advice: don't get between them and their food bowls (paychecks) without shin guards.

Another shift from noon to 3 P.M. on the phones goes like this:
12:00 Someone hangs up on Brenda just as I arrive—she says it's been busy today; 12:08–18 X-dresser back from yesterday, even cruises for ladies in femme attire, jack off to b.j., transsexual, on meds now, surgery in six to seven months., can't know if men turn him on, bisex in my life, plain old American, feels wrong when dressed as male, suggest contact magazines; 12:22–28 man wants ass-fuck, me beneath in traditional missionary, man behind him balling his ass; 12:28–31 hears climax above then wants kinky which I interpret as group sex; 12:32–36 swing-shift worker, headed for shower, is pussy eater, likes tasty twat; 12:49–58 looking for Brenda, James, very good talker re: social roles, men needing stimulation, i.e., even one dance at a club, says to tell Brenda "to use her birthday" but won't explain that to me "yet" (but better not be a contact game); 1:10–19 X-

dresser/TS again, X-state for surgery, has little tits, wants to know how fucking feels, suggest balls at cunt position for alternative stimulation; 1:28 silent; 1:29–36 Frank, Irishman, dirty jokes; 1:36–43 new caller, loved the laughter; 1:4?–51 Greg, the X-dresser/TS, change is cultural as much as sexual, even now can pass in bathing suit or underwear, thinks his reconstructed vag will operate 100 percent normal including taste, via implanted glands; 1:53 hang-up; 1:57 silent; 2:04 silent, lots of connections but no talkers; 2:06–16 great call, single male just turned thirty, loves the talk; 2:20–2:22 great standup head; 2:39–?? Mark, piss dude, I suggest a private enema which fascinates him; 2:44–47 suck my dick; 2:52 hear but can't decipher, suggest he call on a better line; 2:55–56 Mark, the pisser above, wanted to do it in my throat I guess (but no go, evidently); 3:00 Kelly arrives.

"...is Jamie, now who in the heck is calling in at 5:15 in the A. of M.? Could it be Farmer Bob?"

"No, this is Greg. I figured it'd be a good time to call, nobody gets up early unless they have to."

"True enough, it quiets down from 4:30 to 6 during the week, so you've got me all to yourself."

"So, tell me, do you ever get off on the calls?"

"Sometimes. Not usually, it just accumulates, you know, I remember things the callers have said, or memories I've shared. My style emphasizes the caller's pleasure."

"It turns me on to hear a woman come."

"Well, Greg, let's do it together. I go off duty at 5:30, so this might be my last call. This darlin' cunt is all wound up, she wouldn't mind a little attention."

"Touch yourself, OK? Put your fingers right on your clit."

"I usually stimulate my clit by putting my fingers on the lips and pushing them around. I find it works better. I use three fingers, one on either side and one pressing right over the clit, it feels good."

"Do you have a dildo around?"

"Here in the drawer, the classic white plastic vibrator. I'll press it along my cunt, there, I like that."

"Put it inside, in your vagina."

"I can't just slam it in there, Greg, I'm too tight. I have to work it in slowly, just like you would nudge me with the head of your cock, it's in about two inches, ohh, make that three and a half and, ummm, I'm pulling it out, it's all wet, ahhh, see, now it slides in, imagine it, wet from my juice, opening that tight hole."

"I'm going crazy here, thinking of it, in and out of your hole, ohh, rub your clit hard."

"I am, baby. I feel so good, my legs are tense and my belly is tight, I flex my ass to tighten my cunt…"

"Pretend it's me fucking you, me inside you."

"In and out of me, honey, slow and easy to start, sliding in and out of me, then a little faster, just slightly harder, easy but firm, firmer and faster, all the way in me, all the way."

"I would screw you to the bed, Jamie."

"The dildo is in to the base, it feels good when I resist it, clamp the muscle tight around it like I would that cock of yours, it's so tight and hot, and my clit is screaming. Oh, Greg."

"Get off with me, please…I can tell you're excited."

"You talk to me then, darling—tell me what you'd do to this sexy bitch in your bed."

"I'd be all over her, my head between her legs, reaching up to pinch her nipples, licking back to her ass, I'd kiss her and hold her and fuck her."

"Ohh, sweet talk…yes, tell me, love…let me hear you."

"Do it, girl, come on, do it for me, let me hear you getting off, yeah, you turn me on, you really get me going…I'd like to lick your nipples, nurse on you…so pretty…rub it, Jamie, come on, do it, girl."

"Ohh, yes, talk to me, I'm so close, it feels so good, my legs are stretched straight, ohh, I feel tight all over…it's hard to talk."

"Do it, honey, do it for me. I'd put my cock inside you so deep…"

"Yes, fuck Jamie, fuck her."

"I'd drive that cock home, Jamie, deep into my Jamie, yes, Jamie…I know you can't talk…I know, honey…rub that clit for me, baby, do it for me…."

"Oh, yes, here, right here, here it is, I'm so close…so close…"

"Love yourself, Jamie…do yourself, girl, do it for me, do it for both of us, let me hear you, I'm excited by your breathing, by your silence, I know what you must be feeling."

"There…there it is…oh, yes…right, right there…Greg! It feels so good…"

"Me, too, Jamie, I'm there, too, with you. We're together in this, oh, yes, completely."

"Yesss, yessssss. Ooooooh, wow, you did it, Greg, you talked me off…thanks, my friend, it's a rare pleasure."

"I owed you. I listened in last week, you did a thing with a guy about fucking in his car, I'll never forget it, so I vowed I'd catch you alone sometime and see if I could, you know, like repay you for what you do. I've listened to other girls, but you really got to me. They're OK—the other guys get off on it—but I guess I'm a little tougher."

"You're fine by me—more than fine, the finest. Thanks for the compliments, I remember that car scene. Don't give me credit for being creative, though; that really happened to me."

"I don't doubt it, but the way you describe things, you're truly fine. Talk to you again, I've got about 45 seconds left."

"You time it?"

"Yeah, with my long-distance timer, well, good-bye Jam—"

Click.

"…call again anytime, glad to answer your questions."

"Thanks. I may call again, now that I know how it works."

"We'll be here."

Click.

"My name is Jamie. If you feel like talking, just let me know, I'm right here…"

"Can you speak up?"

"Sure. Is this better? Are you far away?"

"No, just old. Don't hear so good no more."

"So, what's on your mind today?"

"Sex, today, yesterday, tomorrow. My ears are shot, but my cock's still working, when it gets the chance."

"How often is that?"

"Beg pardon?"

"How often do you get the chance?"

"The wife says once a week, max, but it's up to me to pick the day."

"Some men get less sex than that."

"Maybe so, but I get hard more often than that, so I do myself, you know, with my hand, like when I was a kid."

"How old are you anyway?"

"Sixty-eight, how old are you?"

"Thirty. Would you be thinking of a lady my age?"

"Honey, a woman is a woman once she's past about twenty-five, she's either going to do it or not. Age isn't the point, is it?"

"To some it is, but I think you're right. I've had men twice my age but at the moment they were like all men, full of feeling, giving and taking love."

"I like talking about sex."

"It's nice, isn't it?"

"Tell me a story."

"I'm in the bathtub, soaking in clear water, my hair is piled up on my head, some curls have fallen loose along my neck and over one shoulder, my nipples are just below the water's surface, my knees are raised so the water swirls between my thighs."

"Nice."

"You are kneeling next to the tub with a soft cloth in your hand. You reach into the warm water and wet the cloth, then move it slowly over my body, from toe to shoulder, softly, slowly, only the cloth between your hand and my skin."

"Keep your eyes closed while I wash you."

"You gently spread my legs and wash the lips of my vagina. The cloth stimulates me while the water relaxes my entire body. You let the cloth drop away and use your hand directly against my pussy. Your other hand is stroking your cock, rapidly up and down."

"Young lady, I thought you had your eyes closed!"

"I can hear your hand moving on it, that peculiar slipping sound of a man masturbating, and it turns me on, my nipples darken and rise out of the water. You are amazed at how pointed they are now when they seemed so smooth and round before."

"You have to get out of the tub. I would want to do oral sex with you."

"On the big rug on the bathroom floor, you towel me quickly even as you put me on my back and open me for yourself. I spread wide and you bury your face, drink me in, yes, lick me, sweet man, you know what to do, oh, yes, I can hear your excitement."

"Don't mind me, keep going."

"You put your hands under my ass and lift me, my legs fall farther apart and my beautiful vagina glistens there, wet from your tonguing me. You kiss my clit, firmly pressing your lips against it, and you feel me climax."

"You'll have to stop. I'll have to call back another time. I can't absorb this all so fast—this is enough for me for today."

"It sure was steamy in that bathroom, right?"

"Oh, yes, steamy is the word for it. You did a nice job, thanks."

"Glad you called. Think of me, OK?"

"Try to stop me, and thank you for speaking up so clearly, I could hear every word."

"Something tells me you were listening extra hard."

"Good night."

"Sweet dreams."

Click.

I sometimes see retired operators and they shake their heads when they remember "those" days. It was a cross between Woodstock and an AA meeting in reverse—you're still anonymous but you speak for indulgence.

"...I can hear your goofy friends giggling in the background. Why not find some smarter people to hang around with, or is this all you could come up with? You sound like nerds in heat."

Click.

"...is Jamie. If you feel like talking, just say..."

Click.

We believe that the institution of a "just talk" CHAT line by our parent corporation with us as managers would help feed business to the Sweet Talker line. We would be freer to advertise general CHAT services and, with our experience, believe it would be a lively one, as we would provide an operator to keep the conversation going and override abusive callers. We know it could be used to stimulate interest in the sex line because in the past our callers have announced our number on competitors' CHAT lines and it brought in new business. ("Hey, guys, let's meet on 976–####. They get really crazy, there's this lady on there…") Our ethics precluded doing this ourselves, but we sure didn't mind when the callers did it. On our own CHAT line we would be able to direct the interested traffic in that direction very naturally (ditto recruiting operators who would earn more money per hour on the adults-only line).

In the alternative, it may be what we evolve into as the phone company hunkers down over us and prepares to take a great big shit on our business. The irony is that such a CHAT line allows callers (not the operator) to meet each other, to arrange meetings with who knows who listening in and inviting themselves along, with the attendant risk of emotional and physical mayhem…our "sex-talk" line is all fantasy, CHAT lines become all too real to some of the people, and, as usual, snare the innocent, victim-type people. To be "conceptually good," we have to do something I think is "actually bad"; facilitate exchange of actual personal data like names, phone numbers, addresses between unscreened strangers.

We'd play a CHAT line straight, not try to sneak get-off calls in between the clean stuff. Acting as a "grapevine," we would offer a bulletin board for messages, providing an interesting and talkative hostess-operator who would work downtown at the central switching machine so she could disconnect harassing callers, and use the community bulletin board. Work-at-home was necessary to have phone-sex operators of any quality at all…with easier advertising for general CHAT operators we believe we can get them into the office for about the same pay.) As for callers, we could target a larger market as we would have access to TV and newspapers that wouldn't let us advertise our Sweet Talk service.

"Hi, this is Jamie. Wondering what you're doing tonight, how you're feeling, do you want to talk?"

"Wanna listen."

"OK by me. Any special topic?"

"Just talk."

"I'm a strong healthy sensuous woman. I like to ride my man, really shove my body up against him, straddle his lap and rub my crotch against his, press my chest against his, smother him with kisses. I grab his hands and put them over his head, holding his wrists together, so his upper body is stretched tight and I can lay on him, feel his meat deep inside my body, enjoy the thrust of his penis. But sometimes I take my cunt away and scoot up so my breasts are at your lips and I groan as you suck the entire tip of my breast into your mouth, while your wet prick feels the night air on it, strange after being enclosed in a warm box."

"Don't take it away—leave me in there."

"Don't fret, baby, you get to feel it plunge back in, that velvet-smooth vagina, the silken thighs and belly, the closeness of my cunt surrounds your cock, you roll me on my back, drive it in, do it the way you like it, move the way you want."

"Move with me."

"Slam right up to you, lift my hips to meet you, grinding tight against you, arms wrapped around you, legs flexing, crying out for you to fuck me, ball me, come on, do it, harder, move for me, move it deep inside me."

"That's enough, I can finish myself."

Click.

"...is Jamie, feeling wild and crazy tonight. Love to hear what's on your mind tonight."

"Who are you talking to?"

"Nobody, anybody...you somebody to talk to?"

"I might be, what do you want to talk about, I mean, at a buck a minute it better be good."

"Hang up anytime, the charges stop. It's hard to pinch your pennies and stroke your cock at the same time."

"I never do that, myself I mean, if it isn't real I don't bother. I can wait."

"I admire your willpower but hope you aren't missing out on a very natural part of your sex life. I think you can bring yourself a lot of pleasure by celebrating the way your body works."

"Don't try to convince me it's normal. I suppose it is for some guys, I just don't like it. Without a woman there, it's nothing."

"Like I said, I admire your strength. How is your love life? Have you been lucky in love?"

"I've had my share, yeah, but it isn't like I'm Hugh Hefner or anything. I once went 7 months between, uh, episodes."

"Was that your choice?"

"Sure, I could have picked up something in a bar...hear that, some*thing*, not some*one*...that's what I don't like about sex, how you sometimes do it just to do it."

"It's true sometimes we all think with our crotches instead of our heads, but you say you didn't do that for 7 months."

"Only because I did it so much when I was young."

"How old are you anyway?"

"Twenty-four."

"I'm 30—you ever gone for an older woman?"

"Nope. No confidence, probably, figured I couldn't satisfy them."

"But by then they know how to satisfy themselves and the pressure is off you. Another advantage of self-stimulation."

"Intriguing...what do you, as an older woman, think of a guy like me?"

"You're educated, ethical, and very guarded, to my way of thinking. I'd rather believe you lie about not masturbating than contemplate you being so uptight you'd deny yourself that joy."

"You're half-right, but so am I. I hate it so much I only do it when I'm desperate and it feels desperate."

"Lighten up, buddy...just whack it around in the morning instead of glorifying your willpower. To me, masturbation is like combing your hair and brushing your teeth—bodily mainte-nance—you're making too big of a deal out of it."

"How can you act like it's, well, an ordinary thing to do?"

"Because for so many people it is, that makes it sound sort of ordinary to me. Man, these lines are the best evidence that men are quite capable of being self-sufficient, can regulate their own desires with an imaginative approach."

"Well, I'm not so sure I like being lumped in with a bunch of guys who choke the chicken."

"No obligation, I'm just letting you know, between you and me, it's quite a habit among your peers, almost an art with some."

"So far I'm OK this way. But if I ever do, I'll certainly remember this conversation."

"What will be, will be. Thanks for calling."

"You're welcome. And thank you."

Click.

Bad operators are usually funny, because the situation is harmless; unskilled doctors are terrifying, cabdrivers can be a threat to life and limb, an inadequate teacher can slow you down forever after...but a bad phone sex operator is no worse than an inept waiter: you probably won't starve to death even if you feel at the time that she has breached some sacred trust by failing to serve you as expected. In our case, we regret the failure of the operator to give a customer his money's worth, yet it is impractical to give refunds as the callers are nameless/faceless to us. (Being anonymous has its price.)

Listening in, I wince at the dropped cues, the stumbling delivery, the ignorance of basic psychological and motivational theory. Once a prospective operator musters up enough gumption to do her qualifying interview, she may have given her all; the men arrive in a staggering collision of style and intent, and she must be of sufficient energy and flexibility to accommodate them, which cannot be known unless and until she succeeds or fails live.

The key is getting into it, letting go, being there; this is more crucial than accurate information. One woman recited her fantasies like a procedure manual, "then I would proceed to lick your penis, afterwards I touch your testicles," correct but uninspiring. Another insisted she had a cock in her mouth and was licking his ass as if the inches-long stretch of sac and crack didn't intervene. A caller says, "Gonna jam it," and she says, "Have I got a jacket?" It's like a quiz show and the clock is ticking away. Will she guess right? Can she remember the magic sequence? Has she got good clues? And is he trying? Monologues are hard, dialogues easier.

Sometimes it's a howl. Even the callers laugh at themselves and the situation, one politely told a tepid operator to sit on a light bulb and brighten up! Another endeared himself to me when he suggested that the operator who said she'd swallowed a foot-long dick ought to rent space in her empty head. Mostly the guys slam down the phone. Many never call again. If they do, they may tell the current operator all about it, especially if they thought the bad operator was lazy rather than simply unable to do the job right. Some operators commiserate with the caller's frustration but remark that the job is harder than it sounds. Others lap up the gossip like the cats they are.

We've rehired some operators who we had terminated, or who had self-destructed. Most usually there was a long gap in service, several months, and we never instituted the reconciliation. In these cases, there was sincere interest in another try, it had not been (with them) a lack of skill but usually of reliability, time, or truth. We allowed them back for short hours at first on easily-substituted-for time, and let them know we would forget the past as long as it wasn't repeated in the future. So far, these rehires have worked out fine.

"Baby, I don't like coke. Even if it were OK to talk about illegal drugs on the line, I wouldn't like cocaine. It's bad news, so don't go bragging to me about it, OK?"

"I ain't bragging, just telling you how it is. My friend who I ran into at the bar had this date who he met at his dealer's, and they had this coke. I didn't even buy it, really, so we did it in the car. We had the tunes on, windows open, all the way home, God, she was so fine, and they dropped me at my door and so here I am...flying high."

"Honey, you're flying alone. You're talking so fast I can hardly understand you. Why don't you call when you come down a bit? It won't take long with coke...fucking fast and furious drug."

"Sex is great with coke."

"Look, my friend, we don't talk about drugs on this line, so either drop the topic or hang up the phone—your choice."

"I want to jerk off while I'm...in this mood...you know?"

"The mood's your business, that erection is mine...got your cock out?"

"It's rockhard, get it? Never mind, I don't feel like coming right now, it feels so good just being hard...it feels good in my hand, it feels fine to me, hard..."

"I've got a soft cunt to match that big old dick of yours."

"Oh, he isn't so big as all that, but he sure is hard."

"Sturdy and reliable, my two favorite words for dicks."

"I like a hairy snatch—do you mind me saying that?"

"No, honey, especially since I've got a thick patch of curly black hair, I trim it back so it's a soft bush, easy to eat me that way, fun to look at the pretty pink lips framed in softest black."

"I could lick you all night, give my mouth something to do besides babble."

"You're coming down. Focus on your dick, its hardness, the head, the throbbing of the vein, your balls...are they loose or up close to your body?"

"Hanging low, really low...jeez, I didn't notice until you asked but wow, it's kind of strange."

"Your body temperature is up—that's normal—your balls are retreating from the heat, spread your legs far apart, now tighten your ass, pull in your belly, see how much bigger your cock looks standing up that way? I can just imagine you stroking it."

"I think I'll call back later—this could take forever, I keep losing my concentration or something. I just want to stroke myself. It's like he'll never die."

"Hey, babe, put on some music, drink some water, and relax with yourself. Play with yourself, appreciate your body, your legs and back and shoulders, everything."

"I'm going to dance naked!"

"Great, wear yourself out. Call later if you like, I'll be here until two and after that you can talk to Ginger."

"I figure since I didn't buy the you-know-what I could afford a call...maybe two. Talk at you later."

"'Night."

Click.

"...I won't be shy with you if you're not shy with me. Speak right up, mystery guest, this is Jamie, and I'm your sweet talker tonight. Any topic, anytime..."
Click.

I am greatly disturbed by the people who insist that children's potential exposure to these sex lines is reason enough to stop them. Kids see thousands of murders on TV, lobbyists lobby and the video violence continues. (I'd rather see a kid with his cock in his hand than pointing a gun at me.) In point of fact, the sex lines have every reason to lobby against parents who cannot or will not control their offspring who taint the line with their immature giggling. Phones are an adult device. A child cannot order phone service; adults are responsible for all uses of the phone in their names. I know some kids call in once or twice, are mystified by the appeal of the line, think it's weird, disgusting and/or boring and go on to other more appropriate activities. The kids who rack up the $4,400 phone bills are evidently out of control. I doubt we can be blamed for that inadequate supervision, lack of moral fiber, whatever you call it; the home seems the likely target for investigation, not one fragment of the outside world.

More than any other excuse, this one propels me to an adamant pro-adult posture. Childbearing and nurture are choices fraught with perils to your young far more serious than overhearing heavy breathing on the phone. Attacking the underlying boredom and lack of purpose in such a child would seem to better advantage. *Advice to parents*: If your kids are using adult lines, block the entire 976 extension with a cheap electronic device that stops it from being dialed or contact your phone company. Many of them will block the exchange for you for a nominal fee. It's your kid, it's your duty. I have every right to complain when they steal from my cookie jar, no matter how tempting the contents, because until you succeed in teaching them to behave, you are obligated to control them. Your election to clone yourself isn't my concern; keep your little as-yet-untamed products out of my ear until they are socially functioning units.

The easiest way to control this is the Dial Seven and Stop rule; the kid can dial seven (7) digits—that's a local non-toll call; any more digits, and the child must get permission first. This simple rule avoids phone-sex calls, joke-line calls, dial-in "guess-that-tune" contests, long-distance calls, ordering from 800 numbers seen on TV. This rule doesn't involve sex-specific warnings, so squeamish parents can avoid particulars. Proof of breaking it is on the phone bill in black-and-white (you owe some green) so it can be a "discipline" point, a specific promise made by a child the status of which, without spying, can be routinely verified by the parent. It is a simple rule to remember: Dial Seven and Stop. And if a child cannot count to seven, it is doubtful that the child should be free to dial the phone.

A TV magazine show investigated phone sex and to no surprise found that the sexually related lines account for more than 60 percent of the revenues of the "976" pay calls while things like dial-a-sports-score account for 6 percent—the increased revenues contributed to the phone company's profitability thus reducing general ratepayers' costs. If a company voluntarily forgives $12 million (!) in supposedly unauthorized calls (one such gesture per household which pleads ignorance), it does this to protect how many millions in revenue? The stickler for the phone company is that the popularity of this service among adults cannot be ignored; they call and call again. It isn't just some small band of depraved maniacs satisfying bizarre desires, it is a fleet of bill-paying Americans who think to whom and about what they talk is their private business. They will follow whatever procedure is needed: credit cards, callbacks, registration numbers, they'll listen to stern warnings and ominous statements on greeting tapes intended to deter kids, but they call and call again. They don't band together to lobby like the Morality Gestapo because it doesn't occur to them that their obvious rights could be abridged by a vocal minority.

This business is not establishing any new freedoms, it is relying on the old faithfuls: freedom of speech, association and religion. If you can dial a prayer, you should be able to dial a moan—otherwise you're supporting one philosophic belief and denying another. The callers are having fun at an expense only to themselves and of some benefit to their present and future love partners if the call results in reduced tension or increased knowledge. What's so awful about that?

Some men have nicknames for their penis, from the whimsical, like Moby, to the practical, like Rod. Some say that since it has a mind of its own, it may as well have a name. Others claim it's a fathead or a bonehead, it's the anticunt, the heat seeker, it's his personal barometer, his rebellious flesh, it's the beaver cleaver.

"...that's right, lover man, run your hands up and down my legs, long, luscious, smooth flesh stretching out, spread wide, smooth and cool, inside the thighs, behind the knees, down the calves, the soft heel and long curving instep, the delicate toes...you massage my feet, kiss them, stretch your arms up along my legs and feel their strength, kiss my delicate feet, suck on my toes. I shudder at the pleasure, your mouth surrounds each toe one by one. I can't describe how good it feels, baby, but don't stop."

"I can look up between your legs from there, see your cunt, especially if you bend one knee. I like that view."

"I'll touch myself while you watch, I'm still squirming from you playing with my feet so my fingers really work between my legs, rubbing the clit, moving down to tease my hole, you watch as my pussy gets ready to take you."

"I can see the wetness, the parted lips, and that beautiful clit...now, listen, I'm going to take an ankle in each hand and slowly lift your legs for you, until your legs are straight up in the air, then I'm going to pull you to the edge of the bed so you can scootch up onto my dick, OK? See, then I can still kiss your feet while I make love to you, I can see those legs spread for me, I'd have a hard time holding my come back, I'd want to get off inside you, one pretty foot in each hand."

"Do it, lover man, spread me wide and pile into me. I can feel the pressure on my legs as you force me open so you can get in deeper. You want to be in all the way when you come, in all the way and that little bit deeper. Come on, open me up, my toes are curled tight. I'm so excited, I'm so turned on....you need to come in me, fill me with your sex, empty your love into me..."

"Yes, that's it, empty myself...yes...."

Click.

"Jamie, I dress as a man only to go to work; the rest of the time I'm fully feminized."

"You never told me—how do you get your clothes?"

"Remember, I'm 5'6", 140 lbs., so I can get them anywhere. It's the big guys who have that problem. I really do pass. I shop like any other woman. I try things on, have the clerk hold things I'm going to buy...I'm not peeking into other dressing rooms, I'm interested in the clothes, you know?"

"I get your point. It isn't done for sexual excitement, it's done to buy things you need or want. But is that enough, to wear it, don't you want to be a person to somebody, acknowledged?"

"By other women. That's what I want: to blend with them, to join them, like a sisterhood."

"You may be idealizing the feminine experience. We don't all join hands and cavort in the meadows together. It can be a vicious combative experience where essential femininity is challenged all the time. You'd be helpless against the cutting accusations of sterility and undesirability."

"See, this is what I want to learn! What it's really like, it isn't all perfume and pantyhose, is it? It's comparing tits and getting diamond rings and houses, it's periods and pregnancy and having men want you. I know I'm missing these things. I read the women's magazines and stuff which made me more understanding of it, but still some of this stuff is alien to me, I admit it, just to you, that if anything convinces me I can't ever truly be female, it is that I don't understand the things that worry you...will "he" like it, will "he" approve? Men will say or do anything to get in your pants just because you've got those holes there—they won't accept my love even if I'm nicer, sweeter and more giving just because I have a cock, you see?"

"But you don't want men's love—isn't that what you said?"

"Maybe because my male side knows I can't have the love of

the kind of man I'd want to love me—he cannot love another man that way, he can't or he wouldn't be him. I mean, the pussy is magic, it's the great tamer, he'll do anything for the woman who has the one he wants, for whatever reason he fixates on it. Frankly, I'm not all that sexual. I cook a lot, always in an apron, or I knit—I'm really a homebody."

"So, what's the future hold for you, do you think?"

"I hope a lady who can understand this in me, who won't be turned off to my love just because of this. Maybe a career woman who'll let me raise the kids...it's good to talk to someone who can talk about it, I'm not all freaked out because I do this, I've done it since I can remember. What bugs me is not being able to talk about it except to people who want to cure me as if it were a sinus problem. It was good talking to you again, but I gotta go, Jamie, I'm saving up for new boots, burgundy, high heeled, classy, so this is my last call tonight."

"I'd probably envy your wardrobe—you sound quite stylish to me, I remember some of the outfits you've described."

"I just love clothes, I really do. *Ciao*"

"Au revoir, my dear."

Click.

I talk about condoms a lot. I encourage their routine use in no uncertain terms, I tell the guys to buy lubricated latex condoms as they are less likely to tear. I tell them to use foam if they can, to wash before and after contact, to learn to splash come outside their partner during oral sex, to appreciate erotic adventures like mutual masturbation or extended foreplay, to use adult videos and steamy music and candles and all the classic enhancements to the sexual experience. Some tell me they always do wrap it up. Some ask if I really think it is so important. I tell them yes, yes it is. It's a sign of caring, a sign of thoughtfulness. It is an admission of vulnerability, of the urge to protect even as you ravage, the wish to add rather than drain; it is the fate of our generation to learn a new kind of restraint, a new kind of sharing. Dennis Miller, the comedian, says in answer to those who claim that condoms kill sensation that he wears *two* all the time and when he prepares for sex he takes one off and feels like a wild man! It's all in the attitude. Elegant men wear love gloves when the occasion arises.

You can even buy little fortune cookies which contain a condom and the prediction you may get lucky, so you should be prepared. Not surprisingly, women's purchases of condoms has increased dramatically lately.

AIDS is scary. AIDS kills. But most of us will die of the same old things: car wrecks and cancer and heart disease...the things we don't stop doing to ourselves. The stigma of a sexually transmitted virus cripples the fight against it, the squeamishness of the government lost precious time in the early 1980s when effective education would have made some difference. We couldn't have stopped it, but we could have better contained it as we studied it.

AIDS is understood better each day. Medicine advances in the wake of frenzied research into all aspects of the body as its immune system fails; it is a study of our sexuality. It is hopeful that we will find a way to deal with AIDS, to incorporate it like we do all the other grotesqueries we deal with every day. (Are you as careful about being in cars with others? You're much more likely to maim/kill each other that way.) My personal attitude is that this is the time of maximum risk and not the time to be physically free with your body. It's better to hang back for a few years and see what's going on out there. In a year, two, three, we will be able to make better choices.

In the meantime, I talk a lot about condoms.

"Hi, this is Jamie."

"This is Jimmy."

"Not Jimmy, Jamie."

"No, *I'm* Jimmy."

"Oh, I'm sorry."

"I'll change it! Don't be sorry, you sound hot. I heard you with another guy the other day. I couldn't even speak up, I was flabbergasted. Who taught you to talk that way?"

"It's a gift, babe, I really think it is. I just surrender to it, I'm glad you liked the way I roll those words over my pretty pink tongue."

"There you go, it's so natural to you, like when you say a hard prick, it sounds sexy."

"Jimmy, love, stretch out, relax, close your eyes, listen close-ly, this is Jamie. That voice gets inside your head, not pretty, better than pretty, it's real, vibrating with feeling. Use your hand for me, just brush it lightly over your cock for me, get a sense of it, thick and full, spread your legs for me, think of me next to you, naked, my hands running up and down my body, you can feel me moving next to you just as I feel you."

"Describe your pussy, Jamie, describe it in detail. I've been so curious."

"It's a strong cunt, Jimmy, a healthy beautiful cunt, the hair is thick, black, curly, I trim it so it's a soft bush. My mound is fleshy, think of it against the palm of your hand, the lips are full, strong, they guard my tender hole—it jumps when I talk about it, it is very responsive, even to the tip of your tongue or finger, the lips seem to curl around your cock when you get inside me, my muscles are strong, you can feel them."

"Good-night, Jamie. I'm going to think about what you said. I'm too curious. If I hear any more, I'll forget what you already told me."

"'Bye, Jimmy. Nice talking to you."
Click.

"Jamie, I like sex two, three, seven times a day, I like '69' five, eight hours at a time...did you get those numbers?"

"Did you know we are supposed to report phone numbers given to us, no matter how cleverly, to the police for investiga-tion into solicitation to incite prostitution? Now, what were those numbers again? It was 237-69...what?"
Click.

Instant gratification (sounds like one of those diet drinks that pretends to be a milkshake) is an aspect of our culture that takes into consideration the pace of our lives. We like the quick and easy, damn the long-term expense such as "saving" money by eat-ing junk food then paying for a coronary bypass. As in all things, balance would help, a little of this, some of that...but, nooo, we are creatures of habit, we go to the known, seek a routine, prize the familiar.

Something else again is condition-specific response; some behaviors are natural at certain times and inappropriate at others. In our phone-fantasy environment, the focus is not on seduction-of-a-person, but rather the celebration of a phenomenon, the re-creation through verbal cues of actual events or the simulation of fantasy occurrences common to the sexually active (in fact and/or imagination). The main attraction is not only what an operator says, but the fact that the caller may time that conversation to his convenience, may make preparations for the call, may dial our number as his housemate backs out the driveway on his way to work. He may watch a sex video, look at sexy magazines or erotic books, if he's a cross-dresser he often dons his best outfit, the slave boys oil their anal dildos...we talk in overtly sexual terms at the moment he's feeling intensely sexual. The whole idea is laughable out of context, the "oh, baby" litany loses its charm when broadcast to a nonresponsive audience; but when it accompanies a sense of personal indulgence and parallels private actions, it is right in tune.

I generally like the guys who call. I launch myself into the call from his perspective: he's alone, he's nervous/agitated, he's willing to try new things, he's suspicious of me, he won't necessarily believe what I say, but he'll be intrigued by my choice of images and acts, he can always hang up. Of course, he might have a partner there; his buddies might be cracking up across the room, he might know the service and/or me quite well, he might be loaded and surly. Change-ups occur based on clues provided.

I can't stress enough to people that these are real men, men who make your planes and fill your teeth and prepare your pie a la mode, they have lives and lovers (some more of each than others). They tell me all kinds of stories, they cooperate, they have fun, they listen, they talk, they give in to the fantasy of the moment; sexuality is a deeply abiding love of the body, yours and your partner's/partners'. These callers are using their ears to gather stimulating stimuli; they bring air from their lungs through their throats and shape it into sounds they want me to hear.

We talk on the phone: peculiarly fragmented conversations, so much implied, so much in the vernacular, that it would be hard to translate to an alien intelligence. The responses themselves vary widely: some guys mumble "yeah, yeah," while you spin out a story; others moan wildly at every sexplicit word; others are positively hushed once their desire is made known. Contrary to men's ideas, we can't always tell which is his moment of climax. Some guys cry out as the excitement mounts, then splash in silence. Some just click off, and you don't know if they got bored or had a heart attack. Endearingly enough, many say "Thanks, good-bye, I'll call again, you're one sexy lady, you talk good, I loved it, I came, I'm gone, thanks, thank you, much obliged, ooo-weee, wow, that was just great, you killed me, I'm done, I got off, we did it, I got my nut, it's over, thanks, thank you, damn, girl, Umm-ummmmm, thanks ever so much, I owe you one, *gracias*, wow, good-night, good-bye, good job."

"Where's Ginger?"

"She went off duty an hour ago."

"Well, get her back."

"No can do, I'm here now, this is Jamie; I think she works again Thursday morning, 6 to 10 A.M., you might catch her then."

"I'm in the mood to talk to her now—just call her for me."

"Wouldn't if I could, but we're all independents here anyway, so I don't know how to reach her off the line."

"Oh, sure…you probably don't want to call her for me."

"Thursday, 6 to 10 A.M., I think she'll be on duty, but I can't promise. Now get on with a conversation or get off the line—she's not here now."

"This sucks. I want Ginger, not you…"

"I'm glad you like her, but on this service you don't order people from a menu, you talk to who's here or you hang up. Sorry you're disappointed, man, but whining won't help."

"Fuck you!"

"Cool it! She isn't here—that's it, buddy. Being a jerk won't bring her back; being a nice guy won't do it, either. She's not here—can you understand that—gone, *adios*'d, out of here."

"Tell her Ray called."

"Look, pal, I don't talk to her unless we cross paths on the line, I'm not her message machine, and I'm getting real tired of telling you good-bye. Even you should get the idea by now. Give it up—she's not here."

Click.

"Jamie, this is Vince. I talked to you last week, about water sports."

"I remember, I had that little accident while you were eating me."

"I did it! What you suggested: I asked my girlfriend if she'd pee for me, just let me watch her pee, I put a big towel underneath her and had her spread her legs and told her how beautiful her pussy was. She spread her lips with her fingers and then she just let go. It was wild! Then I licked her, Jamie, I put my face right there…"

"Did she like it?"

"She said it was hard to do it, to pee while she was excited, but, yeah, I'd say she liked it—she came all over my face while I licked her out."

"You evidently enjoyed yourselves."

"Are you kidding? We fucked like animals, she was all over me, Jamie, she was wild—come to think of it, so was I."

"Sexual adventuring can do that to a couple. You're lucky to have such a partner."

"She says she never did anything like that, she said it was a wild feeling, that I accepted her totally. Jamie, it was great, we reached a new level of something, trust or excitement, or I don't know what…but we got there together."

"Trust is exciting, don't you think? You told her a secret desire, and she fulfilled it, and that exists between you now. Tell me how you felt about it, I've heard what you say she said— what have you got to say?"

"Well, let's see. I *love* her pussy anyway. I love when she shows it to me like that in the first place. Then the towel reminded me this wasn't just any night, but I tried to be cool in case she changed her mind, you know? No pressure, just opportunity, like you said. So she's got herself spread open and I can tell she's excited, which turned me on even more. I could see the first moisture at her vagina and her clit was standing out a bit, then I saw her whole cunt shift, it sort of moved…is it hard to pee?"

"Lying on her back in bed with your face between her legs…yeah, we women have inhibitions about pissing under those circumstances. She was probably trying to relax her muscles so she could let go."

"Then a little trickle came out, it just ran down her cunt and was absorbed in the towel, she was breathing hard so I reached up and stroked her breasts, so we'd both relax, and, uh, Jamie, I could smell it…it smelled, well, fresh…mixed with her wetness, it was great, I just watched it trickle down…I gently kissed her vagina although what I really wanted to do was bury my face in her. She said she had to pee some more, so I drew back to watch and she really pissed, it was a steady stream this time, I couldn't take my eyes off of it, running down, blending with her pussy-juice, soaking the towel. She actually came from that—I saw her vagina close tight, then burst open. It was so beautiful."

"You make it sound beautiful…so what happened next?"

"I dabbed between her legs with the corner of the towel, gently blotting up the moisture, then I wadded up the towel and threw it into the hallway…she was perfectly still, she looked so beautiful to me right then I could have eaten her alive, which is what I tried to do, I guess. I mean, I never munched a cunt like that—I rubbed my face right in it, and that made her come again. She creamed all over my face. I was licking and sucking at her, drinking her, really drinking her juice as it ran out of her. I'd have to say it was the wildest thing she and I, or me and anybody, ever did."

"So you think maybe you might like it, huh?"

"What had me worried me was this: sure, I loved it, but what if she had second thoughts, decided it was too weird or something? But when I got to her place the next night she had a gift box for me, inside were two thick towels, His and Hers, one for her place, one for mine…we ended up fucking right there in the kitchen, which is another first for us! So I had to call and say thanks, from both of us. I told her about our talk on the phone, and she said as long as you didn't steal me away, you could give suggestions all you liked."

"Tell that little vixen that the best way to hold a man's attention is to pay attention. You're a sweetheart, I can tell—she's a lucky woman. Now take care of each other, you hear me?"

"Loud and clear, thanks again…"

Click.

A few of the operators volunteered (as in, for free) to meet callers on the line at specific times they were not scheduled to work, usually because the caller had arranged a date with a woman-in-the-flesh and intended to do something wild. These rarely worked out…most often the men simply didn't call at (or near) the specified time. Probably couldn't work out the details according to their carefully laid plans.

Some of the operators are phone-freaks: they'll pull a shift for us and then call into another phone service and pay to talk to people. They also call the date-line type chat lines which sometimes worries me as I don't want them trading on their Sweet Talker personality or confusing men with their motives. I understand they are revved up from working, in the mood, like a musician who finishes a show then "relaxes" in a club with live music. A good operator is gifted in this kind of contact, so of course she is drawn to it as a means of exploring the world on her free time.

I'm not lonesome when I get off the line, I'm not looking for new friends, I'm not interested in more anonymous contacts. Of course, I'm the boss, and my motives/skills are distinct from the average operator. I'm enjoying a life structured for maximum freedom and expression of my sexual self. Many of our operators have small children at home (if the dad is part of the family he's working a lot), and they crave conversation with adults, not only adult conversation.

I also channel my energies to paper, which alleviates some of the tension. The job is an odd one: you get close to strangers, yet are separated from even the most familiar caller. You have a curtain drawn, but you're naked behind it…you can be free with your thoughts because they can't be connected to y.o.u. in "real" life. Sometimes I arrange to have sex right after my shift; I'm definitely aroused by some of the goings-on on the phone and other times I want to be alone (sleep). After a mid-day shift, I'll often dash out to do errands, reflecting on things I've heard or said on the line while waiting in the bank or while some clerk bags my groceries. I sometimes laugh to myself as I'm driving down the road. After this job, I'll never feel the same about life.

I knew I liked men, but I wasn't sure why. I think that talking to hundreds and hundreds of men in these circumstances confirmed my impressions of them as a group: they are inventive, curious, tolerant, forceful, polite, and dedicated to the appreciation of women. They speak frankly of their frustration because they want to love somebody, admit they've had just about enough casual sex to know they want serious sex, use their daily erections as a chance to focus and release stray energies. They want to be accepted. Women fail to appreciate the upside of this reflex sexuality; it provides a foundation for the repetitive love of long-term associations, creating in him a need to express his fluctuating desires rather than a woman's fluctuating desire to express her needs.

Some men are unpolished gems, others high-gloss plastic; not all are attractive to me, but on the whole they are. There are traits this society lodges in its males and upon which our service is based. Our callers like saucy talk, prefer bad girls when they want to be bad boys, fantasize about things they admit they will never do, thrive on challenge and provocation, enjoy boasting. They notice women at home, on the job, while driving, walking, biking. They consider women a part of nature to be observed and appreciated. They are trying to figure out their new roles in our modern age. Chivalry vs. chauvinism, humanism vs. genderism, seduction vs. manipulation…please notice that most games have rules (which are bent and/or broken as part of some games) but the liveliest game of all is guided by unwritten unspoken conflicting agendas.

Right before payday, a man might use the phone-sex service for a "treat" that doesn't use up his dwindling cash. He can boost the cost from the moment of the pleasure to the paying of his phone bill, thus allowing him to do something if he feels stuck at home with nowhere to go.

Men who wouldn't pay $100 for physical contact will pay ten dollars for verbal contact, judging (correctly, in my opinion) that from one you are buying sensation and the other you are buying feelings.

Prostitution should be sanctioned and taxed; it is a legitimate exchange of life force, healing and challenging, evening out the cycles in a person's life, allowing buyers to take a sexual "vacation" from the known by sharing the energies of someone physically, culturally or psychosexually different from his usual pool of partners; or it may be to obtain throughout a long life the sexual services of one particular type, a late-twenties blonde with slim hips and painted toenails, seeking comfort in this stage of womanhood throughout the passage from novice to elder.

In the words of someone as matter-of-fact as Ann Landers, masturbation is no longer self-abuse. In my words, it is playing with yourself, stopping "production" to relax, to experience release. (Some enjoy the tension before release as much or more than the momentary release.) It is intrinsic to our coming to peace with our sexual pace; it is important that we reserve the right to express ourselves to ourselves.

It is too bad that we can't share our feelings with others. If a couple strolls into a party beaming big smiles, it is OK to say you made a killing on the stock market, your kid got an A in science, the weather is so fine, etc., but if you say you just had some great sex, you'll be considered rude braggarts with no sense of privacy.

"...is Jamie. I wonder what you're doing up so late tonight—all the good boys and girls are sleeping."

"I'm hoping to get off—what do you think?"

"I think I can help you, if you're in the mood for some fantasy interaction, if you want me to pump your head full of thoughts, close your eyes and open your mind."

"This is going to be fun, I can tell."

"Your fantasy female tonight is a large-breasted long-legged soft-skinned beauty. Her pretty lips smile when she sees your body, it arouses her when you handle your prick in front of her, when you tug on it. She opens her blouse and you catch your first glimpse of her lovely breasts, full and round, the cleavage deep between them."

"I love this."

"Her skirt unfastens on the side, and you see the curve of her waist and hip as she drops the skirt. She bends forward a bit and her breasts tumble out of her blouse, you stop stroking yourself and just admire her. She steps close to the bed, and you can see her soft thighs above her stockings, and the bush of hair beneath her garter belt—these seem to emphasize her nakedness to you and you groan with desire."

"Ohhh…"

"She slides onto the bed, positions herself over you, her knees around your hips, her pussy very close to your hot cock. It twitches from the heat of her body so near to it and bumps against her crotch. She rubs against it, causing her breasts to jiggle in your face. You can't help yourself—your cock is up under the hood. She pushes her breasts together and you suck first one then the other tit, as she rocks gently above you."

"Let me in there."

"She slides down your cock, smooth wet cunt surrounding you…you strain to go in deeper, deeper, and she opens wide, spreads for you, you're giving her all you've got and she's taking it, baby, she's taking it all."

"Talk to me, mama."

"Ball her, baby, do her right, shove that cock inside where it belongs, give her what she wants, what she needs, what she's waited for, come on, hot one, come on, baby, deliver that cock like the prize it is, shove it in, all the way…"

"Ohh, darlin', ohh, dear…"

"Now concentrate on sliding it in, smooth and steady, in all the way, all the way, deepest, deepest fucking, she's wringing you out, honey, twisting that pussy right around your dick, you can't stand it…"

"I can't stand it!"

"You're going to come…"

"I'm coming…"

"…inside me, darling, shoot it inside me, oh, baby, I wanted it so. You did so good, made me feel so good, yes, honey, you'll sleep tonight."

Click.

"Jamie, I'm naked in bed, stroking my cock, I've got a pair of my sister's panties in my other hand..."

"I can't go with the sister angle. Sorry."

"Well, they're the only pair I could get on such short notice. I'd rather they were yours!"

"A-plus answer. Think of those panties with me in them, curving over my ass, clinging to my cunt. What color are they?"

"Red, with black lace edging...real sexy. I like the feel of them in my hand, later I'll put them around my cock and stroke myself with the silk."

"Think of slipping your finger inside the leg of those panties, brushing against my clit, it's warm, slightly moist, the panty crotch is damp from my excitement."

"I like to explore you with the tip of my finger, feel up under the hood there to your little button, past your peehole and all the way back. You know what I'd really like?"

"No, can you tell me?"

"I'd like you over my knee, wearing only panties, they stretch tight over your buns, your tits are crushed against my leg, your tummy across the other, I rub your rear and slide my hand into your crotch from the back, still over the panties. You flex your butt for me, I like watching it, touching it."

"They'd be soaking wet by now, I like to be fondled."

"I slip the panties down, just a bit, just so the crack of your butt shows, and you wiggle in my lap, against my cock. I slide my hand into the panties and track the crack forward to your wet pussy. You're all wet for me, aren't you, honey?"

"I want you to finger me—please put your finger in me."

"I can feel the folds of skin around my finger. I can see your ass and back, so beautiful, so smooth, you wiggle in my lap as I finger you. The panties are around your thighs now, your buns are bare, I can see you, I put my thumb against your asshole as I finger-fuck you. I want you to come this way, to wet my hand with your come."

"I want your finger deep in my cunt. I raise it up, shake it, you use your other hand on my asshole, first wetting your finger with the juice from my cunt, then I feel the first part of your finger violate my hole, it is tight, you slowly work your finger into me, finger-fucking me with the other."

"Ohh, yes, I'd use both hands, you'd go crazy in my lap, across my knee, panting and heaving, frantic with desire, needing me to please you."

"I push my ass back against your hand, your finger is in all the way, you are using the palm of your other hand against my mound, fingers at my cunt-hole, stretching it open."

"I can't stand it. I have to fuck you, I want to ball you."

"Fuck me? *No.* You're going to butt-fuck me, you're going to shove that cock into my ass, you fucker. I'm too hot for an ordinary fuck, I need more than that, I need you to take my ass."

"Jesus, yes, oh, yes, spread your cheeks for me."

"I'm kneeling, forehead on the pillow, hands on my fleshy ass, spreading myself for you. You see the tiny hole and can't believe your cock will fit but you slide it in, easy now, gentle now, be my sweet fuck, take me slowly."

"Yes, slowly, yes, take your ass, fuck your ass."

"Thrust it, you're in now, it's all yours, I'm yours, you know this is the most intense love of all, this is the wildest love, come on, sweet fuck, fuck me, come in me, fill my ass."

"Fuck you in the ass, in the ass, yes, fuck you."

"Shoot yourself into me, darling, come on, daddy, yes, fuck me, fuck my ass, I spread it for, take it from you, you're my bad boy, my ass-fucking man."

"Damn it all to hell, lady, you took my breath away."

"Yeah, we did get the kinks out, didn't we?"

"How would I meet a woman like you? I'd be so good to you."

"You talk to strangers at parties, you strike up conversations in elevators. Women like me notice men who are involved in life, who are on the lookout for women like us…you see?"

"You won't tell me where you go, where you live?"

"No can do. But I'm real, and if I'm real, then there really are others, right?"

"Yeah, I guess so. But I doubt there are any just like you."

"Aren't you sweet? That kind of talk works on a lady like me—just remember that to get attention you have to pay attention. Now, mop up that bed and get to sleep."

"Another use for the panties...don't suppose you'd consider send—"

"Don't even suppose it, honey bear. Sweet dreams."

"Good night, and thank you so much. I won't forget this."

"Sleep, sleep, you're falling to sleep."

Click.

At times I wanted to tell some whiny guy who wanted a new sensation to put his prick in a blender, or boil it before I ate it. Thankfully, I found that when I clipped on my headset, I became "Jamie," and my problems weren't on her mind...

I've also been bone-tired at times, most often during the afternoons when the sun is out and the world is busy and my eyes are closing.... I'm so aware of an all-night shift that I always grab a nap, but I forget it's the midday that leaves me drowsy and dull...thinking the sleep I plan to get that night will get me through the preceding afternoon. I'll walk around my room, play with the kittens, imbibe some caffeine. If I start yawning, I'll walk in place, lifting my knees high, raising my arms overhead, until the blood fills with air again. It isn't fair to the callers to have to rouse the operator before she arouses them.

I've never fallen asleep on the line, never. Not even a few winks, but I admit I've had to fight it. Other operators lose that fight and nod out, most usually just a catnap; we've actually had to get on the other line and holler for her to wake up, and if *that* didn't work we'd access and reaccess the line until it bumped her off (a handy glitch)...all the while their sleepy breathing rattled over the line. This is usually discovered at shift-change time when the new operator can't clear her off the line and in frustration calls us, although we do catch them when monitoring, too. (In those cases, we might pull her off the line if we have a substitute or otherwise startle her awake and check in frequently to keep her awake.)

Sexplicit. Sexotic. Erotic. All terms to describe the depiction of sex. These categories seem simple enough: the sexplicit is any work that describes in particular detail the mechanics and/or emotions of sexuality, be it textbook or novel. Sexotic works may or may not be sexplicit, but they all focus on the sexually odd, the kinks and quirks of passion. Erotic material is judged by the intent and effect of evoking a sex-specific reaction; it is not merely informational or interesting, it is keyed to the arousal of response.

The book on Sweet Talkers is intended to document a modern tele-phenomenon, while describing an ageless desire for the release of pent-up energy. For some it will introduce detail about hitherto-disregarded aspects of sexual expression. For some it will represent a masturbatory aid.

As the writer of this book, what do I expect? In terms of "personal" recognition I don't care if people know "I" wrote it as much as I want it out and being read, seeping into the minds and hearts of others, counterbalancing all the speculation about the phone sex industry. As for "compensation," I already earn enough to live on. I don't want to buy a villa or invest in silver on the side, I merely want to be paid for working hard and providing information of interest in an informative, interesting way.

I believe the distinction in my writing style and method is its effectiveness, which is not a snide remark. Most "artists" are not seeking to communicate with the masses, they are not truly trying to communicate with anyone. They are living a personal vision and must be content with personal satisfaction. The best analogy is cutting your lawn with a manicure scissors. You could hardly make a living doing that, but it may gratify you to have what you consider to be a perfect lawn. If you want others to purchase your services, you must provide a service of value to them which gratifies *their* needs, not yours.

"...name is Jamie. Anybody feel like talking to a pretty lady on a beautiful day?"

"I do. This is, um, David."

"Hi, babe, you got something special on your mind?"

"Someone, this person at work, so I had this idea, like, if

you were this person's girlfriend and you two were on a date and ran into me and we all got drunk and did it together, see, like a fantasy thing…it'd have to be something wild like that."

"You're straight, right?"

"I used to think so, but this guy at work—I don't know, he's real sexual, I'd like to see him with somebody, like maybe I'd learn something."

"So I get you two dudes to a hotel room and what happens?"

"He tells me to sit back and let him warm you up. He stands behind you to undress you, which is something I wouldn't think to do—you see what I mean?"

"But you did think of it, right, for this fantasy?"

"Because I'm thinking like him, see? Now, listen, he's got you naked and like you're really sexy, small, round, and his hands are all over you. I've got this big hard-on and so does he. You're turned on and you lay sideways, so I can see him when he puts his dick into you, you let me watch and I'm seeing his dick go in and come out of you, I can't take my eyes off the way he moves, it's quick and surefire—he doesn't miss a beat."

"Can't I suck your cock while he balls me? Maybe he'd like to see you get some head."

"Well, sure, maybe he would, I've got a nice one, I think, anyway, that's what women tell me. They say it's very straight and very thick—is that the kind you like?"

"Sounds tasty, slide it between my lips, you can feel my body being shoved by your friend, he's fucking me and I'm sucking you, we're all connected."

"He comes and when you respond to that, you pull off my cock so we can all watch me come. I do it all over your boobs, we're all watching."

"I feel him come again inside me, you getting off got him off again."

"Yeah, and I shoot my last bit, too. We're both finished."

"But I'm not, I roll onto my back and put my hand between my legs, you both watch as I masturbate, you each take one of my breasts, stroke it, tug on the nipple. I move my hand between my legs, closer and closer to climax, you both lean forward, suck my tits into your mouths, and I have my orgasm between the two of you. You can feel the power surge through my body. We all feel great."

"Yeah, wild! And I see that next time I could fuck you while he watched. It didn't sound weird to me at all to talk about it, you seem to know what I meant, I don't even want to touch him, I just want to be there."

"Some guys like to team up with somebody and really satisfy a woman—it's a turn-on to be with two virile men, we ladies have such capacity for sex sometimes we wear out a man. What a delight to have two of you to satisfy me."

"If I come up with another weird idea, I'll call here. You sure satisfied this one. I don't know how you did it, I was afraid you'd think I was gay or something."

"You would have approached it all different if that were the case—then so would I. You just relax—this is hardly a weird fantasy. I get all kinds of buddy-fucks described, and part of it has to be the watching each other do it, experiencing sharing a woman, stereo rather than mono, that's all."

"I'm ready again, but this I have to do solo, no more dinero this week. When do you work next week?"

"I'm all over the clock but you can always find me late-night Fridays, after midnight…until five. Until then, pleasant dreams."

"Back at you. 'Night."

Click.

"Jamie, my man's here eating my pussy. It feels great, he's doing a great job."

"How can I help?"

"We called the other night. I ate him while he talked to you, so this time I get to talk and he's eating me."

"Sounds fair to me. Tell me, what kind of cock has he got?"

"It's long and smooth. The head isn't real big, but the whole thing is thick, it's a pretty one. Ohh, I forgot he was listening, he just, ummm, pressed his tongue, ahh, on my clit, uuuuoo…"

"Spread for him, honey, open wide, let him have that delicious box of yours. I'm jealous of him, I'd love to lick a clit right now, move for him, sweetie, let him know you feel it. I love a responsive woman."

"You sound so sexy, Jamie, I want to eat you while he eats me!"

"Yes, darling, but first press your body against mine. Let me feel those tender breasts against my own, kiss me, sweetheart."

"Jamie, call me Karen, please, talk to me."

"Ohh, Karen, let me hold you close, let me touch you, you feel so soft and smooth, so beautiful...ahh, Karen, your naughty nipples are getting so hard, is my darling excited?"

"Yes, Jamie, darling, yes..."

"Let me touch that sweet pussy, let me feel you, Karen, imagine my fingers teasing at that delicate flesh. Kiss me while I slide my finger into the hole, ohh, dearest, you are so sweet."

"I'm coming, over and over, when you talk to me."

"That man between your legs is helping, Karen, he's doing what I want to do, he's licking your juice, he's tasting your flesh, he's making love to you, Karen, like I would, devouring you."

"May I touch your breasts, I remember you said that they were big, mine are, too...I would kiss them and squeeze them, lick them all over, press my lips to your nipples, ohh, Jamie, it would be so beautiful."

"Our boyfriends could watch us, we could make love to each other right in front of their eyes."

"And, Jamie, when they got really excited we could let them fuck us but we'd kiss and hold each other while they did."

"And we wouldn't let them come in us, would we, ohh, no, Karen, because I want to eat your box after a man's churned up those juices but before he changes your taste...I want that cunt of yours streaming wet and juicy, like mine will be."

"Oh, if only we could meet you..."

"Baby, I'm not the only woman who knows the pleasure of another woman's sex. If you want it, Karen, you'll find it for real."

"But you make it sound so romantic."

"Between women, it seems it always is. They're so cuddly and kissy and sexy together, you obviously know that."

"We'll call again—I'll be thinking of you."

"Karen, female callers are rare, so you can bet I'll be thinking of you, too, and you're lucky to have such a good dude to be with. Be nice to each other, you hear?"

"We are, you can bet on that. Good night, sweet Jamie."

"Good night Karen, and, hey, what's the muncher's name—you know, your silent partner?"

"Oh, right, it's Joe, a good old Joe."

" 'Bye, lovebirds."

" 'Bye."

Click.

There are calls that consist of 98 percent operator monologue...the caller's 2 percent is a peculiarly rasping gasp and an intent silence (after their voice ID for age, which ID can range from "I'm old enough," to "Hit it, Mama."). There is a ragged edge to their breathing, a yearning in their sighs that is unmistakably the sound of a man masturbating. When they approach their climax (one to eight minutes, depending on budget and mood and nature of monologue) I will deliberately key myself to that sound, talk about that sound, about that sexy hiss and sexier silence, then focus on their prick, on the clenching ass and tightening thighs, on the belly held down and in so that the cock juts up, on their yearning and burning.

At these times I do feel connected to the caller, most likely from a sense of empathy rather than the sympathy offered in conversation with them. I know they want to be knocked over the edge, kicked back on their butts, drained dry. They are in an extreme state of arousal, straining to spill over. Anyone who's ever heard it wouldn't mistake it.

As I hit certain details, a man might punctuate my monologue with remarks like "Oh, yeah," or "Yes," or "God, God," or "Oooh," which escalates my performance, and if he signals by sound or word that he's near his climax I will encourage him to let me hear it, I get more emphatic, more demanding. "Do it, damn it; fuck it, eat me! Give it up to Jamie, angel, come on, that's right, stroke that heavy prick and think of creaming deep inside me...pump it out of that hot cock, lover, push it, clench it, *do* it."

The women I've brought to climax seem more fluttery, more delicate, with that characteristic cooing that men want so much to hear the operator simulate, a sigh with the rising lilt of sensation. I show them no mercy. I tell them I know what they're doing, I can feel the same things. I make them spread for me and show themselves, give those delicious tits a toss, arch her back so she thrusts her breasts up and out, come for me, don't hold back, give it up, the softness of her pussy on my smooth thigh, the wetness of her cunt on my tongue, her nipples against mine, oddly right.

The guys who connect in the midst of this sort of call never ever interfere.

What is the future of the phone sex phenomenon? As of early 1988, upcoming changes in telephone company billing policies will throttle the market, returning it to the credit-card-type exchange that discriminates against legitimate phone users who don't happen to qualify for major credit cards. Until those changes, it is in a boom period: inexperienced investors see the potential income and ignore the social reality. It takes a rare combination of operator talent and business management to make a successful enterprise, the salacious ads offering "live nude girls" contribute to the sleazy atmosphere that makes such a handy target for the repressionists. In fact, we made ours a "sweet-talking" operation to forestall the grosser elements of the business, which we gladly send to our competition. We concentrate on real women discussing fantasy sex. Crusaders cry out but are on shaky ground constitutionally and culturally: the safe-sex argument is on our side and it is a powerful one. My main argument against repression is the obvious—it hasn't worked yet. Consider that the following sentence, "Phone-y sex should be banned because it is distasteful to some people," sounds a lot less reasonable if you substitute the nouns "football," "sushi," or "rock and roll."

What's really behind this business? The basic freedom to pursue sexual fantasy is established by our right to view and read erotic materials—how can it be that the "sensory traffic" is a one-way (inbound) stream? Where else can men say what they want to say and hear what they want to hear? What better place than the privacy of their own homes? Their best argument is that they are not a small number; the fact so many wish to do so is proof enough that some combination of factors in our society has created an appreciation for this kind of conversational adventure.

Why do the guys call? Because they want to. Not one single caller has reported coercion. I've heard no pistols cocked, no whips snapped. I certainly would have included that here!

I cannot speak for other services but we have never, in a year of twenty-four-hour a day operation, been approached by a parent whose minor child had run up a horrendous phone bill—we've had them concerned over a three dollar call, mad about forty dollars, upset just for the fact the kid called at all, but we have structured the service to be hostile to children, and then we happen to have a call pace that would make a repeating nontalking customer stand out, alerting the operator to possible intrusion by an unwelcome guest (either child or adult acting like child and refusing to even acknowledge presence to allay operator's sincere concern it could be a kid; old enough, but not man enough).

Advertising continues to close tighter and tighter around us; we aren't sure what to do. We play it straight, don't go where we're unwelcome, but do wonder if it is healthy in the long run that the big companies lobby moral values based on one vocal subset of their consumers. Of course their image is vital to them but if Hitlerian methods (be my idea of pure or you die) are used to defend that image isn't the company's very integrity sacrificed? One of what we considered our prime advertisers (since it was often mentioned by the caller by name) dropped the entire 976-sex line advertising due to pulled ads [lost revenues] by "bigger," more "right" advertisers and our call rates went *up!* Figure that!

In point of fact, it is difficult to find a "grown-up" medium of exchange not invaded by kids whose parents can't or won't control them. We don't mean small-circulation "adult" outlets, but an exchange system of information for people who (a) don't have children, (b) have children but control them, and (c) desire to know what really happens in the world. Everything is so filtered as to be unreliable.

Pretend it is two years from now. Phones can be keyed to certain services for certain users. It is impossible for an underage child in any circumstance to ever access this adult activity at all. Period. What is the objection to phone-fantasy services now?

Will I miss it when it's over? Sometimes. You'd have to be there to understand how interesting men can be when freed of their daily realities. They are purely male, all man on the phone. Their car doesn't matter, their size isn't an issue, they know the operator is predisposed to cooperate—yet they also know she's a mirror of their own intent. It isn't for everybody, we all know that; but it is the choice of some. We make converts all the time: guys who get the number by chance, a buddy mentions it, it's in a magazine he never read before, he's seen the advertisement 100 times, but today he feels like finding out what it's all about and dials, one finger near the disconnect button. I won't miss the scheduling problems, the late-night "My relief didn't show up" calls, the knee-jerk negative reaction of people who never gave the idea of the actualities of sex other than their own one serious thought.

I'll admit that after my first few hundred hours on the line, the largest temptation was to sell my sexuality more directly. Guys spend on this stuff! In my greediest dreams, I figured then I wouldn't have to split my dollar a minute with the phone company, but in a flash of reality I realized then I couldn't use their wires as a web to protect me, either. I'd go from no-risk to all-risk. I'd have to put up or shut up. Honestly, I've had men say they'd build a duplex house if I'd just live next door and be their neighbor. They'd do my dishes and hand-paint my car. I've been offered money, trips, companionship, unlimited sex, no sexual obligations, clothes, jewelry, jobs, a life of luxury. I could have sold my panties, my shoes, my unlaundered jeans, letters, tapes....

Why did I write this book? I had to do something in between calls. I produced over two-thirds of the rough draft while actually on the line—remember I was wearing a headset, so both my hands were free. I was steeped in the atmosphere of the line as I re-created the calls. I'd like to think that this book gives you better information about the nature of the business. Sure, it can be tawdry and depressing; yet it can glow with life and wit and feeling and compassion. Some days I'd look in the mirror and ask myself what I was doing. But I plugged in and did it. I can see now that it enriched me to experience the unfiltered sexual emotions of these familiar strangers, one after another after another, each different, all the same: they come from the heart.

we come like a heartbeat
a rolling pulse
emptying one chamber to fill another